D0559913

DISCARD

THE DYNAMICS OF ISRAELI-PALESTINIAN RELATIONS

THE DYNAMICS OF ISRAELI-PALESTINIAN RELATIONS

THEORY, HISTORY, AND CASES

Ben Soetendorp

THE DYNAMICS OF ISRAELI-PALESTINIAN RELATIONS
© Ben Soetendorp, 2007.
rsoetendorp@cs.com

First published in 2007 by
PALGRAVE MACMILLAN™
175 Fifth Avenue, New York, N.Y. 10010 and
Houndmills, Basingstoke, Hampshire, England RG21 6XS
Companies and representatives throughout the world.

PALGRAVE MACMILLAN is the global academic imprint of the Palgrave Macmillan division of St. Martin's Press, LLC and of Palgrave Macmillan Ltd. Macmillan® is a registered trademark in the United States, United Kingdom and other countries. Palgrave is a registered trademark in the European Union and other countries.

ISBN-13: 978-1-4039-7172-2
ISBN-10: 1-4039-7172-2

Library of Congress Cataloging-in-Publication Data is available from the Library of Congress.

A catalogue record for this book is available from the British Library.

Design by Newgen Imaging Systems (P) Ltd., Chennai, India.

First edition: April 2007

10 9 8 7 6 5 4 3 2 1

Printed in the United States of America.

Transferred to digital printing in 2007.

CONTENTS

INTRODUCTION

UNTYING THE GORDIAN KNOT

This book deals with one of the main puzzles of contemporary history and international relations: the question of why has the Israeli-Palestinian conflict proved so intractable, and why is an Israeli-Palestinian settlement so problematic? To answer these questions I construct in the next chapters three separate "lenses," akin to the levels-of-analysis.[1] Each lens section is divided into two distinct chapters: a theoretical chapter and an empirical one. The theoretical chapters draw on a range of different and sometimes competing international relations and foreign policy perspectives. The first conceptual lens takes the individual decision-maker as the central focus of foreign policy analysis, and concentrates on the important impact of human cognition on the way individual policy-makers see the world and the actions they take. The starting point for the second lens is the assertion that international politics is rooted in domestic politics, and is explained by internal political structures and domestic political processes. The third lens concentrates on theoretical approaches that conceive the choices of leaders and the actions of states as resulting from the characteristics and nature of the international system.

I employ these three conceptual lenses as organizing frameworks for three empirical "cuts" of the Israeli-Palestinian conflict. Across lenses I look at the same cases of decisions, but from different angles. In other words, I apply three different theoretical lenses to explain the same events in three empirical cuts. That way the three cuts produce three alternative interpretations of the choices Israeli and Palestinian have made regarding two central issues in the Israeli-Palestinian conflict: the dilemma of partition in 1947, and the adoption of a two-state solution in 1983. The first case focuses on the decision of the Jewish community in Palestine in 1947 to accept the two-state solution as proposed by the United Nations (UN) partition plan for mandatory Palestine, and the decision of the Palestinian community to reject partition. The focal point of the second case is the decision to sign the Oslo agreement, which implied a decision of the Israeli government and the Palestinian Liberation Organization (PLO) leadership to recognize each other's existence and to accept the principle of a two-state solution to settle the Israeli-Palestinian conflict. Each decision is historically situated and deals with the preceding period as well its aftermath.

I do not assume any of the three conceptual lenses and the range of theories that go with each to have more explanatory power than the others, as every theoretical perspective has strengths and weaknesses. I do not consider any of the three alternative empirical cuts to be predominant, as each highlights some aspects and leaves others out. They simply demonstrate that the Israeli-Palestinian conflict is a multifaceted conflict, and that one's position on it depends a great deal on which lens is used to interpret it. In other words, there is more than one story to tell about the Israeli-Palestinian conflict. Does this mean that I am agnostic with regard to the different perspectives offered by the three levels-of-analysis? My answer is that the level-of-analysis approach usually involves a level-against-level notion of causation that fails to do justice to the complexity of the Israeli-Palestinian conflict. As Graham Allison has demonstrated in his classic study of the Cuban missiles crisis, alternative conceptual angles present significant differences in emphasis and interpretation to the same question.[2] Inspired by Allison's approach my aim is to identify causal factors at all three levels, and to show how different lenses produce different explanations to the same decision. In writing this book I also took as my guiding principle the wise words of Bruce Bueno de Mesquita: "None of us can be better scholars or teachers than those who seek to understand and convey to others the motives and principles governing individual choices and their consequences for world affairs."[3] Thus, in the construction of the conceptual lenses and the analysis in the empirical cuts I will take as my unifying concept the choices of individual leaders and other key foreign policy decision-makers, and will explain how these choices were influenced by factors originating from all three levels.

However, before I turn to the next few chapters I have to address briefly the problem of whether the theories discussed in the three theoretical lenses apply to two dissimilar actors. While in the first case one may doubt weather the two parties can be treated as state actors, in the second case one party to the conflict is a state actor, whereas the other party is considered to be a non-state actor. The easy escape route is to argue that what international relations really means is: *inter national* relations, that is, relations between nations. Following this argument one may say that the Israeli-Palestinian conflict was, and indeed still is, basically a conflict between two *nations* with a *national leadership* acting on behalf of the people of the two nations. My answer, however, is different. Following Robert Gilpin, I consider in the first case the Jewish and the Arab Palestinian communities in Palestine, to be two conflict groups.[4] Such conflict groups may, or may not, take the form of states. I argue that in the first case both Jews and Arabs in Palestine did not confront each other as individuals, but as members of two competing groups that organized themselves into political groups and were loyal to these groups, which got into conflict with one another. As Randall Schweller asserts, conflict groups that do not have sovereign control over a given territorial jurisdiction can be regarded as major actors.[5]

In the second case, although both parties may still be considered as conflict groups, the international status of the Jewish and Arab Palestinian communities in former Palestine has changed. While the Jews have organized themselves in a nation-state and enjoyed from that time international legal sovereignty, the Arab Palestinians failed to do so. Nonetheless, with the foundation of the PLO in 1964 the Palestinians established a political body that gradually developed into a state-like-actor. Although the PLO was not a state as it obviously missed the essence of a state, which is its territoriality,[6] it nevertheless gained in a step-by-step process the status of a political entity in the international system, that is, international legal sovereignty. While a basic rule for international legal sovereignty is, according to Stephen Krasner, that international recognition is granted to entities with independent control over territory and formal juridical autonomy, an exception was made for the PLO.[7] The PLO was given observer status in the United Nations in 1974, and this status was changed to that of a mission in 1988 immediately after the declaration of Palestinian independence. The international status as a state-like entity was further reinforced by the creation of the Palestine Authority as a result of the Oslo accords in 1993. Although the Palestinian Authority had only some sort of formal juridical autonomy and exercised a limited form of sovereign control over some parts of former Palestine in the occupied West Bank and the Gaza Strip, it clearly enjoyed international legal sovereignty. Throughout this period the PLO can also be conceived as a diplomatic actor that fulfilled many diplomatic functions without being a state.[8] The PLO established and maintained formal and informal relations with other political entities, usually states and international organizations, through which it pursued its respective goals and interests. The PLO Chairman and later president of the Palestinian Authority Yasser Arafat also operated slowly but surely as a representative head of state with a clearly defined foreign policy.

In the remaining of this introductory chapter I will establish a brief historical framework that will serve as a common historical context for the alternative empirical cuts discussed in the next few chapters.

THE FIRST ISSUE: THE UN PARTITION PLAN

The decision of the United Nations General Assembly in November 1947 to divide Palestine in two states, a Jewish state and a Palestinian state, was an attempt of the international community to solve a conflict between two national movements driven by diametrically opposed objectives toward an inescapable war between Jews and Arabs for the exclusive ownership of Palestine. The UN had to take this decision because the British government which governed Palestine from 1917 decided in February 1947 to turn over the Mandate it received in 1922 from the League of Nations to the UN. After three decades of British rule over Palestine in which the British government tried to reconcile the conflicting claims of the two national movements, it had come to realize that compromise between Arabs and Jews was impossible. They draw the conclusion that war between Arabs and Jews was unavoidable as only war could decide who will control the country or how much of it will be part of a Jewish or an Arab independent state. This proved to the British government that the costs of maintaining its rule over Palestine was not worth the limited strategic value the country offered. In fact, both the conservative opposition and the labor government shared a consensus against the continuation of the British presence in Palestine.[9]

In the preceding years the British authorities in Palestine had to deal first with a revolt of the Arab population which they managed to suppress, but were then faced with a Jewish resistance that was still going on when they decided to withdraw. The Arab uprising against the British, which started in 1936 and lasted until 1939, was a violent expression of the increasing frustration of the Palestine Arabs about the British policies that in their view favored the Jewish community and stimulated its massive expansion. Under the terms of the League of Nation's Mandate by which Britain was to govern Palestine, the Jews enjoyed indeed a privileged position. The Mandate recognized the historical connection of the Jewish people with Palestine and obliged the mandatory power to establish a Jewish national home in Palestine. It also recognized a Jewish Agency representing the Zionist world organization and the Jewish population in Palestine, which had the task to advise and cooperate with the British authorities in

Palestine in matters that may affect the establishment of the Jewish national home. The only reference the Mandate made to the Palestine Arabs, who formed at that time the vast majority of the population, was in connection with the British obligation to facilitate Jewish immigration and settlement. In implementing this requirement the British authorities had to ensure that the rights and position of other sections of the population were not prejudiced.[10]

The British inquiry commission that was set up to study the causes of the Arab Revolt, named after its chairman, Peel, acknowledged in its report that the British government could not deny national self-determination to the Palestine Arabs, and transform Palestine into a Jewish state against the will of the Arab population. The national home, as the commission said, could not be half-national. The Peel commission came to the conclusion in 1937 that it was impossible to reconcile the national aspirations of the Jewish and Arab communities. As a way out of that dilemma the Peel commission established in its final report the principle of partition and proposed to divide Palestine in two states, an Arab and a Jewish state.[11] But the British government decided against partition. In a policy paper (a so-called White Paper) published in 1939, it promised to establish an independent state in Palestine in which Arabs and Jews share in government within a transitional period of ten years. It was clear that such a state would have an Arab majority as the prospect for any important growth of the Jewish community—at that time about a third of the population—was further restricted by the severe limits that were imposed on the immigration of Jews to Palestine.[12]

The British intention to calm the Palestine Arab's fear that they would become a minority under the impact of massive immigration of Jewish refugees fleeing Hitler, turned the Jewish community in Palestine against the British authorities. The closure of Palestine on the eve of the Second World War to the Jewish refugees who faced extermination in Europe and the British retreat from its obligation under the terms of the Mandate to enable the building of a Jewish state, were seen by the Jews as a cynical attempt of the British government to appease the Arabs in order to win their goodwill in the coming war against Germany. Because of the war the Jews postponed their intention to organize a strong opposition to the British policy, but as the war ended and the British government did not change its prewar policy the Jews started an open confrontation. Besides violent clashes between Jewish underground units and British troops, the Jewish leadership began an intensive illegal immigration campaign.

They succeeded in making the fate of the displaced Jews in Europe who survived the Holocaust and wanted to immigrate to Palestine a sensitive international issue, and mobilized in particular the support of the United States who put the British government under pressure to allow a significant number of these displaced persons into Palestine. Faced with the unwillingness of the Arab and Jewish leaders to agree on a formula that would satisfy the national aspirations of both communities, and its inability to control the growing tensions and hostility between the two communities that were clearly heading toward a civil war, the British decided to give up. As mentioned earlier, the whole problem of Palestine was brought by Britain before the UN that decided to set up a special committee of inquiry, the UN Special Committee on Palestine (UNSCOP). In its report a majority of its members recommended, as the Peel commission did ten years earlier, to divide Palestine into independent Arab and Jewish states, while a minority of its members proposed an independent federal state. The UN General Assembly adopted on November 29, 1947 the partition plan by a two-third majority. Thirty-three members of the UN, including the United States and the Soviet Union, voted in favor of the UN resolution for the partition of Palestine (UN General Assembly resolution 181), while thirteen members voted against and ten abstained.[13]

The Jewish community accepted the UN partition resolution and saw it as the international legitimization for the creation of a Jewish state in Palestine, which was established when the British left Palestine in May 1948. The Palestine Arabs rejected the resolution and started immediately fighting the Jewish community, with the support of volunteer units from neighboring Arab countries and the Arab armies who invaded Palestine after the British departure. The war ended in January 1949 with the signing of armistice agreements between the new state of Israel and its neighboring Arab countries. As a result of the war the newborn state of Israel extended its territory to the cease-fire lines, which were beyond the original partition lines of the UN partition resolution. The Palestine Arabs failed to establish a Palestinian Arab state in any part of Palestine, and a large number of Palestine Arabs was forced to leave their houses in cities and villages that came under Israeli control. The Arab armies also managed to keep only small parts of Palestine. Egypt maintained control of a tiny area in the south around Gaza, and Jordan occupied some parts of Palestine that were allocated in the partition resolution to the Arab state in Palestine. That area would become in 1950 an integral part of the Hashemite Kingdom of Jordan.

THE SECOND ISSUE: THE OSLO ACCORDS

The core significance of the Oslo accords is the mutual recognition by Israel and the Palestinians of each other's existence, and the readiness to negotiate with each other on a settlement of the Israeli-Palestinian conflict. Although the Oslo accords do not mention the establishment of a Palestinian state, the two parties to the Oslo agreement expected that a final-status agreement would be based on the principle of a two-state solution. The road to Oslo was a step-by-step process in which both Israelis and Palestinian removed one by one major obstacles for a resolution of their long-standing conflict. The first substantive building block was actually UN Security Council resolution 242, adopted in November 1967. The resolution emphasized the inadmissibility of the acquisition of territory by war; called for a just and lasting peace in the Middle East; demanded that Israel withdraw from territories it occupied in June 1967 (the French version spoke of all the territories); and demanded that the Arabs and Israel terminate the state of belligerency and acknowledge the sovereignty, territorial integrity, and political independence of every state in the area and their right to live in peace within secure and recognized borders. The resolution also affirmed the need to solve the refugee problem.[14] Resolution 242 would be complemented by UN Security Council resolution 338. Both resolutions would be the cornerstone of all future peace efforts in the Middle East including the Oslo accords.

The second major substantive building block, and the first serious implementation of the principles for a negotiated settlement laid down in resolution 242, were the Camp David accords between Egypt and Israel in September 1978. The Camp David accords went further than resolution 242. An integral part of these agreements was namely, a detailed framework for negotiations on the Palestinian problem. Israel recognized for the first time the legitimate rights of the Palestinian people and their just requirements, accepted that representatives of the Palestinian people should participate in negotiations on the resolution of the Palestinian problem in all its aspects and take part in the determination of their future. Menachem Begin, the Likud prime minister who negotiated and signed the Camp David agreements on behalf of Israel, also agreed that negotiations on the final status of the West Bank and Gaza would be based on the provisions and principles of UN Security Council resolution 242, which emphasized the inadmissibility of the acquisition of territory by war. This was also the first time that an Israeli prime minister made a commitment to cooperate in establishing agreed procedures for a prompt, just, and permanent solution of the refugee problem, and to decide on modalities of admission of persons displaced from the West Bank and Gaza in the 1967 War. Although the Camp David agreements did not refer to the establishment of an independent Palestinian state, it already mentioned the replacement of the Israeli military government and its civil administration by a self-governing authority that has been freely elected by the inhabitants of the West Bank and Gaza. It also referred to a withdrawal of Israeli armed forces into specified security locations, as well as the establishment of a strong local police force to assure internal and external security and public order.[15]

However, the groundwork laid in the Camp David accords did not lead to full autonomy for the Palestinians in the occupied territories. Israel and Egypt could not agree even on an interim agreement, given the Israeli restrictive view of autonomy. The Americans also were unable to find any common ground that might lead to some form of self-government for the Palestinians. The talks were postponed as a result of the Israeli invasion of Lebanon in 1982, and never revived. In the meanwhile the Likud government built as many settlements as was possible in the occupied territories to change the Arab nature of the territories and to prevent the establishment of an autonomous Palestinian entity. The creeping annexation and the Likud government's occupation policy triggered in December 1987 a Palestinian uprising that would continue until the signing of the Oslo accords.

The PLO laid a crucial substantive building block for the Oslo accords in November 1988. In a significant move, the Palestine National Council (PNC) approved in November 1988 the proclamation of an independent Palestinian state based on the partition resolution of 1947. The PNC also endorsed the acceptance of resolution 242 as basis for a negotiated Middle East peace settlement, and condemned (later this would be revised to renounce) terrorism. This implied that the PLO accepted the existence of Israel, and was willing to reach an agreement with Israel based on the principle of a two-state solution, as the independent Palestinian state would be established only in the occupied territories.[16]

The last building block for the Oslo accords was the Madrid Middle East peace conference of October 1991, sponsored by the United States and the Soviet Union. But this time, right from the beginning, the United States had no intention of functioning as a mediator, and limited its role to that of a convener. The American idea was that the participants would express in the opening ceremony their commitment to further negotiation, which were to take place on two different tracks: a bilateral one and a multilateral one. The bilateral track consisted of a sequence of carefully arranged meetings in which the parties were expected to present their positions. But the Americans had no intention of intervening in the substance of the negotiations in the initial stage of the negotiations. They were simply facilitators and were prepared to present some workable compromises only in a later stage to bridge the differences between the parties.[17] The Madrid peace conference did not produce any substantive results. But the significance of the Madrid peace conference, and in particular the bilateral negotiations between the Israelis and Palestinians that followed the ceremonial opening, was that the Palestinians participated for the first time in a peace conference. Although the PLO had to accept that only inhabitants of the occupied territories represented the Palestinians as part of a joint Jordanian-Palestinian delegation, the Palestinian delegates operated nonetheless independently and in close cooperation with the PLO leadership. Israelis and Palestinians were sitting for the first time at the same negotiation table on equal footing and were expected to come up with ideas of their own for a settlement of their conflict. Ultimately this happened, but not in the formal bilateral track of the Madrid peace process. As the PLO leadership signaled to the Israeli Labor government that if they want a deal this had to be done directly with them, the two parties opened a back door with the help of Norway that functioned also as a facilitator rather than as a mediator.

The Oslo accords consisted of a mutual Declaration of Principles for Interim Palestinian Self-Governance Arrangements in the West Bank and Gaza Strip, the so-called Oslo agreement; a number of protocols that stipulated arrangement for withdrawal of Israeli forces from the Gaza Strip and Jericho area, and Israeli-Palestinian cooperation in economic and development programs as well as regional development programs. It also included minutes to the Oslo agreement that comprised an annex with an exchange of letters between Yasser Arafat and Yitzhak Rabin in which the PLO recognized the right of Israel to exist in peace and security; accepted UN resolutions 242 and 338; committed itself to the Middle East peace process and to a peaceful resolution of the conflict between the two sides and declared that all outstanding issues relating to permanent status will be resolved through negotiations. The Israeli government on its part recognized the PLO as the representative of the Palestinian people and expressed its will to start negotiations with the PLO within the Middle East peace process.[18] The Oslo accords were in fact an interim agreement rather than a comprehensive agreement and avoided linking such initial practical arrangements with the nature of the final peace settlement. It was followed by the Cairo agreement of 1994, that specified concrete arrangements for the withdrawal of Israeli military forces from Gaza and the Jericho area; the transfer of authority in these territories to a Palestinian Authority; the powers and responsibilities of the Palestinian Authority; as well as arrangements for security. Further implementation of the Oslo accords was agreed in the Interim Agreement on the West Bank and Gaza Strip, the so-called Oslo II agreement, signed in 1995. It arranged the further withdrawal of Israeli forces from the Arab cities and other densely populated Arab areas in the occupied territories, as well as additional measures for the transfer of authority and the building of a political system within the territories controlled by the Palestinian Authority.[19] The Oslo accords as well as the subsequent Cairo agreement and interim agreement on the West Bank and Gaza Strip established the principle of Israeli withdrawal from the occupied territories, and set out concrete arrangements for the establishment of a Palestinian interim self-government authority.

1

A First Lens

Individual Influences in World Politics

It is common sense practice to see nations, states, and governments as abstract entities. In everyday language when we write about international events we conceive states as unitary actors, thinking and acting collectively. We speak of a nation's decision, a state's action, or a government's policy. It is, for example, the Palestinian decision to sign the Oslo accords, the Israeli action in Gaza, and the United States' policy toward Iraq. But in fact nations do not act, it is their leaders who do.[1] This view was proposed already in the early 1950s by Richard Snyder, H. Bruck, and Burton Sapin who argued that in explaining governmental behavior we should focus on the behavior of its official decision-makers: "State action is the action taken by those acting in the name of the state. Hence, the state is its decision-makers."[2]

Many international relations scholars have expressed similar views. In order to explain foreign policies and international politics, they say, it is necessary to study human decision-makers. Charles Kegley, for example, has argued that in theorizing about the sources of foreign policy behavior we should begin with individuals, the people who occupy the decision-making roles at the highest levels of government, because only persons think, prefer, and act. Referring to Snyder and his two colleagues he says that nation-states are incapable of acting or thinking; decision-makers alone do this. Neither do national conditions nor international circumstances make decisions and form foreign policy.[3] More recently Jerel Rosati has echoed these views saying that in reality countries do not act, only people act; states are made up of individuals who act on their behalf.[4]

Following this reasoning, I consider in this chapter national leaders and other key foreign policy-makers to be the true actors of international relations. It is they who make a difference in determining the course of international events. As Snyder and his two associates have argued: "the key to the explanation of why the state behaves the way it does, lies in the way its decision-makers as actors define their situation."[5] However, as Kenneth Boulding has pointed out in one of the pioneering articles on the role of individuals in international relations, the people whose decisions determine the policies and actions of nations do not respond to the objective facts of the situation but to their image of the situation. It is what they think the world is like, not what it is really like, that determines their behavior.[6] Also Ole Holsti, in one of the first seminal studies on the relationship between belief systems and decision-making in international relations and foreign policy-making, has indicated that decision-makers act upon their definition of the situation and their images of states. But these images, he says, are in turn dependent upon the decision-makers' belief system, which may or may not be accurate representations of reality.[7]

The claim that the personal beliefs and images of leaders and other key foreign policy-makers about the world are of overriding importance in shaping a country's foreign policy is influenced by psychological theories of human cognition. Cognition is the representation of reality that the person experiences as reality itself. It involves processes like thinking, problem solving, and memory.[8] Cognitive psychology studies the dynamics and processes of the human mind, which can be seen as information-processing system and the ultimate locus of decision-making. It argues that much of an individual's behavior is formed by the particular ways in which he perceives, evaluates, and interprets incoming information about events in his environment.[9] Cognitive psychology applies in the first place to the individual qua individual, but knowledge about the way individuals process and interpret information about the world is vital if we want to understand why leaders and other key foreign policy-makers hold different belief systems. All leaders, for example, do not think about power and interest in the same way. To know how different leaders perceive power and interest, the beliefs and the reasoning processes of individuals are important. As Michael Young and Mark Schafer argue, both concepts are cognitive in nature: "Neither power nor interest is objective; rather, each emerges from the beliefs individuals hold about these concepts."[10]

As I will illustrate in this chapter a number of international relation scholars regard various assumptions and findings of cognitive psychology very relevant and useful for the study of international relations and the analysis of foreign policy. They refer to several cognitive principles that help national leaders and other key decision-makers to handle the complex environment they face in international relations. Such cognitive principles explain how policy-makers organize their beliefs about the world or how they develop their images of other actors in the international arena. Yet, as Janice Stein states, there is no single cognitive theory or a dominant cognitive principle that explains how people make sense of their environment. Instead, she says, cognitive psychologists have specified the cognitive filters and the cognitive short cuts, that are the simplifying mechanisms, through which people process information to make sense of their surroundings.[11] Moreover, principal advocates of the use of the cognitive approach in the study of international relations and foreign policy analysis, like Holsti and Alexander George, have cautioned against the drawing of direct causal correlations between an individual's beliefs or images and foreign policy outcomes. They propose to concentrate on the effects human cognition have regarding the two basic tasks in foreign policy-making that precede and accompany the decision-maker's choice of action: first, determine the specific policy problem with which policy-makers must deal, that is, the diagnosis of the situation, and second, formulate and evaluate the alternative policy options for dealing with the problem they face.[12] Following this suggestion I will turn now to consider implications and consequences of some basic cognitive principles and psychological constructs that political leaders are likely to employ for the process of foreign policy-making.

THE NEED FOR COGNITIVE CONSISTENCY

The starting point for my discussion is the observation that "the mind is a belief-seeking, rather than a fact-seeking apparatus."[13] A fundamental principle of cognitive psychology is the recognition that in order to cope with the complex confusing reality of the surrounding, every individual acquires during the course of his development a set of beliefs about the nature of their physical and social environment. A belief may be conceived as lens or prism through which information concerning the surrounding is processed. It acts as a sort of filter deciding what information from the outside world is to be selected and how this information should be interpreted. Beliefs provide an individual with an important tool to clarify and impose meaning on the complex and uncertain environment and help him to simplify and structure the external world, to perceive others' behavior and form judgments about their intentions. Decision-makers' beliefs about the world are therefore necessary mental constructs that facilitate an individual to make sense of what would otherwise be an amorphous and puzzling collection of messages received from the environment. It serves as a guide to information processing and a starting point from which an individual is able to analyze and understand others' behavior.[14] An individual does not hold a random collection of beliefs. Belief systems are organized in concentric rings from more central to more secondary or peripheral beliefs. A belief about whether the political world is one of conflict or harmony, which is conceived as a central belief, is connected with many other beliefs, such as the willingness to compromise with political opponents.[15]

The human mind organizes relations between beliefs according to some general cognitive principles. A well-established cognitive rule holds that the mind operates in such a way as to keep internal belief relationships consistent with one another. The mind produces coherent and stable systems of beliefs, which form an interdependent and hierarchical system whose elements are consistent with one another and resistant to change. Hence, individuals are consistency seekers; they have a strong need to maintain consistency among beliefs. As a result decision-makers try to avoid information that is inconsistent with their beliefs. They have a strong tendency to see what they expect to see and assimilate incoming information to preexisting images. They tend to ignore and even reject any new information that is inconsistent with existing beliefs, in particular their most central beliefs.[16] As Robert Jervis explains, by this tendency of belief structures toward consistency we are inclined to believe that countries we like do things we like, support goals we favor, oppose countries that we oppose; and countries which are our enemies make proposals that would harm us, work against the interests of our friends, and aid our opponents. According to Jervis there is little doubt that this simple principle does organize a large number of our cognitions. Individuals feel more comfortable when collections of beliefs are balanced; they learn them more quickly, remember them better, and interpret new information in such a way as to maintain or increase balance.[17]

The cognitive principle of consistency striving has an important impact on the quality of a decision-maker's diagnosis of the situation and evaluation of the policy options for dealing with it. Cognitive consistency causes decision-makers to fit incoming information into preexisting beliefs. They ignore information that does not fit, twist it so that it confirms their beliefs, and deny its validity; while confirming evidence is quickly and accurately noted.[18] This leads to distorted judgments about the situation and increases the chances of error in the assessment of alternative options. Two major international fiascos, the surprise attacks of Japan on the United States' Pacific fleet at Pearl Harbor in 1941 and the Syrian-Egyptian surprise attack on Israel in October 1973, illustrate how a failure to recognize the influence of preexisting beliefs results in biased information processing. The American key decision-makers expected the outbreak of war with Japan any time. But they assumed that the Philippines or Guam, not Pearl Harbor, would be a target of Japanese attacks. Because they did not believe Pearl Harbor was vulnerable, they neglected many military warning signals during the ten days before the large-scale destruction of the United States Pacific fleet at Pearl Harbor, at that time the most important American marine base in the Pacific. The explanation for that behavior lies according to Roberta Wohlstetter in the fact that for every warning signal there were several plausible explanations; decision-makers were inclined to select the explanation that fitted the assumption which placed all the possible targets of Japanese attacks somewhere else.[19] In a similar way, Israeli key decision-makers believed in October 1973 that war between Israel and an Egyptian-Syrian coalition was unlikely before 1975 because of Israel's military superiority and the Arab lack of capability. In spite of detailed information from different sources indicating the possibility of a full-scale coordinated Syrian-Egyptian surprise attack on Israel's northern and southern fronts, they stuck to their original evaluation that the probability of war was low. The Egyptian and Syrian military preparations were not interpreted as a military threat but as part of an Egyptian military exercise and a Syrian defense alert in response to the shooting down of Syrian military airplanes by the Israeli air force.[20] In both cases the tendency of key decision-makers to disregard information that was inconsistent with prior beliefs clearly influenced the errors they made in their assessment of the situation.

The Operational Code Belief System

A cognitive construct that is based on the principle of cognitive consistency and that links a leader's beliefs and decisions is the operational code. It describes a coherent collection of beliefs that is bound together by some form of constraint or functional interdependence.[21] An operational code refers to the central beliefs an individual leader holds about international politics. An individual acquires, according to George, a set of generalized principles about political life that he applies in information processing for the purpose of exercising judgment and choice in decision-making. This applies in particular to political leaders who are assumed to be informed and interested in political life and have a high level of political awareness. George identified two categories of operational code beliefs about political life. The first one concerns philosophical issues and relates to the basic objectives of political interaction and the potential for their realization; the second one refers to instrumental issues and involves the strategies and effective tactics required to realize the political goals. The beliefs in the two collections are internally consistent. The two sets are also interconnected in the sense that philosophical beliefs have their counterpart in instrumental beliefs.[22]

The philosophical beliefs deal with the essential nature of politics and political conflict; the fundamental character of one's political opponents; the prospects for realizing one's fundamental political values and aspiration; the extent to which the political future is predictable; the degree to which political leaders can influence historical developments and shape desired outcomes; and the role of chance in human affairs and in historical developments. Instrumental beliefs have to do with the best approach for selecting goals for political action; the most effective way to pursue those goals; the best approach to calculation, control, and acceptance of the risks of political action; the best timing of action to advance one's interests; and the utility and role of different means for advancing one's interests.[23]

This set of operational code beliefs captures political leaders' core beliefs about fundamental unchanging issues of politics and political action. But, as George notes, a leader's operational code is not a set of recipes or rules for action that he employs automatically. Neither his diagnosis of situations nor his choice of action for dealing with them is strictly dictated and determined by these beliefs. Rather, George says, the operational code belief system serves as a prism that influences the leader's diagnoses of political events and his analysis of particular situations. It also provides norms and guidelines that influence the leader's choice of strategy and tactics as well as his structuring and weighing of alternative courses of action in specific situations.[24] For instance, a leader's belief that the political universe is essentially one of conflict and his belief about the opponent as being fundamentally hostile, encourages him to see interaction with that opponent as presenting dangers to his side, to define ambiguous situations as threats, to interpret intentions of the opponent as evidence of hostility, and to ignore discrepancies in the information that questions the existing belief about the opponent as being basically hostile. A leader who believes that the political future is predictable and that an individual can control and shape historical events, is more likely to carry out an extensive search and evaluation of the various options.[25] But his search for information is directed more toward facts that are relevant to deal with the situation rather than controlling the situation. A belief that an individual can control events will also influence his risk taking behavior. In threatening situations or events decision-makers who believe in the possibility of controlling events are more likely to take risks.[26]

A number of scholars applied the operational code approach in an attempt to reveal a link between a leader's operational code and a country's foreign policy. One of the most significant studies is Stephen Walker's examination of the connection between the operational code beliefs of Henry Kissinger and the conduct of the negotiations that ended the U.S. involvement in the Vietnam War. Walker found a close relationship between the operational code beliefs of the former national security adviser and secretary of state and his bargaining behavior in the negotiations with North Vietnam from 1969 through January 1973. The rationale for negotiations was consistent with his beliefs that an individual lack of control over history makes the deliberate process of negotiations the best means to maximize the chances for realizing one's goals throughout a conflict. Kissinger's negotiation strategy also corresponded, according to Walker, to his beliefs that threats and force should be used during negotiations only to counter their use by an adversary; and that force has to be applied in combination with generous peace terms so that the opponent is faced with an appealing peace settlement versus the unattractive alternatives of stalemate or the necessity to escalate the conflict.[27]

THE NEED FOR SIMPLICITY AND STABILITY

In addition to the principle of consistency two other cognitive rules, the principle of simplicity and the principle of stability, are important for understanding the impact of cognition on foreign policy-making. According to these two principles, cognitive inference mechanisms work to keep the structure of beliefs as simple as possible and to resist change in the core structure of beliefs.[28] Since the human mind has a limited capacity to process information and lacks the ability to deal with every stimulus from the environment, these mechanisms help the mind to manage the process of information selection and to deal effectively with the enormous burden of information processing. Such mechanisms also avoid a major restructuring of beliefs, which is likely to impose severe burdens upon the information-processing system. As John Steinbruner notes, the human mind is highly selective about the information to which it attends and that which it uses; it remembers some things of importance but forgets a great deal of the information it receives.[29]

Hence, political leaders and other key decision-makers, like all individuals, build simplified mental representations of the world and adopt a number of short cuts that help them to impose some degree of simplicity and stability on a complex and uncertain reality. Once formed, these cognitive constructs become filters through which information passes upon which diagnosis of the situation takes place and policy choices are made.[30] Several of these simplified mechanisms and cognitive shortcuts have been described by the use of concepts like image, stereotype, schema, and analogy. These cognitive constructs serve the need of decision-makers to simplify reality very well, and make the problem of information overload manageable. But, they are also the source of biased patterns in the processing of information and the origin of significant errors in foreign policy-making.

Images and Stereotypes

Images are substantive beliefs that describe the conceptualization that individuals have about the world and especially of other individuals or another country. It can include, for instance, information about the values other leaders hold, describe the relative military power and economic capabilities of another country, and express judgments about a specific other actor regarding the threat it represents. Images also include information about the self, like the idea a country has about the role it plays in the region or in the international system.[31] The image concept is designed, according to Richard Herrmann, to capture the understanding of relationships. A perception of another actor as stronger or weaker than the perceiving actor defines both the view of the other and the view of the self.[32]

A special sort of images is stereotypes. These are images that characterize all elements of a particular group. Individuals may have racial, ethnic, or religious stereotypes or posses stereotypical images such as enemy or ally. Stereotyping is an inevitable by-product of the tendency of the human mind to categorize. It refers to the process by which people, when they perceive new stimuli, first try to categorize the stimuli as another case of some familiar group.[33] The image of the enemy is the stereotypical image that is mostly discussed in international relations literature. This stereotype indicates a felt threat and combines, according to Herrmann, a number of perceptions about the opponent. The stereotyped enemy is characterized as aggressive and motivated by evil intentions. Its leadership is assumed to act with the perceiver as the primary target, but it is presumed to respond to the perceiver's actions. The stereotyped government takes advantages of opportunities presented by the perceiver's weakness and retreats in the face of the perceiver's strength and resolution.[34]

The stereotyped enemy image helps to simplify reality but it also creates cognitive predispositions that influence information processing and consequently lead to errors in the judgment by political leaders and other key decision-makers of the intentions of an opponent. As individuals have a basic bias toward the preservation of an individual's prior beliefs and existing images, individuals tend to pay attention to confirming evidence and close their eyes to contradictory evidence. Because of this selective attention to information, individuals are more inclined to perceive the opponent's aggressive actions as confirmation of the initial aggressive image of the adversary, while restrained or conciliatory behavior on his part is seen as reflecting its response to the perceiver's resolute and strong actions. In other words, if another state is believed to be hostile, contradictory indicators are ignored, dismissed as propaganda ploys, or interpreted as signs of weakness.[35] The effects of selective attention are reinforced by mirror images that exist when each party in a conflict maintains a negative image of the other party but holds a positive self-image; they are aggressive, we are defensive.[36]

Many historical examples illustrate how leaders and other key decision-makers often preserve their stereotyped images of the enemy in the face of what seems in retrospect to have been clear evidence to the contrary, and as a result have missed opportunities for conflict resolution. The most cited study in this respect is Holsti's pioneering research of the relationship between the former Secretary of State John Foster Dulles's image of the enemy, in this case the Soviet Union, and American decision-making during the cold war. Holsti demonstrated that Dulles perceived and interpreted information concerning the Soviet Union in a manner that was consistent with his inherent bad faith image of the Communist leadership. Although Dulles clearly perceived Soviet hostility to be declining, he attributed decreasing Soviet hostility to factors such as increasing Soviet frustration in the conduct of its foreign policy and decreasing Soviet capabilities, rather than to any real change in the character of the Soviet regime.[37] These findings had, and in fact still have, important implications for the problem of resolving international conflicts. They indicate that as long as decision-makers on either side stick to rigid inherent bad faith images of the other party, there is little likelihood that friendly proposals and even real offers to decrease tensions will achieve the desired effect of reduction of tension. To put it in Holsti's own words: "They suggest the fallacy of thinking that peaceful settlement of outstanding international issues is simply a problem of working out good plans."[38]

Schemas and Analogies

The tendency of the human mind to categorize leads also to the construction of schemas. A schema is an abstract memory structure that represents a hierarchical organization of knowledge about a particular type of stimulus or concept. It usually includes a category label, specific attributes of the stimulus or concept, the relationships among the attributes, and particular instances of the category.[39] Schema-based processing is cognitively efficient because organizing material schematically increases the limited ability of individuals to store information in their memory. Individuals can ignore, as well, the details of new stimulus when it is perceived as another instance of some preexisting schema and can make decisions faster. Moreover, as schemas represents past experience or are based on historical knowledge, schemas enable political leaders and other foreign policy decision-makers to use stored knowledge about situations and events with which they had prior experience, to interpret similar situations and events with little processing of information.[40] Thus, schemas clarify the relationship between policy-makers' memories and their decisions on current issues. But as the use of schemas involves selective attention it also foresees a tendency of policy-makers' to draw conclusions about current situations unjustified by the available information, and then to maintain these erroneous assessments in the face of discrepant facts when they diagnose a situation and select policy options.[41] This is especially the case in the use of analogies, which is a specific example of how schemas influence perception.

Individuals use analogical reasoning as a cognitive shortcut to give meaning to current events by perceiving new situations as being comparable to some other event in the past. To put it in another way: "History does not repeat itself in the real world but it does repeat itself in the 'reality world' of the mind."[42] Firsthand knowledge of situations that individuals have experienced earlier in their life, especially major historical events that have made a strong impression on decision-makers or were important for their nation, are used by individuals as an analogy for a contemporary one. Political leaders and other foreign policy-makers, in particular, assume that there are lessons to be drawn from the past and therefore have a tendency to force the present in constructs of the past. As a result, analogies determine the images that influence decision-makers' interpretation of the present situation and their decision about the best response. Reasoning by analogy provides decision-makers a useful shortcut to cope with a complicated current event, but it also hinders decision-makers to see aspects of the present event that are different from an earlier situation.[43]

One of the most obvious examples of analogical reasoning is the frequent use of the Munich analogy. It refers to the agreement of the British Prime Minister Neville Chamberlain and the French Prime Minister Edouard Daladier during a conference at Munich in 1938 to allow Germany's leader Adolf Hitler to occupy parts of Czechoslovakia so that ethnic Germans in this territory could unite with their homeland. Yielding to Hitler's pressure, Chamberlain and Daladier believed that this concession would prevent a major armed conflict with Germany and save the peace in Europe. However, this appeasement policy provoked further territorial demands by Hitler and turned out to be the run-up to the Second World War.[44] Different political leaders expressed on many occasions their determination to avoid repeating the mistakes of the Munich sellout. Since Munich was a failure, any attempt to solve a crisis by concession and compromise should be avoided; only firmness will avoid a major war. For example, successive American presidents and other policy-makers used the analogy of Munich to defend and justify the American continuous military involvement in the conflict between North Vietnam and South Vietnam. A retreat from South Vietnam was seen as surrender to North Vietnam's blackmail that would result in increased Communist aggression in neighboring Asian countries.[45]

However, this example also illustrates that reliance on historical analogies that compare past and present situations can lead to incorrect diagnosis of a new situation as one analogy does not hold in other historical cases. The causal linkage that is supposed to be present in the earlier historical case of the Munich Agreement between a policy of appeasement and a major war may be only one of a number of causes that have led to such an outcome. Moreover, in the comparison between the two cases no careful examination was made to see whether all these causes were also present in the later case. Since the two cases differ in important features and details it is doubtful whether a policy of appeasement toward North Vietnam would have caused a major war in Asia.[46]

THE ROLE OF PERSONALITY

The cognitive dynamics discussed so far characterize the pattern of foreign policy-making by political leaders and other key foreign policy-makers nearly all the time. But as Rosati reminds us: "Although cognitive predispositions and tendencies are likely, similar cognitive patterns for individuals do not automatically trigger similar outcomes."[47] Among the many reasons that may explain such dissimilarities psychologists assume that these differences are rooted in personality characteristics.[48] Since personality traits differ across individuals, they can affect perceptions of the policy environment and therefore result in some variation in the diagnosis of new situations or response to foreign policy problems. According to this assumption a change in leadership, which brings to power a new personality, would have an observable effect on a country's foreign policy. However, a number of foreign policy analysts have cautioned against the assumption that personality characteristics explain an individual's behavior. Drawing on research results that examined such a relationship Michael Sullivan concludes: "changes in individual leadership does not appear *systematically* related to changes in major trends of nation-state behavior."[49] The obvious exception might be the coming to power of the Soviet leader Mikhail Gorbachev who generated a fundamental shift in the foreign policy of the Soviet Union and made the ending of the cold war possible. But even in the case of Gorbachev, Sullivan says, "still no central set of personality characteristics that he may have possessed have been established as having triggered the transformational phenomena often attributed to him."[50]

Nevertheless, advocates of the personality approach assume that personality traits are underlying and are essential dispositions that exert generalized effects on foreign policy outcomes. Reviewing the literature on this topic David Winter concluded that a war disposition in foreign policy (advocacy of the use of force and perceiving the enemy as a threat) is associated with a powerful and dominant behavioral style, along with simplistic cognitive structures involving nationalistic beliefs and distrust. Peace dispositions in foreign policy (against the use of force and in favor of cooperation and arms limitation) result from a trusting and extroverted behavioral style along with cognitive complexity and self-respect.[51] Other researchers have argued that under some conditions and in specific circumstances personal characteristics explain for a large part a particular foreign policy outcome. This is, for example, the case when a leader is the head of government; when power is concentrated in the hands of an individual leader; when there is a crisis; when the situation is ambiguous; or when the international circumstances are fluid.[52] Margaret Hermann and Thomas Preston have focused on what happens when a single leader has the power (by a constitution, law, or general practice) to make the choice regarding how to deal with a particular foreign policy problem.

To understand the impact of the personality of predominant leaders on a government's foreign policy, Hermann and Preston distinguish first between two types of leaders: the more goal-driven leaders and leaders who are more responsive to the current situation. The more goal-driven leaders come to foreign policy with a particular perspective or set of priorities. Such leaders, Hermann and Preston say, perceive information from their environment selectively; they will see what they want to see and, consequently, will reinterpret situations and are determined to find information which supports their definition of the situation. Goal-driven leaders are more likely to engage in conflict, using tactics such as "rally around the flag" to reduce the effectiveness of domestic opposition that may disagree with a particular action. The more contextually responsive leaders modify their behavior to fit the demands of the situation. In their definition of the situation and their response to foreign policy problems, they are relatively open to incoming information and guided by evidence they receive from the environment. According to Hermann and Preston, such leaders are predisposed to seek support for their international decisions and are therefore less likely to pursue extreme policies such as confrontation and war or peace initiatives and international agreements, unless the choice enjoys the support of important constituencies.[53]

By combining the leaders' openness to information and responsiveness to political constraints Hermann and Preston describe several leadership styles: crusaders, strategists, pragmatists, and opportunists. A leadership style refers to the political leader's preferred methods of making decisions. For example, when leaders are closed to information from the environment and challenge political constraints they become crusaders. They are convinced that available information supports their position and do not wait to take action until the time is right. By contrast, when leaders are open to information and respect constraints from the political setting they are usually opportunistic. For such leaders inaction is preferable to action that has the potential of losing support and building opposition. To understand the different reactions of leaders to what is essentially the same foreign policy problem, Hermann and Preston incorporate in their analysis, in addition to the leaders' differences in openness to incoming information and responsiveness to political constraints, the leaders' difference in motivation for action. A leader can be motivated to act by a specific interest, an ideology and a particular problem and cause, or by the desire for a certain kind of acceptance, approval, and support from others in their environment. The first kind of leaders are more concerned with the issues facing the government, while the second sort of leaders are more interested in the responses of relevant constituencies. This additional distinction makes it possible for Hermann and Preston to differentiate further between leadership styles (expansionistic, evangelistic, incremental, charismatic, directive, consultative, reactive, and accommodative), and argue that each type of leadership style has different effects on the kind of foreign policy such a leader pursues. However, as Hermann and Preston emphasize, these leadership styles are ideal types, and in practice a leader can move between different leadership styles or manifest in the same situations more than one leadership style.[54]

LEADERS ARE COGNITIVE ACTORS

My discussion of the basic psychological principles and cognitive constructs underlying a leader's diagnosis of the situation and evaluation of the policy options for dealing with the foreign policy problem he faces, has pointed out that political leaders and other key foreign policy-makers must be treated as cognitive actors rather than rational actors. Allison has illustrated in his classic study of the American and Soviet decision-making during the Cuban missile crisis in 1962, that the rational actor approach is widely used in thinking about foreign policy behavior and international relations.[55] Those who employ the rational actor approach assume that foreign policy-makers base their response to an international event upon a rational process of decision-making, using a specified procedure to produce a decision. Once foreign policy-makers have recognized a problem and have clarified their goals, they are expected to search for relevant information and identify alternative courses of action. To evaluate the options they identify, decision-makers estimate the consequences that each of these alternative courses of action is likely to produce in terms of costs and benefits. An increase in the perceived costs that will follow from an alternative course of action reduces the likelihood of that action being chosen, while a decrease in the perceived costs of an alternative increases the likelihood of that action being chosen. Ultimately decision-makers choose that alternative which promises the greatest gain and is considered the optimal course of action with regard to the objectives pursued.[56]

However, actual patterns of decision-making do not follow a rational process of decision-making. Advocates of the application of the assumption of rational behavior have already acknowledged that decision-makers use a satisfying rather than an optimizing decision rule. Because of the limited capacity of individuals to process information and the fact that an optimal diagnosis of the situation and evaluation of options requires enormous quantities of information that is not available, the search for an optimal course of action is not practical or simply not possible. As a result decision-makers do not search for all options and do not consider all possible costs and benefits, but settle for a course of action that offers a sufficient rather than an optimal outcome. What is more, when decision-makers employ an incremental strategy of policy-making, they consider a narrow range of policy alternatives that differ only slightly from existing policies.[57] Herbert Simon, for instance, has concluded that: "to understand and predict human behavior, we have to deal with the realities of human rationality, that is, with bounded rationality."[58]

Furthermore, as prospect theory suggests, under conditions of risk when individuals define the situation and evaluate the risky options before they make a choice, losses have a greater impact than gains. Since decision-makers are more concerned about prospective losses than prospective gains, they tend to accept a risk for avoiding losses. In addition, the choice between options will be influenced by the way in which the alternatives are framed. Individuals will choose the risky option when the choice is presented in terms of avoiding losses.[59] Framing choices in terms of potential losses or gains becomes therefore crucial to the conduct of foreign policy. For example, during the Kosovo crisis in the late 1990s, American and European policy-makers expected that the Serbian leader Slobodan Milosevic as a result of political, economic, and military pressure, would change his oppressive policy toward ethnic Albanian Muslims in the Serbian region of Kosovo and would accept a compromise that would allow the holding of a referendum on Kosovan independence. But Milosevic considered the loss of Kosovo as an intolerable loss. He was willing to accept considerable risks and bear significant costs, in order not to lose Kosovo.[60]

The notion of bounded rationality and prospect theory touch upon the psychology of the rational actor and as a result have turned the rational actor into a bounded rational actor and have raised some doubts about his rational behavior under conditions of risk. But both modifications have not really challenged the picturing of foreign policy-makers as rational actors. The cognitive approach, on the other hand, is a real deviation from the rational actor approach. As I have described in this chapter, those who make foreign policy decisions are likely to employ in the processing of new information a number of cognitive constructs and mental shortcuts that help them to deal with uncertainty and complexity. Yet, the filtering of information through beliefs and images that are already programmed in the individual's mind and the use of stereotypes and historical analogies that result in biases and errors in judgment, distorts their diagnosis of the situation and evaluation of options, and consequently influence their choice of the appropriate course of action. Hence the many cognitive limits imposed on the possibility of rational information processing makes political leaders and other foreign policy-makers not even bounded rational actors but cognitive actors.[61]

2

A First Cut

The Relevance of Leadership

In this chapter I approach the two issues under consideration in this book from the perspective of the national leaders. As I have argued in the previous chapter, the personal beliefs, the individual images, and the personality characteristics of these leaders are crucial for determining the specific policy problem with which policy-makers must deal and the way they formulate and evaluate the alternative policy options for dealing with the problem they face. In order to describe these beliefs and images I will identify in each issue the key political leaders and explore the content of their beliefs and images, which I will then link to a particular decision. However, in an attempt to increase the explanatory power of these beliefs and images, I introduce some restrictions in establishing such a linkage.

First of all, as George suggests, there must be a correspondence between the content of a leader's beliefs and the content of his decision. As he explains, if the characteristics of the decision are consistent with the leader's beliefs, there is at least a presumption that the beliefs may have played a causal role in this particular instance of decision-making. To increase the causal significance of the consistency between beliefs and actions such coherence must also be encountered repeatedly in a sequence of interrelated decisions taken by a leader over a period of time. Secondly, following Walker's argument, the scope of these linkages is restricted to decision-making situations with characteristics that permit a leader to exercise his personal influence. Walker maintains that to make it possible to establish a connection between a leader's belief and his foreign policy behavior, he must conduct personally or dominate indirectly all stages of the policy-making process, that is, the decision-making as well as the action or implementation phase. This is a very important restriction. However, it does not mean that a leader must have absolute control over the policy-making process, or that he must be a predominant leader in the sense that he is the only one individual who has the authority to commit or withhold the resources of the government with regard to foreign policy problems. To improve further the explanatory power of a leader's beliefs and images, I will also try to meet three conditions that Holsti considers to be important for the establishment of a connection between a decision-maker's beliefs and his policy choices. He suggests that the likelihood of such a linkage may be greater in nonroutine decision-making situations, like decisions to initiate or terminate major international undertakings, including wars or interventions; in circumstances that require decisions at the top of the government hierarchy by leaders who are relatively free from organizational and other constraints; and in unanticipated events in which initial reactions are likely to reflect cognitive constructs.[1]

With these restrictions in mind I will turn now to explain the relationship between the beliefs, images, and personality characteristics of Israeli and Palestinian leaders and the decisions regarding the dilemma of partition, and the issue of a two-state solution. Both issues involved certainly nonroutine decision-making situations and required decisions at the highest level of government. But in order to make the correspondence between the content of a leader's beliefs and the policy outcome meaningful I will limit my choice of relevant leaders in both cases to those leaders who conducted personally or dominated indirectly all stages of the policy-making process. Other leaders who were involved in the policy-making process but do not meet this decisive condition are excluded from my analysis. This means that in the first issue I will deal only with the Israeli leader David Ben-Gurion. As I will explain later, the Palestinians lacked any serious form of leadership and certainly a leader who controlled the Arab policy-making regarding partition. In the second issue I will consider on the Israeli side two leaders, Yitzhak Rabin and Shimon Peres, and on the Palestinian side the PLO leader Yasser Arafat.

THE DILEMMA OF PARTITION

The Jewish acceptance of partition was without any doubt the achievement of Ben-Gurion. This founding father of the state of Israel was the charismatic dominant leader of the Jewish community during the period in which the Jewish policy on partition was decided. As leader of the mainstream labor Zionist movement in Palestine, he served in the 1920s as secretary general of the trade union movement, the Histadrut, and became in 1935 chairman of the Jewish Agency

Executive (JAE) that made him the most important leader of the organized Jewish community. From 1946 he also held the defense portfolio in the JAE, which gave him the power to lead the military effort of the Jewish community in the decisive confrontation with the British authorities and the Palestine Arab community after the Second World War. As the first prime minister and defense minister of the state of Israel he was the strong leader of the newborn state and served as its minister of defense in the war of 1948 and kept this position, with a short break in the early 1950s, until his retirement in 1963.[2] Ben-Gurion can certainly be identified as the leader who was the major political strategist behind the Jewish policies regarding partition. Although the formal decision-making was made by the JAE, as I will discuss in chapter 4, he had absolute control over the policy-making process. Ben-Gurion was able to concentrate and keep the responsibility for the Jewish military preparations for the struggle in Palestine and the conduct of the military operations during the war of 1948, in his own hands. He was also very influential in determining the diplomatic course of the Jewish community and the formulation of the foreign policy of the newborn state.

In what follows, I will therefore focus on the beliefs, images, and personal characteristics of Ben-Gurion. This means that I consider other Jewish leaders involved in the formulation of policy about partition as less relevant. Moshe Sharett, for instance, head of the Political Department of the Jewish Agency and the first foreign minister of the state of Israel, took part in the decision-making process that led to the decision to accept partition and to establish the state of Israel. But the influence that he was able to exercise on the political and military policy-making process, compared to Ben-Gurion, was quite marginal. Moreover, as Shlomo Ben-Ami argues, Ben-Gurion and Sharett shared a common worldview. Ben-Ami disagrees with those analysts of Israel's foreign policy who picture Ben-Gurion and Sharett as poles apart. The two leaders represent in these studies two contrasting views of the world and embody different strategies for dealing with the Palestinians and Arab neighbors.[3] While Ben-Gurion is seen as the activist militant leader who did not believe in a peaceful accommodation with the hostile Arab enemies that surrounded Israel, Sharett is described as being a more moderate politician who stood for a policy of peaceful coexistence with the Arab world. Ben-Ami argues that the assumed division expressed itself more in Sharett's intimate reflection in his personal diary than in real life and actual policies. He refers to Abba Eban, a close associate of Sharett, who claimed that the difference in their approach was "trivial to the point of being microscopic."[4]

Ben-Gurion's definition of the situation was based on a number of interrelated beliefs and images about the fundamental nature of the conflict between the Jews and Arabs and the image of the adversary; the utility of military force; the need for the support of a western power and the importance of self-reliance; the control a leader has over historical development and the importance of timing of action to realize political goals.

Nature of the Conflict and Image of the Adversary

Like many other members of his generation of founding fathers of the Zionist movement Ben-Gurion had almost no knowledge of the Arab civilization and Arab language. He had clearly no intention of integrating into the Arab Middle East. As he admitted: "we want to return to the East only in the geographic sense, for our objective is to create here a European culture."[5] It is therefore no wonder that Ben-Gurion, who arrived in Palestine as a Zionist pioneer in 1906, had the tendency to be blind to the native Arab population. Like many other Zionist leaders he was initially indifferent to the presence of Arab Palestinians, ignored their national aspirations, and had no knowledge of writings on Arab nationalism. As most other Zionist leaders Ben-Gurion had a stereotype image of the Palestine Arabs as primitive and tribal, who lacked any sense of a national community. In his perception they could only benefit from the progress brought by the Zionist pioneering enterprise.[6]

At first Ben-Gurion also misperceived the Arab-Jewish conflict. Like many Zionist socialist leaders who on their arrival to Palestine adhered to a Marxist logic, he initially interpreted the problems between the Jewish settlers and the local Arab population in Palestine in class terms. As the Jewish pioneers and the Arab peasants were both seen as proletariat, the clash was in essence a class conflict between the Jewish pioneers and the Arab landlords. It could be solved, in his view, by approaching the Arab masses directly and uniting the Jewish and Arab proletariat against the Arab landlords and reactionary Arab middle class. Such a perception entirely underestimated the national sentiments of the Palestine Arabs.[7]

However, gradually Ben-Gurion became aware of the basic enmity of the Arabs of Palestine toward the Jews, and developed a deep belief that the conflict between Jews and Arabs in Palestine was a zero-sum game. He saw no solution to the Arab-Jewish conflict. He said already in the early 1920s: "I do not know what Arab will agree that Palestine should belong to the Jews—even if the Jews learn Arabic."[8] When the

Arab riots in 1929 took place he was quick to realize that this was the beginning of a violent movement against the Zionist presence in Palestine that will not disappear. From his discussions with local Arab leaders he also drew the conclusion that a comprehensive agreement was not possible. As the Arab revolt in 1936 began against the British, Ben-Gurion was convinced that the Arab aggression was actually aimed at the entire presence of the Zionists in Palestine. It reinforced his certainty that there was no chance for any agreement with the Palestine Arabs, and that a military confrontation between the Jewish community and the Arab community in Palestine was inevitable. As he said in May 1936: "we both want Palestine, and this is the fundamental conflict."[9] He never believed that the Arab community would settle for a political compromise that would allow the establishment of a Jewish state in Palestine. Since this was the ultimate Zionist goal it was obvious that both parties moved toward a violent military clash rather than a peaceful political solution.[10] This deep conviction about an unavoidable war between the two groups of people, in combination with his belief in the use of force, on which I elaborate later, was an important drive behind Ben-Gurion's effort to make sure that the Jewish community was well prepared and strong enough for such a war.

But the zero-sum conception of the conflict had also another important consequence. It created a mindset that was open to the idea and implementation of transfer and expulsion of the local Palestine Arab population from the Jewish state. As Benny Morris illustrates Ben-Gurion was not the only Jewish leader who considered the option of transfer seriously in order to create a Jewish majority in a future Jewish state in Palestine. In fact, the topic of transfer was discussed intensely among the Zionist leadership in the 1930s and early 1940s. Many Jewish leaders, including Sharett, considered the question of transfer not as a moral or immoral problem, but more as a practical and tactical problem. Morris, who studied the birth of the Palestinian refugee problem extensively, has concluded that there was no direct causal connection between this thinking about transfer and the creation of the refugee problem in the course of the 1948 War. He could not find any indication for the existence of a Jewish plan to expel the Arabs of Palestine. He has emphasized that the Palestinian Arabs and Arab countries started the war of 1948, and that a large number of refugees did not flee their homes under direct Israeli threat. But Morris has also stressed a readiness to resort to compulsory transfer which was preconditioned by the idea that after the Palestinians and Arabs had initiated the war, transfer was what the Jewish state's survival and future well-being demanded.[11] As Morris says: "Expulsion was in the air in the war of 1948 . . . with Ben-Gurion himself setting the tone and indicating direction, usually resorting to a nod and a wink if not actually issuing explicit orders."[12]

The fundamental belief about the nature of the conflict did not change after the Jewish victory in the war of 1948. Ben-Gurion believed that Arab hostility did not die with the signing of the armistice agreements with the surrounding Arab countries in 1949. It gave Israel only time to prepare itself for the next military round. He was convinced that the Arabs would never forgive their humiliating military loss and that once they recovered from their defeat they will seek revenge. Their aim was and remained the destruction of the Jewish state. On many occasions Ben-Gurion expressed the view that he had no illusions about peace with the Arabs as long as they considered Israel to be an illegitimate entity and insisted on two conditions for any settlement: the return of the Palestinian refugees to their original homes and the retreat of Israel to the 1947 partition lines. Ben-Gurion's first priority was to ensure Israel's sovereignty and security in the 1949 armistice borders, not a peace treaty. As he had already declared in the 1930s peace with the Arabs was not an end in itself, only a means to realize the establishment of a Jewish state. The armistice lines created by the 1948 War offered Israel a better defense than the 1947 partition lines, and the departure of a large number of Palestine Arabs liberated Israel from the burden of dealing with a big hostile Arab community within its own borders. During indirect contacts with Arab leaders about a peace settlement Ben-Gurion therefore ruled out any change in the territorial and demographic status quo created by the 1948 War. He actually preferred a status quo without peace than peace without the status quo. In this connection it is important to note that Sharett was also unwilling to pay the price of such concessions in exchange for a peace settlement.[13]

The Utility of Military Force

Ben-Gurion strongly believed that the building of Jewish military force and the use of military power to advance political goals was critical for the establishment of a Jewish state in Palestine. After the British retreat from its commitment to establish a Jewish state and the brutal repression of Jewish immigration to Palestine, Ben-Gurion did not hesitate to begin an armed resistance against the British as he believed that it would put pressure on the British government to end the British rule over Palestine. As a show of force he ordered the beginning of an illegal immigration campaign from Europe to Palestine in spite of a British blockade, and authorized military actions against British strategic targets in Palestine, although he realized that this would result in a direct confrontation between the British military in Palestine and the underground forces of the Jewish community.[14]

Ben-Gurion firmly believed that the conflict between the two national movements would be decided by force. He was convinced that only Jewish military strength would prevent the physical destruction of the Jewish community in Palestine. Ben-Gurion was also certain that Jewish military power would be decisive in shaping the territorial dimensions of the Jewish state, and that the outcome of military operations during the war in 1948 would determine the size of the territory of the state of Israel. For these reasons, in 1946, he assumed responsibility for the military preparation of the Jewish community in Palestine for an inescapable war with the Arabs, and made the crucial strategic decisions before and during the war. It was Ben-Gurion who decided on the priorities of military operations, and sometimes overruled his military commanders. Ben-Gurion, for instance, decided against the wish of some of his military commanders to leave large parts of the West Bank in the hands of Transjordan to avoid the inclusion of heavily Arab populated areas within the borders of Israel, and to concentrate instead on the occupation of the thinly populated southern part of Palestine, the Negev. He also ordered his generals to change from a defensive to an offensive strategy, and to attack on one front while holding the other fronts.[15]

But military power had for Ben-Gurion another vital function. As mentioned earlier, for Ben-Gurion the maintenance of the status quo was more important than peace. But this did not mean that he was not interested in peace, as it was impossible, in his view, to build a country in a permanent state of war. However, since Ben-Gurion believed that the Arabs understood only the language of force, he was sure that ultimately only Jewish military power and deterrence will compel the Palestine Arabs and the Arab states to come to terms with the emergence and existence of a Jewish state. Only when the Arab leaders were convinced that they couldn't destroy Israel they could be persuaded to make peace.[16] This belief was an important motivation for Ben-Gurion's decision to produce an Israeli nuclear weapon. As Aronson maintains, the reason for that decision was not just to deter the Arabs from starting another war. Ben-Gurion also hoped, according to Aronson, that the Arabs needed a reason to reconcile themselves completely to the presence of Israel among them. Once the Arabs saw Israel as indestructible, positive incentives could be added to the nuclear one.[17]

Support of a Western Power and Self-Reliance

A crucial element in Ben-Gurion's strategic thinking was the basic belief that the Jewish community in Palestine, and later the state of Israel, should never operate without the support of a western superpower. From the very beginning of his leadership he was convinced that the diplomatic support of a major western power is vital for the complete realization of the Zionist objectives. In first instance Ben-Gurion followed the pragmatic moderate diplomatic course of Chaim Weizman, the preeminent Zionist leader who was the driving force behind the formation of the Jewish connection with Britain, which was based on keeping the British commitment to a Jewish homeland in Palestine. When the British government retreated just before the Second World War from its initial support for the Zionist objective of establishing a Jewish state by its decision to ignore the recommendation of the Peel commission in favor of partition, and published instead a White Paper that imposed strict limits on the number of Jewish immigrants, placed restrictions on the purchase of Arab land, and declared the British intention to establish in Palestine one state in which Arabs and Jews will share authority but where the Jews would remain a minority, Ben-Gurion was reluctant to adopt an anti-British course of action that could result in a definite loss of the British support for the Zionist project.[18] While the British policies were seen by other Jewish leaders as a critical blow for the Zionist aspirations and a betrayal of the Jewish cause in an attempt to appease the Arab governments, Ben-Gurion proclaimed: "We will fight with the British against Hitler as if there were no White Paper; we will fight the White Paper as if there were no war."[19]

However, after the war Ben-Gurion lost complete faith in the goodwill of the British government toward the Zionist enterprise. As the British government continued its rejection of large-scale immigration to Palestine, even for displaced Jewish survivors of the Holocaust, and refused to promote the establishment of an independent Jewish state against the will of the Arabs, he saw no other choice but to fight back and start a rebellion against what he perceived a brutal British rule.[20] In search for a new western power, Ben-Gurion turned toward the United States. During the war he already thought that the Zionist movement had to proceed in a new direction. He foresaw a major change in the international order as a result of the war and expected the United States to play a vital role in shaping the new world order. He therefore believed that the support of the rising superpower for a Jewish state was crucial and the key to a Zionist success. As he said: "The moment we succeed in convincing America to support the

Zionist solution of the Jewish question, all our problems today . . . will be diminished."[21] But although he was sure about the change of course, it did not mean that he had full confidence in the readiness of the United States to assist the Jewish community in Palestine. He certainly had his doubts. Referring to the Munich Agreement of 1938, in which Britain and France allowed Germany to occupy part of Czechoslovakia in attempt to avoid war by appeasing the German Nazi leader Adolf Hitler, Ben-Gurion said: "America did not stand up for the Czechs, will it stand up for us? Will it quarrel with England because of us? As far as we know, Roosevelt does not believe in Palestine as a haven for Jewish immigration."[22]

It is against this historical background that Ben-Gurion developed a strong belief in the need for self-reliance. This belief is summarized in his well-known statement: "Our future does not depend on what the gentiles say but on what the Jews do."[23] Self-reliance was the cornerstone of his foreign and security policy, as he believed that neither the UN nor any other external power would protect the life of Israeli citizens. This explains the disregard that Ben-Gurion repeatedly showed for the UN. Although he acknowledged the role the UN partition plan had in the creation of the Jewish state, he always emphasized that it was only due to the Israeli defense forces that Israel existed, not the UN which failed to implement the UN resolution on partition. After the Arab states' invasion of Palestine and the Israeli counterattack that resulted in the occupation of areas that were beyond the partition lines, Ben-Gurion officially declared the death of the UN resolution. Sharett, by the way, supported Ben-Gurion's policy of keeping the conquered territories under Israel's control. He admitted that this was contrary to UN resolution 181, but he considered this to be a bitter necessity.[24]

Ben-Gurion's indifference toward the UN was clearly demonstrated in his first clash with the UN at the end of 1949 over the status of Jerusalem. Under the UN partition resolution the city of Jerusalem was treated as a separate entity with a special international regime. But in the 1948 War Israel and Jordan divided the city among themselves. When the UN General Assembly adopted a resolution that placed Jerusalem under UN rule, he declared that Israel would never accept foreign rule over Jerusalem and to underline his rejection of internationalization decided to move the parliament and government offices of the newborn state from Tel Aviv to Jerusalem. Ben-Gurion's deliberately chose the confrontation with the UN because he considered the question of Jerusalem to be an important test case. He was convinced that if he would have complied with the UN resolution it would be followed by more international pressure to retreat behind the 1947 partition lines and to take back the refugees. On the other hand, if Israel was successful in resisting the international pressure regarding the internationalization of Jerusalem the problems of borders and refugees were solved as well. Ben-Gurion would show the lack of concern about the UN again in the early 1950s when Israel was faced with the armed infiltration of Palestinian commandos across the armistice lines who carried out attacks on Israeli civilians. He did not rely on the UN to stop the infiltration, but implemented a policy of military retaliation against civilian and military targets in Jordan and Egypt to persuade their leaders to end the infiltration.[25]

Control over Historical Development and Timing of Action

Ben-Gurion had a deep messianic drive to establish a Jewish state in Palestine. He strongly believed that people can influence historical developments and shape desired outcomes. He therefore stressed that the salvation of the Jewish people could only be achieved through the creation of facts on the ground, as only those who settle and work it possess the land. But Ben-Gurion was also pragmatic. He believed in the importance of timing of action to advance one's interests, and had an intense conviction in the obligation of a leader to seize the historical chances that can change the fate of a nation. Ben-Gurion believed in the fundamental right of the Jews, like any other nation, to self-determination and he emphasized the justified Jewish historical claim to the whole land of Palestine as the Jewish homeland. But he took a practical attitude toward the idea of partition every time he saw an opportunity to create a Jewish state in a part of Palestine. Sovereignty was, in his view, more important than territory.[26]

Ben-Gurion's decisions to endorse the idea of partition when the Peel commission suggested it for the first time in 1937 and again when UNSCOP proposed it in 1947, were determined by his strong sense for timing and his deep conviction that a leader should grab the opportunity that can decide history. He supported the Peel commission's plan to create two states for the simple reason that it offered a unique opportunity to establish a sovereign Jewish state. Even if such a state was small in size, it could open the possibility of unlimited Jewish immigration from Europe and serve the immediate need to absorb as many Jewish refugees as possible from Europe who wanted to escape the threat posed by the rise to power of Adolf Hitler in Germany in 1933. He emphasized that accepting partition does not mean that he gave up the territorial claim for the whole of Palestine. Such a modest Jewish state was only a first stage in implementing the Jewish claim for a much larger territory and provided therefore, a possible springboard for future expansion.[27] To put it in his own words: "Erect a Jewish state at once, even if it is not in the whole land. The rest will come in the course of time. It must come."[28]

Ten years later Ben-Gurion followed a similar rational and supported the UNSCOP partition plan mainly for tactical reasons. By approving the establishment of a viable Jewish state along the lines suggested by UNSCOP, he explained, the Jewish community gained time until it was strong enough and well prepared to fight the Arabs. Once again he stressed that the borders of the Jewish independent state as laid down in the partition plan were not final, since he believed that "there are no final settlements in history, there are no eternal borders, and no political demands are final."[29] He declared that he would respect the UN resolution on partition but he also made clear that if the Arabs did not do so, he felt no obligation to be bound by the borders of the Jewish state as specified in the UN resolution. During the war of 1948 when successful military operations made it possible to extend the territory of the new state beyond the proposed partition lines, Ben-Gurion indeed renounced the UN resolution and declared that the political borders of the state will be determined by the limits of military force.[30]

However, the best illustration of Ben-Gurion's strong belief in the ability of political leaders to influence historical development and shape desired outcomes by taking risks and choosing the best time for action, is the historic decision to establish the state of Israel. On May 14, 1948, the very day the British left Palestine, he declared the creation of an independent Jewish state. He did this in spite of the certainty that such a decision will cause an all-out war with the Arab Palestinians and the neighboring Arab states. Ben-Gurion was determined to go ahead with the declaration of independence despite the concern among some members of the provisional government about the ability of the Jewish community to resist an invasion of the large and well-equipped Arab armies. He even took the risk of taking a vote within the provisional government on the immediate declaration of independence that he only won by a tight majority of six to four. He also ignored the American pressure to postpone the establishment of a Jewish state, and the American warning that the newborn state could not expect any military help from the United States against the invading Arab armies. As Ben-Ami notes, the decision of Ben-Gurion was the move of a leader who decided against all odds not to miss his and his people's encounter with history.[31]

His sense for the best timing for action was also visible in the views he expressed regarding the sensitive issue of a forced transfer of Arab inhabitants from the areas that would make up the territory of the Jewish state. As I have mentioned earlier, Ben-Gurion like many other Zionist leaders wanted a Jewish state with as few Arabs remaining as possible. This could mean a compulsory transfer, but as Ben-Gurion emphasized, it could take place only during a war. As he indicated, what might be impossible in normal times is possible in revolutionary times.[32] The war of 1948 was probably such an opportunity. As Morris has argued the Palestinian refugee problem was born of war not by design. Referring to Ben-Gurion's role he says that there is no indication that he adopted a policy of expulsion, but he had certainly set the tone that encouraged the military commanders to clear from the areas conquered all hostile elements, or as it was sometimes formulated to assist the inhabitants wishing to leave the conquered area.[33]

THE ABSENCE OF A PALESTINIAN LEADERSHIP

As I mentioned in the introduction to this chapter it is impossible to identify a Palestine Arab leader who controlled on the Palestinian side the policy-making process during the decisive period in which the Palestine Arabs had to deal with the issue of partition. As a result of the failure of Palestinian institution formation during the years that the British ruled over Palestine, as I will explain in chapter 4, the Palestine Arabs missed an institutionalized decision-making process that could cope with the problem of partition. In fact, the Palestine Arabs surrendered the policy-making and the diplomatic effort concerning Palestine to the Arab League that was founded in 1945. As a consequence the Arab Palestine leaders could exercise little influence on the political discussions and the collective decisions taken by the Arab leaders who tried to conduct a common policy and present a common political front on the issue of partition. This does not mean that members of the Arab elite in Palestine did not claim the leadership of the Palestine Arab community. The most prominent person in this respect was Hajj Amin al-Husayni, who is seen by many analysts as the dominant political leader of the Palestine Arabs. He drew his political influence from two functions. The first one was the post of *mufti* of Jerusalem that made him also the head of the Supreme Muslim Council (SMC), a body of Muslim religious dignitaries, which supervised and controlled religious courts. It gave him an important political and economic power base for the building of a huge and countrywide patronage network. The second function was the presidency of the Arab Higher Committee (AHC) a permanent executive body which represented various Palestinian political organizations.[34]

In 1936 the AHC initiated a general strike and organized a nationwide demonstration against the British authorities. When this political protest was taken over by more militant local leaders who intensified the rebellion and turned it into a military guerrilla war, the British suppressed the revolt by brutal military actions against the Palestine Arab populations and arrested and exiled many of the nationalist leaders. Al-Husayni managed to escape to Lebanon. When he also collaborated with Nazi Germany during the Second World War, the British did not allow his return to Palestine after the war. It removed him further from the negotiation tables and the international forums where the future of Palestine was debated after the war. He had also little influence on the decision-making process within the Arab League, where he clashed frequently with the Arab leaders about their true intentions regarding Palestine and criticized the Arab League policies. However, his unconditional rejection of partition was fully shared by all the leaders of the Arab countries.[35]

From his exile in neighboring Arab countries Al Husayni tried to maintain his political influence on the political developments in Palestine and resist any challenge to his dominance of the national movement. But as Rashid Khalidi observes, in exile farther and farther away from Palestine Al Husayni was increasingly out of touch with events on the ground, and was unable to lead the national movement effectively from a distance. This brings him to the conclusion that when the Palestinians faced their most fateful challenge in 1947–1949 they were practically without any leadership.[36]

MUTUAL RECOGNITION AND ACCEPTANCE OF A TWO-STATE SOLUTION

The peacemakers who made the conclusion of the Oslo accords possible were Rabin and Arafat. Although Israeli and PLO officials conducted the actual negotiations in a location near Oslo, these two leaders controlled every stage in the negotiations, approved every detail in the agreements, and used their authority to legitimize the outcome. It was their definition of the situation, based on a set of interrelated beliefs, which led to the making of the historical breakthrough in the Israeli-Palestinian relations. Since Peres fulfilled a crucial role in initiating the negotiations that led to the Oslo accords and the

successful conclusion of the Oslo agreements I will include him as well
in my analysis. All three leaders meet the restrictions I have discussed
in my introductory remarks to this chapter, regarding the relationship
between a decision-maker's beliefs and his policy choices.

Rabin's Changing Perception of the Conflict

Before Rabin entered politics, in 1973, he had served most of his life
in the army. His beliefs regarding the conflict with the Arabs and the
Palestinians were deeply influenced by his life's experience as warrior.
Rabin considered the Arab–Israeli conflict as fundamentally given but
felt deep responsibility for the many soldiers who gave their life to preserve what he called the right of the people of Israel to live in its own
state, free, independent, in peace and tranquility. As soldier he had
faced all the suffering of the Arab-Israeli wars. He expressed these
painful feelings when he received from the Hebrew university in
Jerusalem an honorary Doctorate of Philosophy after the June War of
1967. Rabin contrasted the excitement and happiness of the home
front with the somberness of frontline soldiers "who had seen not
only the glories of victory but also its price—the friends who fell next
to them, covered in blood."[37] As Michael Oren comments: peace and
tranquility would become a lifelong and elusive goal for Rabin. This
desire forms the foundation for the achievement of the historic reconciliation with the PLO in 1993.[38] The traumatic experience of war and
the desire for peace was indeed echoed in the speech that Rabin held
during the signing ceremony of the Oslo accords in September 1993.
Addressing the Palestinians he said: "We, the soldiers who have
returned from battles stained with blood; we who have seen our rela-
tives and friends killed before our eyes; we who have attended their
funerals and cannot look into the eyes of their parents; we who have
come from a land where parents bury their children; we who have
fought against you, the Palestinians, we say to you today in a loud and
clear voice, enough blood and tears. Enough!"[39]

Rabin's attitude toward the Palestinians was also shaped by his military experience. As a young military leader he commanded the Israeli
forces during the war of 1947–1948 in the battles around Jerusalem
and shared with other military commanders the responsibility for the
expulsion of Palestinians from their original homes. At that time he
considered it to be a solution to Israel's Palestinian dilemma. It was
not a human solution, he said later, but war had never been a human
business. As an experienced chief of staff he led the Israeli army in the
June War of 1967, and again, during the war he kept the main bridge

between the West Bank and the East Bank of the Jordan River open to facilitate the flight of Palestinians from the occupied territories to Jordan. However, as Ben-Ami observes, Rabin was a military man who responded to political challenges that were not likely to be influenced by military solutions. He told his prime minister that it was impossible to expel half a million Palestinians from the West Bank. Since it was also unfeasible, in his view, to annex the West Bank because it would transform Israel into a South African apartheid state, he proposed to his prime minister the creation of a Palestinian state.[40] Twenty years later when he was minister of defense in a national unity coalition government and the Palestinians began a popular uprising in the occupied territories, the so-called first *intifada*, his first intuitive reaction was also that of a military man. The disturbances, as he first called the outbreak of violence in the occupied territories, had to be pacified by the use of massive force. As the shooting led to a growing number of Palestinian casualties he ordered the Israeli troops to stop shooting and to start beating. However, he rejected all the extreme proposals made by Likud ministers for ending the uprising, as these measures were in violation of international law and violated the Israeli army's regulations and norms.[41]

It took Rabin some time to understand that, besides the legal and moral restrictions that limited his freedom of action, there was not a military solution to the uprising. As he believed that the occupation could not go forever and that the Palestinian issue would finally require a political solution, he concluded that the only way out of the confrontation was a political answer. In 1989, he drew up a plan that was based on the assumptions that negotiations were needed to change the status quo, and that Israel had to choose between two negotiation partners: the PLO or representatives from the territories. As the only viable option at that time was to deal with local Palestinians, Rabin wanted to promote the negotiations process by holding elections among the Palestinians in the occupied territories, to elect a delegation to negotiate with Israel over an interim period of self-rule. He also suggested negotiations at a later stage on a final settlement, in which all proposed alternatives would be considered. As a result of the collapse of the Labor-Likud coalition government and the outbreak of the Gulf War in 1990 no attempt was made to implement this plan, but the idea was adopted by allowing the participation of Palestinian residents from the territories in the Middle East peace conference that convened in Madrid in October 1991.[42] However, as Ben-Ami rightly argues, Rabin did not come to peacemaking because of lofty idealism about the human and national rights of the Palestinians. Peace was for

Rabin in the first place a means to security and a tool for economic expansion.[43]

Seizing the Window of Opportunity

In his analysis of the Middle East peace process Dennis Ross, the chief Middle East peace negotiator in the presidential administrations of George H.W. Bush and Bill Clinton, concludes his description of Rabin's personality with the observation that Rabin was a man preoccupied with history, always thinking about the possibilities of change for both better and worse.[44] Rabin was indeed a man who believed in the duty of a leader to make the right decision when the historical development and timing for action was there. In the 1967 crisis leading to the June War when Rabin served as chief of staff of the Israeli army and believed that the power of Israel's conventional deterrent was at stake, he supported the launch of a preemptive attack against the Arabs and led Israel to a decisive victory in that war. In 1975, during his first term as prime minister he exploited the historical opportunity created by the momentum of the step-by-step diplomacy of the American mediator Henry Kissinger, and signed a separation of forces agreement in the Sinai with Egypt. It was the basis for the later peace treaty between Egypt and Israel.

When he returned in 1993 as prime minister he believed that it was a time of opportunities, which were related and connected. He thought that the end of the cold war had decreased the likelihood of war and increased the possibility of peace. The survival of the United States as the only superpower and the disappearing of the Soviet Union as a superpower the Arabs could rely upon had created a real window of opportunity to make peace. He also saw the opportunities offered by globalization. He believed that peace would help Israel break its international isolation and overcome its sense of siege so that it would be able to exploit its technological capabilities and profit from the emerging markets offered by the changing global economy. Rabin valued the military strength of Israel but he believed that the real backbone is Israel's economy, its standard of living, its social fabric, its education, and culture. Economic strength and military power were in his view two sides of a coin. Rabin believed that as Israel becomes stronger economically and socially it would be easier to reach a political solution that, in turn, would reduce the need to face security problems. Besides the opportunities he saw also risks. He saw the strategic threat posed by the development of nuclear weapons by rogue states like Iran and Iraq. He also understood the danger presented by Islamic fundamentalism. But Rabin believed that to cope with the risks of Islamic fundamentalism it was necessary to bring up the standard of living of the people in the Arab countries. Peace was in his view a prerequisite for economic development and regional cooperation.[45]

Rabin perceived peace as a long-term goal, a vision, and was resolved to move ahead toward that goal and turn the vision into reality. Sometimes, he said, it was necessary to put on a helmet and a bulletproof vest and continue moving. Whoever is incapable of doing this will never reach his goal. Rabin was therefore determined to use the framework of the Madrid peace conference that he had inherited from the former Likud government to make peace with Syria, Jordan, Lebanon, and the Palestinians. He emphasized the difference between himself and his predecessor, the Likud leader Shamir who showed the tactics of moderation but did not negotiate in good faith about a political settlement. As he told the Israeli parliament after becoming the new prime minister: the previous government created the tools, but it had never the intention to use them in order to achieve peace.[46]

Since there was a taboo on direct talks with the PLO Rabin ruled out, at first, dealing directly with the PLO. However, as he became convinced that no Palestinian leader from the territories would ever have the authority to make commitments or deliver on them, he believed that he had no other choice but to deal with the PLO which had such authority. Dealing with the PLO became even more attractive when he realized that the PLO was ready to make a deal at a lower price than the local Palestinian leadership. That there was in his view no other choice than to make a deal with the PLO, was also motivated by the increasing power of Hamas in the occupied territories. Rabin believed that only the PLO could contain the growing influence of Hamas and other Islamic fundamentalist groups. As he said, it was either the PLO now or the Hamas later. He realized that giving the PLO a foothold in the occupied territories was a risk, but he believed that it was the duty of leaders to cope with risks and to take tough decisions if necessary. For Rabin the measure of leadership was the readiness to make difficult decisions. The higher you climb, he once said, the higher the wall. A leader had to adjust to realities no matter how painful they might be. Dealing with Arafat and recognizing the PLO, which he blamed for many terror acts in the past, was such a difficult and painful decision. Explaining his decision to negotiate with the PLO he said: peace you don't make with friends, but with very unsympathetic enemies.[47]

Peres's Conception of a Borderless Middle East

Peres had developed his initial ideas about the future of the occupied territories during his close collaboration with Moshe Dayan in the late 1960s, when Dayan was minister of defense and Peres minister without portfolio. Dayan and Peres were both opposed to the establishment of a Palestinian state and pursued a policy that was aimed at maintaining Israeli control over the occupied territories. However, a major feature of Dayan's policy was the so-called open bridges policy. The goal of that policy was to remove the barriers between Israel and the occupied territories and between the Palestinians in the occupied territories and the surrounding Arab countries. Shortly after the end of the June War Israel allowed the Palestinians in the occupied territories to resume their routine commercial relations with Jordan in both directions. This open borders policy made it possible for the Palestinians in the occupied territories to export their products and import goods to and from the Arab countries as they did before the war. Israel also permitted the free movement of persons from the West Bank and the Gaza Strip across the Jordan bridges to the Arab world, which enabled inhabitants from the occupied territories to travel and visit Arab countries almost as they had done earlier. Both Dayan and Peres believed that the open borders approach would lead to a process of economic integration between Israel and the occupied territories and pave the way for a de-facto coexistence between Israel and Jordan. It would cultivate a relationship of cooperation and lower the psychological barrier to formalize such a reality of coexistence in an official peace.[48]

When Peres became himself minister of defense in 1974, he continued the open bridges policy, which was in fact based on a tacit cooperation between Israel and Jordan. However, Peres wanted to push this collaboration one step further. He developed the idea of joint Israeli-Jordanian control of the West Bank and the Gaza Strip, the so-called Jordanian option, as a solution to the Palestinian problem and the future of the occupied territories. The Jordanian option proposed the creation of three political entities: Israel, Jordan, and a Palestinian entity that would be administered by Israel and Jordan jointly. The Palestinian entity, comprising of the West Bank and the Gaza Strip, would fall under no single sovereignty. The Arab inhabitants of the Palestinian entity with a Jordanian passport could vote for the Jordanian parliament, while Jewish residents with an Israeli citizenship would vote for the Israeli parliament. The three entities would form one single economic unit, open to the free movement of goods, persons, and ideas. The Palestinian entity would be wholly demilita-rized, and worshippers of all faiths would have free access to their holy places. As Peres admits in his memoirs this plan was based on his opposition to an independent Palestinian state. He believed that such a Palestinian state led by the PLO, which at that time preached the elimination of Israel, would create a constant threat to Israel's security and to the peace and stability of the region. Jordan, by contrast, lived alongside Israel in de-facto peace and opposed as well the rise of a separate Palestinian state. Moreover, Peres believed that although some inhabitants of the West Bank supported a Palestinian independ-ent state, many others had financial and personal interest in Jordan—which continued to pay the salary of about a third of the civil servants on the West Bank—and would support the return of Jordanian rule to the West Bank.[49]

While critics of Peres called the Jordanian option a fallacy, as it was based on the misperception that King Hussein will accept a program that did not include a full Israeli withdrawal from the occupied West Bank, Peres adhered to the Jordanian option until King Hussein's decision in 1988 to cut Jordan's legal and administrative ties with the West Bank.[50] Peres always denied that the Jordanian option was based on wishful thinking, but a new and creative way of tackling the Palestinian problem. Finding a peaceful solution to the Israeli-Palestinian conflict was, in his view, the key to regional peace and a prerequisite for the building of a new Middle East. Although Peres has called himself in the epilogue to his memoirs an unpaid dreamer, he has argued that his grand vision about a new Middle East was not a pipe dream but a vital necessity in order to raise the living standard of people that, in turn, would reduce the level of violence and tension in the region. Making peace would put an end to the wasteful and always growing arms race, and promote the enhanced generation of wealth. Inspired by the example of the European Union Peres truly believed in the possibility of building a future of peace in the Middle East based on the exploitation of the natural resources of the region. To achieve a borderless Middle East he advocated the construction of key infrastructures like roads, railways, and telecommunications that served the region as a whole and facilitated the smooth and efficient movement of trade and persons between countries in the region. He shared with Rabin a belief that the end of the east-west confrontation and the collapse of the Soviet Union signaled far-reaching changes in the region, as the Arabs lost the diplomatic backing and the military support of the Soviet Union which had aligned itself with the Arab cause. Peres also believed that the Gulf War of 1991 had taught the

Arab regimes that the real threat to their survival did not come from Israel but rather from radical and fundamentalist leaders of certain countries in the region.[51]

Inspired by his vision of a new Middle East and understanding the importance of the global and regional changes that were happening, Peres was determined to use the framework of the Madrid peace conference to advance the peace process, searching for any and every new opening. Since the Madrid peace process had in fact two different negotiation tracks, Rabin and Peres agreed on a division of labor. While Rabin directed the bilateral track in which Israel was engaged in direct talks with the Palestinians, Syria, Jordan, and Lebanon on its borders, Peres was in charge of the multilateral track that was meant to encourage regional cooperation between Israelis and Arabs on common regional problems such as: arms control and regional security, regional economic development, environment, water, and refugees. Peres presented to the arms control and regional security working group a vision paper that contained a proposal for the construction of a mutually verifiable zone, free of surface-to-surface missiles and chemical, biological, and nuclear weapons. Given his beliefs about the importance of economic cooperation to regional peace and stability, Peres gave special priority to the issue of regional economic cooperation. He suggested the establishment of several subcommittees of experts to negotiate practical economic proposals in areas like tourism, agriculture, transportation, energy, finance, and Red Sea development. In order to generate private sector business interest and involvement in regional development, Peres also launched the idea of the so-called MENA summits, based on the concept of the annual Davos conference where leading figures in the world business and political community meet to put together deals. In spite of some initial success in the Arab-Israeli multilateral economic cooperation as a result of the Oslo political breakthrough in the Israeli-Palestinian relation, further progress was stalled by the setbacks in the Israeli-Palestinian peace process after the return to power of the Likud in 1996.[52]

Peres had more success in laying the foundation for the Oslo breakthrough. Although Rabin led the bilateral negotiations with the Palestinians within the framework of the Madrid peace conference, Peres participated in the decision-making process. To break the stalemate in the negotiations with the Palestinians Peres suggested Rabin: talk directly to the PLO leadership and make a substantial offer, which Peres called "Gaza-first." His idea was to withdraw from Gaza, which he believed would be supported by a vast majority of Israelis who wanted to get out of the terror-ridden Gaza Strip, and propose to Arafat to move into Gaza as part of an agreement on interim self-government for the West Bank. As Arafat did not want that "Gaza-first" should become "Gaza-first and last," the "Gaza-first" concept evolved into "Gaza and Jericho first," but it became the basis on which the Oslo agreement was further built.[53]

Arafat as State Builder

The most fundamental belief that influenced Arafat's behavior throughout his whole life was the belief in the return to Palestine. Arafat deeply believed that the restoration of the Palestinian homeland as it was before 1948 and that still existed in the mind of Arafat and many Palestinians, would put an end to the suffering and humiliation of the refugees who were uprooted from their original houses during the 1948 War. He thought that the creation of a Palestinian state would stop the dependency that the Palestinian people experienced in the lands of exile and bring back their self-confidence. This fundamental belief in the need to build a Palestinian state with a territorial base in Palestine, was the driving force behind the founding of the Palestinian Liberation Movement, Fatah, by Arafat and some other Palestinians in 1959. They truly believed that the establishment of an autonomous political entity with independent organizational structures was a necessary key to national survival. Arafat and the cofounders of Fatah shared also some other core beliefs. They strongly believed that the people of Palestine should take their fate in their own hands. This belief was rooted in a deep distrust of the Arab governments, which were blamed for the loss of Palestine in 1948 and the purposeful suppression of the Palestinian will to fight for their independence. Moreover, although some Arab states still controlled parts of Palestine after the 1948 War they did not help the Palestinians establish their own state on the remaining parts of Palestine. The founders of Fatah, which would become later the backbone of the PLO, therefore resisted Arab tutelage over the Palestinians and insisted on the absolute independence of Palestinian organization and decision-making from the Arab governments.[54]

Arafat and the Fatah core leadership had also a strong belief in the primacy of armed struggle as the only way to regain their stolen homeland. In their belief system there was no room for a Jewish state. Since Israel prevented the return of Palestinians to their homeland their main goal was the destruction of Israel, which was conceived by Arafat and the core group that led Fatah as a colonialist Zionist occupation state. They wanted to start an uncompromising war against

Israel and rejected any political agreement that left Israel in existence. They demanded that the Arab governments which controlled the Arab parts of Palestine establish a national Palestinian rule in the West Bank and the Gaza Strip. From this territorial base they wanted to launch an armed struggle for the liberation of Palestine. However, Arafat realized that the destruction of Israel required massive force that only the regular Arab armies could pull together. Since the Arab countries were not inclined to adopt an activist military strategy or start a conventional war against Israel, he considered the Fatah actions to be a first stage in activating such a united Arab effort. Arafat in the 1960s was very active in organizing bases for the armed struggle in Jordan, Syria, and Lebanon and mobilizing and preparing local groups for action. In an attempt to provoke a confrontation along the borders of Israel and its Arab neighbors, Fatah groups conducted many guerrilla raids against Israel before the June War.[55] Their actions were certainly not a decisive cause for the June War, but the guerrilla attacks before the war triggered Israeli reprisals that destabilized the military situation along the Arab-Israeli borders in the period leading to the war.

In spite of the Israeli victory in the June War, Arafat stuck to his fundamental belief that Palestine could be liberated only through armed struggle. Moreover, Arafat and the core leadership of Fatah perceived the removal of Egyptian control from the Gaza Strip and Jordanian authority from the West Bank as a unique opportunity to establish an autonomous Palestinian entity, or as they called it a revolutionary authority, in the occupied territories. Modeling their effort on those of the Chinese, Vietnamese, and Algerian revolutionaries, they believed that they could use the occupied territories as a territorial base from where they could force Israel to withdraw from the occupied territories and liberate the rest of Palestine. The Fatah leadership hoped to begin a guerrilla war that would repeat the 1936 Arab Revolt against the British. The armed struggle also intented to frustrate any attempt of the Arab leaders to conclude a deal with Israel that would recognize the borders that existed until the June War. Arafat and the other Fatah leaders sensed a readiness on the part of the Arab leaders to accept a settlement with Israel at the expense of the Palestinians. They interpreted resolution 242 of the UN Security Council, which was accepted by Egypt and Jordan, as clear evidence that the goal of the Arab leaders shifted from the liberation of Palestine to regaining the territories occupied in 1967. While resolution 242 implied the Arab recognition of Israel in its pre-June 1967 borders in exchange for Israel's withdrawal from the territories it occupied in 1967, the Palestinian issue was addressed in resolution 242 as a refugee problem and no reference was made to Palestinian self-determination.[56]

Arafat began immediately after the June War to push for the establishment of a permanent popular base for resistance and revolt in the occupied territories. Following a decision of the Fatah to transfer its leadership to the occupied territories and prepare the local inhabitants for military and civilian resistance, Arafat infiltrated into the West Bank in June 1967 to recruit support and establish military bases in the occupied territories. Arafat was formally nominated as Fatah field commander in the territories and was given the task of leading the struggle in the West Bank. He set up headquarters in Nablus in August 1967 but failed to organize the ambitious armed struggle inside the occupied territories that he had in mind. Even worse, the Israelis discovered and dismantled many secret Fatah cells and Arafat was forced to escape in December 1967 to Jordan. Arafat was more successful in building an operational base in Jordan, from where he continued and even intensified the cross-border raids into Israel. He built new bases on the East Bank of the Jordan River and in densely populated refugee camps, which became ex-territorial areas controlled by Fatah. In 1969 Arafat also took over the PLO, which competed, from its establishment in 1964 by the Arab governments, with Fatah. The PLO was transformed into an umbrella organization for the different Palestinian resistance organizations, but dominated by Fatah. Arafat also amended the PLO charter, which already denied Israel's right to exist and posited the establishment in its place of an Arab state, emphasizing the armed struggle as the overall strategy to liberate Palestine and to exercise the Palestinian right to national self-determination and sovereignty. However, the growing power of Fatah and other Palestinian resistance organizations, which began to form in Jordan a state-within-the-state, led to a confrontation between Arafat and the Jordanian king Hussein. It culminated in September 1970 in a major offensive of the Jordanian army against the strongholds of the Palestinian resistance organizations in Jordan that were forced to move to Lebanon.[57]

When Arafat arrived in Lebanon after his expulsion from Jordan he thought he could avoid a repetition of what had happened in Jordan by forging an alliance between the PLO and local Muslim and leftist groups. These groups supported the Palestinian cause and saw the PLO as asset in the traditional power game between the Lebanese Maronite right wing elite that dominated the Lebanese political system, and the opposition of Muslim, Druse, and left wing groups that represented the disadvantaged segments of the Lebanese society. But the growing PLO military presence and its increasing involvement in Lebanese politics were perceived by the Maronite leaders as a threat and resulted in 1975 in a civil war between the Maronite militias and the PLO. This time Arafat and the PLO survived the war and became an integral actor in the new Lebanese balance of power that was negotiated between the Lebanese leaders and Arafat with the help of Saudi, Syrian, and Egyptian leaders. Under the terms of the political settlement the PLO withdrew its armed forces to southern Lebanon, where it enjoyed relative autonomy and was able to continue its guerrilla attacks against Israel. In the next few years Arafat built in Lebanon a Palestinian entity that Rashid Khalidi labeled a para-state. In his view, the PLO chairman Arafat was a head of state in all but name. Sayigh even called the PLO state-within-the-state in Lebanon a state-in-exile, with an autonomy born out of the combination it enjoyed of territorial control in Lebanon, a major military build-up, the availability of non-extractive financial resources, and international recognition. This so-called Fakhani Republic included parts of north and south Lebanon with its capital in the Fakhani area of West Beirut where the PLO headquarters were located.[58]

Moving Toward a Two-State Solution

The consolidation of a state-in-exile in Lebanon did not imply that Arafat changed the fundamental belief in the need to build a Palestinian state with a territorial base in Palestine, recognized by the Arab states and the international community. However, after the end of the October War of 1973 Arafat recognized that he had to adapt his belief regarding the means to achieve this core objective to the changing historical circumstances. Arafat perceived the American effort to broker interim agreements between Egypt, Syria, and Israel after the October War of 1973 as an indication that these two Arab countries would make no further attempts to regain the occupied territories by force. Arafat thought that the end of the war marked the beginning of several diplomatic initiatives aimed at the realization of a negotiated settlement between Israel and its Arab neighbors about the future of the occupied territories. Arafat's main concern was therefore to secure the participation of the PLO as the legitimate representative of the Palestinians in such negotiations, and to neutralize any attempt by Jordan to get back the occupied West Bank through a deal with Israel.

In the first Arab summit after the October War, which was held in Algiers in December 1973, Arafat's major goal was to ensure the participation of the PLO in any Middle East peace conference. He managed to obtain the support of the Arab leaders for the Palestinian resistance and made certain an active role for the PLO in future peace negotiations. Arafat endorsed the joint declaration in which the Arab leaders expressed their readiness to advance peace on the basis of Israeli withdrawal from the territories occupied in 1967 and restoration of the Palestinian national rights. It implied that Arafat accepted the peace for land principle as a basis for negotiations. This crucial shift in Arafat's views became even more evident six months later, in June 1974, when the PLO revised its traditional position regarding the establishment of a Palestinian state and declared that it was willing to set up a Palestinian national authority in every part of the Palestinian territory that would be liberated. The PLO considered this as a stage in the pursuit of its strategy for the establishment of a Palestinian state in the whole of Palestine. In other words, Arafat and the PLO adopted for the first time a policy that allowed the creation of a Palestinian state in parts of the occupied territories and made, in fact, the very first move toward a two-state solution. Arafat and the PLO were rewarded a few months later during the Arab Summit at Rabat in 1974. The Arab leaders declared that the PLO was the sole legitimate representative of the Palestinian people, and approved the right of the Palestinians to establish an independent national authority under the leadership of the PLO on any part of Palestine that was liberated. That way Arafat was assured that the occupied West Bank and Gaza Strip would not return to Jordan and Egypt and that King Hussein was not allowed to negotiate on behalf of the Palestinians.[59]

However, Arafat's political pragmatism and turn to diplomacy as a means to advance the goal of a Palestinian state was dealt a major blow by two successive events. The first setback was the conclusion of the Camp David accords between Egypt and Israel in September 1978. The provisions of the accords that dealt with the West Bank and the Gaza Strip offered the Palestinians only a self-governing authority for a transitional period in which negotiations would take place on a permanent settlement. However, there was no guarantee that the autonomy would be transferred into a sovereign Palestinian state and the PLO was excluded from the negotiations. The second major setback was the Israeli military invasion of Lebanon in 1982. The military offensive resulted in the destruction of the PLO headquarters and the military infrastructure in that country, and the removal of Arafat and his troops from Lebanon. However, the loss of the territorial base of the Palestinian state-in-exile in Lebanon shifted the attention of Arafat back to the occupied territories and reinforced his effort to obtain

Palestinian statehood in the occupied territories. The PLO leadership in the new headquarters in Tunis and the local PLO leaders in the occupied territories were already planning to escalate mass protests and confrontations with the Israeli occupation authorities, when the popular uprising in the occupied territories started in December 1987. Although the timing of the actual outbreak of the riots surprised Arafat, he was quick to capitalize on the *intifada*, as the rebellion became known. He took control of the uprising through local PLO leaders and used the uprising as a means to place the settlement of the Palestinian problem and the Israeli occupation of the West Bank and Gaza Strip high on the international agenda.

But Arafat understood that the main obstacle for active PLO participation in any sort of international conference that would initiate negotiations on the final status of the occupied territories was the PLO exclusion by American diplomacy. The United States had committed itself in 1975 not to recognize the PLO and not to negotiate with it or allow it to attend peace talks, unless the PLO recognizes Israel's right to exist and accepts UN security resolutions 242 and 338. President Ronald Reagan added in 1981 to these requirements the extra precondition that the PLO had to renounce terrorism as well. Arafat, who had always hoped to open a direct or indirect dialogue with the United States, as he believed that the United States held the key to Israel, was willing to meet these preconditions. At the end of 1988 Arafat made a quantum leap. Arguing that at this stage the most important goals were the end of Israeli occupation, self-determination, and the establishment of an independent state under PLO leadership, Arafat declared on November 15 the establishment of an independent Palestinian state. In the declaration that was formally approved by the PLO, he referred explicitly to UN General Assembly resolution 181 as the basis for Palestinian independence, and announced formally the acceptance of UN Security Council resolutions 242 and 338 as the basis for negotiations with Israel within the framework of an international peace conference. The approval of the UN partition plan of 1947 and the willingness to reach a comprehensive and peaceful settlement among the parties to the Arab-Israeli conflict in accordance with resolutions 242 and 338 committed the PLO to the coexistence of Israel and a Palestinian state, hence to a two-state solution. Arafat restated this commitment in a speech to the UN General Assembly in December 1988, but the United States was ready to start a dialogue with the PLO only after a formal statement of Arafat, dictated by the United States, in which he reiterated these assurances and pledged to reject all forms of terrorism, including individual, group, and state terrorism.[60]

With the removal of the American obstacle Arafat had still to overcome a major hindrance to getting a seat at the negotiation table. Israel continued to see the PLO a threat to its existence and a framework for terrorist organizations operating against Israel. Although Arafat repeated several times his willingness to negotiate directly with Israel at an international peace conference under UN auspices, and to exchange mutual recognition, Israeli leaders rejected all his proposals. They outlawed contacts with the PLO and stuck to their traditional rejection of indirect or direct talks with the PLO. Under American pressure Israel suggested in 1989 the holding of elections in the territories for a Palestinian delegation that would begin negotiations with Israel on local autonomy. Talks between the United States and Israel on the one hand and the United States and the PLO on the other in an attempt to find a formula for such elections ended as a result of the Iraqi invasion of Kuwait in August 1990. In the aftermath of the Gulf War the United States was determined to live up to the promise it made to the Arab countries that had joined the American led coalition against Iraq and organized in 1991a Middle East peace conference in Madrid. Arafat was eager to participate in the conference but he had to stand on the sidelines, as the Americans were unwilling to overcome the Israeli opposition to PLO participation following his choice of supporting Iraq during the Gulf War.[61]

However, not being involved directly in the Madrid peace conference did not mean that Arafat had no power to influence the negotiations, first indirectly and later directly. The Palestinian representation to the Madrid peace conference was composed of public figures from the West Bank and the Gaza Strip but he approved each member of the delegation that belonged to the PLO mainstream. Arafat checked personally all the texts and the instructions issued to the delegation members who reported directly to him. Thus, while Israel and the United States did not want to negotiate directly with Arafat, they had to deal with him indirectly as he was able to obstruct or delay the bilateral negotiation process between Israel and the Palestinians in Washington as he wished. Moreover, Arafat personally authorized a second negotiation track, the Oslo back channel, in which he negotiated directly on an equal footing with Israel. It was this secret negotiation track, of which the Palestinian delegation in Washington was unaware, that would produce the Oslo accords. As Sayigh observes, the Oslo accords were a far cry from the PLO's goal of a totally liberated Palestine and was a much-reduced independent state as envisaged in its declaration of independence. The resemblances of the Oslo accords with previous proposals for Palestinian autonomy were strong, but for Arafat the key element in the Oslo accords was that it extended formal Israeli recognition of the PLO, and assured the transfer of its state-in-exile to the occupied territories. As Arafat argued, the Oslo accords offered a means to statehood if properly acted upon.[62]

3

A SECOND LENS

DOMESTIC ROOTS OF WORLD POLITICS

As any review of the relevant domestic sources of international relations and foreign policy illustrates, the domestic factors that account for variance in foreign policy choices made by decision-makers are numerous and diverse. These factors range from national attributes such as geopolitical setting, economic development or type of government, to the influence of bureaucratic politics, societal groups and the effects of the media and public opinion.[1] In this chapter I have no intention of dealing with all these domestic factors. Rather, this chapter examines international relations and foreign policy through the lens of domestic politics. It starts from the assertion that "one fundamental law of international relations is that such politics is shaped by and rooted in domestic affairs."[2]

Many international relations scholars share the view that foreign policy behavior is primarily determined by domestic politics.[3] Building on Richard Neustadt's pioneering work on the politics of leadership, Roger Hilsman, Graham Allison, and Morton Halperin, stressed the important influences of domestic politics on international relations in the early 1970s. They said in various studies that foreign policy decision-making is in essence a political process and that foreign policy actions are in fact political resultants.[4] More recently Robert Putnam has pointed out that an adequate account of the domestic determinants of foreign policy and international relations must stress politics: parties, social classes, interest groups, legislators, and even public opinion and elections, in addition to executive officials and institutional arrangements.[5] Joe Hagan has also emphasized the political nature of foreign policy, and argued that government leaders and decision-makers regularly observe domestic political conditions and incorporate them into their foreign policy calculations.[6] But the most forceful advocacy of approaching international politics and foreign policy-making from a perspective that regards the centrality of domestic political factors essential for any understanding of the foreign policy preferences of political leaders and other key foreign policy-makers is expressed by Bruce Bueno de Mesquita. When we examine international affairs through the lens of domestic decision-making, he says, we provide a way to think about how properties of the international system are shaped by local considerations as part of the larger strategic fabric of politics.[7] He emphasizes that international politics are formed by the aggregated consequences of our individual and collective decisions. "I cannot help but reflect on the extent to which American policy toward the Kyoto Protocols, the Comprehensive Test Ban Treaty, engagement or disengagement in Europe, and commitment to nation-building or defensive security have been framed for at least the period 2001–2005 by the hole-punching skills of a few hundred Floridian voters with diverse interests regarding prescription drugs and, perhaps, little interest at all in foreign policy or international affairs."[8]

As I will illustrate in this chapter, two factors are likely to be critical in explaining and understanding the impact of domestic politics on the foreign policy choices made by political leaders and ruling groups. The first one is the drive for political survival of those who have the power to make foreign policy decisions. The second one is the incentive for consensus building among those who have the power to influence foreign policy outcomes. Both factors are derived from the characteristics of the domestic political context and the institutional setting in which foreign policy is made: the electoral vulnerability of politicians; the challenge imposed on the ruling leadership by a significant opposition outside and within government; the pressure of public opinion; the demands of societal interest groups; and the fragmentation within government. Fragmentation, in turn, results in bargaining among those who are involved in the process of foreign policy-making and influences the likelihood of agreement between competing policy-makers on a final policy choice. As I will further indicate in this chapter, the existence of opposition encourages foreign policy behavior of either accommodation or confrontation, while the need to bargain with one another can lead to different foreign policy outcomes such as compromise or deadlock. The electoral vulnerability and the pressure of public opinion also affect foreign policy choices as it discourages policies that are not acceptable for a majority of the public.

THE DRIVE FOR POLITICAL SURVIVAL

The claim that every leader or ruling group has a strong desire to stay in power is at the heart of arguments favoring a domestic politics approach to international relations and foreign policy. Bueno de Mesquita, for example, says that politicians are keen to retain high office once they have achieved it. He argues that since international relations is a normal aspect of ordinary domestic politics and a place for politicians to gain or lose political advantages, the quest of leaders for personal political survival becomes a crucial motivation for their foreign policy choices.[9] Hagan also says that political leaders and ruling groups, when they make foreign policy decisions, have to take into account the need to maintain and enhance the political base for staying in office. He argues that if a leadership faces significant challenges to its position, it is reasonable to expect that it is sensitive to the domestic costs of controversial decisions and will avoid actions that might help its removal from political office.[10]

Electoral Vulnerability

The concern of political leaders and ruling groups about their political survival, stems, first and foremost, from their electoral vulnerability. Electoral vulnerability arises from the probability that a political leader or ruling group can be removed from office. Such a possibility exists in almost every political system, although the likelihood of not retaining political power varies according to the institutional arrangements of a political system for selecting the ruling leadership. As Bueno de Mesquita, James Morrow, Randolph Siverson, and Alastair Smith illustrate, different political systems have different ways for choosing the country's political leadership. They use the concept of selectorate to indicate all those people who have an institutionally granted right or norm that gives them a say in choosing the government, and the concept of winning coalition to refers to those members of the selectorate on which any leader in office relies to maintain his or her position in office.[11]

In modern contemporary democratic systems, Bueno de Mesquita and his colleagues explain, the selectorate consists of all adult citizens. In such political systems the ruling leadership is formed by a winning coalition that represents one half of the selectorate plus one additional vote, which is the number of voters needed to win elections. However, if any member of the winning coalition defects to a rival leader, then the leadership in office is removed. They further say that politicians attract a winning coalition and keep its support by providing benefits in the form of either public goods like political freedoms, national security, and general economic growth, or private goods such as special privileges and favorable contracts. While the distribution of public goods in the form of public policies affects the welfare of everyone in the state, the private goods are allocated only to the members of the winning coalition. However, to retain political power, they clarify, a leader must provide sufficient benefits to the winning coalition to satisfy its member so that they continue to support the current leadership rather than defect to a political rival.[12]

In fact, as Bueno de Mesquita and his colleagues observe, in all democratic political systems even small policy failures increases the risk of removal of a leader from office. Leaders in democratic political systems have great personal incentives to be careful about their policy choices because democracies, with usually large winning coalitions, do not encourage political loyalty. Key backers of the government are relatively quick to defect into the successor winning coalition in the face of failure, as they derive their utility to a large extent from the government's policy performance rather than its allocation of private goods. Only leaders in authoritarian systems have a high probability of political survival and have to worry less about their performance, even if they fail to increase their nation's welfare, ruin their country's economy, or lead its citizens into disastrous military defeats. This is so, Bueno de Mesqiuta and his associates point out, because the ruling leadership of autocratic systems controls the membership of their winning coalition as it is easier for authoritarian leaders, of usually small winning coalitions, to compensate for policy failures with private goods. Hence, autocratic systems encourage a norm of loyalty by members of the winning coalition toward their leader in spite of policy failures.[13]

Anthony King demonstrates the way electoral vulnerability has a major impact on the functioning of politicians. Focusing on American politicians' electoral vulnerability he states that their conduct in office is continuously governed by electoral considerations.[14] King says that the extreme electoral vulnerability of American politicians is explained in the first place by the fact that American politicians have in many cases very short terms of office. Members of the House of Representatives are chosen for a term as short as two years. Individual members of the United States Senate enjoy a longer six-year term in office. But, as the terms of one third of the senators end every two years, the Senate as a whole, like the House of Representatives, is under permanent electoral pressure. Electoral sensibilities characterize in particular the functioning of the American president. Although he is elected for a fixed period of four years, newly elected presidents immediately start their reelection campaign. As King clearly illustrates, American presidents focus on electoral considerations as much as they concentrate on actual governing, even in their second term when they are not running for reelection. The extreme electoral vulnerability of American politicians is further explained by the fact that in order to attain office in general elections they have to compete first in primary elections to secure their party's nomination. This means that in addition to the prospect of being defeated in general elections, American politicians face also the prospect of being defeated in primary elections, and after being elected they have to worry about renomination as much as they have to worry about reelection. A third explanation for their electoral vulnerability is given by the fact that American politicians have to run for office mainly as individuals and have to raise large amounts of funds for their own election campaigns. The political party is only a background factor and politicians have to fight and finance their own election campaign, which means that they have to be attentive to their constituents as well as individuals and interest groups who make large financial contributions to their expensive election campaigns.[15]

King assumes that politicians in other democratic countries are more secure in office and therefore less worried about their electoral futures and less preoccupied with electoral considerations. Because the elections of politicians usually take place at longer intervals and the mass electorate is not involved in their nomination, politicians are less subjected to continuous electoral pressures. Also the selection of party candidates is actually done by the political parties themselves through some kind of political mechanism, which varies from a selection by party executives or a selection by party delegates to a system where all dues-paying party members are allowed to participate in the selection process. Moreover, being party representatives, the political fate of politicians in other democratic countries depends not on their personal effort but on the party's performance during and between elections. Besides, the party in most other countries is subsidized by the national government that sets limits on the amounts of money that parties are allowed to spend during campaigns, so that politicians are not required to raise large sums of money for the election campaign.[16] However, as King himself indicates, some of the reasons for electoral vulnerability in the United States operate in other democratic countries as well. Political leaders in other countries, for example, can be removed from office not just during national elections, but also during the long intervals between them. As King reminds us, British prime ministers may fall as the result of a political coup inside their party, French prime ministers come and go, and Italian prime ministers rarely stay in office longer than a year or two. Moreover contrary to the legal maximum for the duration of legislatures, the actual period that parliaments remain in existence in almost all democracies is shorter. Most parliamentary democracies have legal arrangements for the possibility of dissolving parliament before the end of its term and the holding of national elections ahead of schedule.[17]

The electoral vulnerability of politicians in other democratic countries is to a large extent caused by the move in the 1970s from party democracy to what Bernard Manin calls audience democracy. In party democracy citizens vote for a party rather than for a person. Individual candidates are nominated by the party machinery and bear the colors of a party. A major effect of party democracy, says Manin, is electoral stability, which results for the most part from the fact that the political preferences of citizens are decided especially by social, economic, and cultural characteristics of the voters. But from the 1970s there is, according to Manin, a transformation toward audience democracy in which citizens do not vote on the basis of party identification but on the basis of the personal image of the candidates and the image of the parties to which they belong, as well as on the basis of the issues at stake in each election. The person of the party leader, not the party program, becomes more and more the focus of election campaigns, who communicates directly with the voter through radio and television without the mediation of a party network. The party leader uses the party primarily as an instrument for fund-raising and the building of a large group of volunteers and activists. In audience democracy politicians are more vulnerable than in party democracy because voters tend to vote differently from one election to the other. A political leader is evaluated by voters on the basis of his personal record in office, and the expectation that voters have about his personal qualities and capability to fulfill the electoral commitments he makes.[18]

Political Opposition

A second major source for the concern that political leaders and ruling groups have about their political survival is the existence of opposition to the political leadership that controls the government. Political rivals are assumed to exist all the time and political opposition is assumed to be present in any type of political system.[19] On the basis of area studies literature on foreign policy decision-making in western parliamentary democracies, authoritarian systems, and political systems in less developed countries, Hagan makes a distinction between several forms of opposition. The most familiar type of political opposition to the ruling leadership and its policies is opposition from other political parties who compete for control of the national government. The strength of such an opposition is usually determined by the number of seats it controls in parliament in comparison to the number of seats controlled by the ruling party or the ruling coalition. An opposition that controls a large number of seats in parliament and presents itself in the eyes of the public as a real alternative to the current government forms, according to Hagan, a significant challenge for the ruling leadership to maintain its current majority in the next elections. Moreover, in parliamentary systems where a minority government is in power, the opposition can remove the present government at any moment and enjoys a veto power over current policies. Such a veto power has an opposition also in presidential systems where the ruling president does not control a majority of seats in parliament.[20]

Opposition to the ruling leadership and its policies may also come from within the ruling party or ruling group. This type of opposition, says Hagan, involves usually leaders of factions in the party or in parliament who want to change the current policies. In parliamentary systems such an opposition, especially when it is excluded from participation in government, presents a real threat to the continuous rule of the present government as it may lose its majority in parliament. But in authoritarian systems, he emphasizes, the ruling leadership also has to be sensitive to the probable loss of political support from powerful individuals or groups in the central leadership, who may remove the current ruling leader or group from power. Groups who have an autonomous power base in the society like the military establishment and paramilitary groups form another type of opposition. The sensitivity of the ruling leadership to the military, says Hagan, depends on their size and the institutional arrangements and norms that define their role in domestic politics. This may vary from subordination to the civilian government, to direct or indirect involvement in policy-making, and sometimes even the selection of the ruling leadership. Opposition to the ruling leadership may further arise from regionally based groups. The strength of such opposition is based, according to Hagan, by the structures that govern the relationship between the national and regional government, the level of access to the national policy-making process and the degree of regional autonomy, while the intensity of regional opposition is influenced by the political orientation of the regional leadership toward the national leadership, and the demands for reforms in the relationship between national and regional authorities.[21]

The Pressure of Public Opinion

The need of the ruling leadership in democratic systems to win elections in order to gain or retain political power, and the necessity of the ruling leadership in almost every political system to control the challenge posed by a significant opposition to continue in office, is closely related to a third important source for the concern that political leaders and ruling groups have about their political survival: the pressure of public opinion and organized societal and interest groups. As Russet argues, foreign policy issues are important to the public and influential to voting in many American elections since the Second World War. Although there are some indications that the mass public is largely ignorant about foreign affairs and usually lacks a sustained interest in foreign policy, he argues that low levels of detailed information should not be confused with lack of interest. Russet admits that the general public is much more interested in domestic political problems and that the level of inflation and unemployment are major determinants of the popularity of an American president with the voters, but he emphasizes that there are also indications that an increase in the public's approval of his foreign policy is linked to its general approval of the president's performance in office.[22] Hagan also argues that the public links more and more the handling of foreign policy issues to the overall credibility of the current leadership. Confrontation with foreign adversaries, says Hagan, are easily perceived by the public as demonstrating the government's willingness to risk war, whereas accommodation is seen as signifying its weakness in world affairs.[23]

The difficulty of conducting foreign policy in a democracy is in particular evident during international crises. James Fearon, for example, highlights the public aspect of international crises. He argues that international crises are public events, carried out in front of domestic political audiences who observe and assess the skill and performance of the leadership. This makes leaders more sensitive to, what Fearon calls, audience costs, which arise from the action of domestic audiences concerned with whether the leadership is successful or unsuccessful in handling such crises. Leaders suffer audience costs when domestic audiences judge them as performing poorly. This happens, for instance, when they first choose to escalate the crisis and later prefer to back down. Backing down after making a show of force is costly for a leader, explains Fearon, because this is perceived as having suffered a greater diplomatic humiliation than standing firm until the other side backs down. It gives domestic political opponents an opportunity to criticize the international loss of credibility, face, and honor, and exposes leaders to the risk of losing authority.[24]

The eminent international scholar Hans Morgenthau, has already drawn the attention to this political phenomenon in his classic study of international politics. Arguing in favor of secret diplomacy, he states, that because of the nature of international negotiations it is impossible to negotiate in public. One of the main characteristics of such negotiations, says Morgenthau, is that they start with each side stating its case with maximum demands, which are watered down in the bargaining process until they agree on a compromise that satisfies both sides. An important disadvantage of public negotiations is, in his view, the fact that leaders have to negotiate under the watchful eyes of their own people. Especially in democracies, he further says, no government that wants to stay in power can afford to retreat publicly from a position initially declared as necessary.[25] As Morgenthau argues: "Heroes, not horsetraders, are the idols of public opinion. Public opinion, while dreading war, demands that its diplomats act as heroes who do not yield in the face of the enemy, even at the risk of war, and condemns as weaklings and traitors those who yield, albeit only halfway, for the sake of peace."[26]

In democratic political systems the pressure of public opinion usually takes the form of opinion polls, demonstrations, and the ultimate power voters have, namely, to send away the ruling leadership. But the pressure of public opinion can also come from the collective opinions of a large number of societal organizations and narrow interest groups, like business and employers' organizations, trade unions, churches, peace groups, and many other sorts of single-issue groups. Such organizations and groups express preferences and are interested in influencing the policies pursued by the national leadership. Societal organizations and interest groups draw their influence from the fact that in many societies, democratic as well as authoritarian, the political leadership depends on their support to rise to power or to stay in office. Political leaders therefore take the policy preferences of such organizations and groups into consideration when they make their policy choices.[27]

Jack Snyder has indicated that narrow interest groups may hijack the state and twist national policy in the pursuit of their private interest. Taken separately, he says, narrow interest groups may be weak. But the power and persuasiveness of these groups lies with the process by which they form coalitions of several such groups. As Snyder points out, narrow interest groups overcome their weakness and hijack national policy by a process of logrolling. They join coalitions by trading favors so that each group gets what it wants most, and the costs are spread to society through taxes imposed by the state. Moreover, Snyder explains, once they gain control over national policy, they can use the instruments and credibility of the state to sell their self-serving ideas.[28]

THE INCENTIVE FOR CONSENSUS BUILDING

The need to secure support for a policy is at the core of many approaches that try to understand how domestic politics shape foreign policy outcomes. Alexander George begins his study of effective presidential decision-making in foreign policy with the observation that "a president must be sensitive to the need to achieve sufficient consensus in support of his policies and decisions within his own administration, in Congress, and with the public."[29] Hagan has illustrated that the need to build domestic support for any foreign policy proposal is not limited to established western democracies. Achieving agreement among a coalition of the various domestic actors that formally or informally share the authority to make foreign policy decisions is also required in authoritarian systems and in less developed political systems.[30] As Barbara Farnham explains, the fact that in almost every political system groups and individuals have some degree of power makes it necessary for political decision-makers to seek acceptability by others, if they wish to achieve various goals. To put it in Farnham's own words: "in almost all societies the ability to get things done in the political arena rests not on authority alone but also on the achievement of consensus of some sort."[31]

Political Fragmentation and Bargaining

The desire for consensus building stems from a very important characteristic of every political system: political fragmentation. It concerns lasting internal political divisions within governments in the form of competing personalities, bureaucracies, factions, or other autonomous groups.[32] Political fragmentation within governments makes disagreement over policy issues unavoidable, and results in debates over alternative courses of action among those involved in the decision-making process. It means that policy-makers have to bargain with one another, and get the approval of other decision-makers for the ultimate policy choices.

That authority alone is not enough to get things done is actually the basic assumption underlying Neustadt's pioneering analysis of the power of the American president. Presidential power, he states, is just the power to persuade. He emphasizes that formal presidential powers are no guarantee that a president can get results simply by giving orders. Because of different responsibilities and different interests politicians and officials have different perspectives on how to deal with a specific issue. The essence of a president's persuasive task is, according to Neustadt, to convince politicians and officials that what he wants of them is what they ought to do in their interest, not his. Thus, Neustadt conceives the power to persuade as the power to bargain, and real power becomes, in his view, a matter of give and take. The authority inherent in presidential office gives a president only personal influence; his ability and will to use it, gives him bargaining advantages in dealing with the individuals he needs to persuade.[33]

Hilsman has further developed these ideas, picturing the process by which governments make policy in defense and foreign affairs as essentially political. He indicates that politics implies disagreement and dispute about the goals a government should pursue and the means for achieving them. Competing groups, such as political parties and special interest groups, as well as different governmental departments and agencies with alternative goals and rival policy preferences, use their relative power to reach an agreement through bargaining, accommodation, compromise, alliance forming, and consensus building. Hilsman therefore argues that in reality policy-making is a process of seeking to reconcile conflicting goals and advocates the accommodation of competing goals and aspirations.[34] In Hilsman's view the test of policy is "whether enough of the people and organizations having a stake in the policy and holding power agree to the policy."[35]

Allison and Halperin also argue that government decisions and actions result from a political bargaining process, which they labeled "bureaucratic politics."[36] Allison presents a governmental politics model that conceives foreign policy-making as a bargaining game among individual members of the government with diverse interests and unequal influence. Individuals become participants in the bargaining game by occupying key positions in the government, and the bureaucracy responsible for decision-making on national security issues. Their preferences and stands on the issue at hand, says Allison, are shaped by different conceptions of national goals as well as organizational and personal interests, as each participant tends to protect and advance the parochial interests and perspectives of his department. Allison therefore coined the phrase: where an individual stands depends on where he sits, meaning that the position an individual takes on an issue is affected by a person's seat in government and placement in the bureaucracy. He further says that the bargaining power, that is the effective influence of individual participants on the outcome of the bargaining game, is determined by a mix of three factors: bargaining advantages (drawn for instance from formal authority and responsibility or actual control over resources necessary to carry out action); skill and will in using bargaining advantages; and other participants' perceptions of the first two elements. Each participant in the bargaining game pulls and hauls with the influence he has for outcomes that advance his conception of the national, organizational, and personal interests. In Allison's view government decisions are made according to the bargaining power and the bargaining performance of those individuals who support or oppose a course of action.[37]

Halperin reasons very much along the same line. He says that each government consists of numerous individuals and groups, who have very different interests and very different priorities, and consequently do not agree on what course of action should be taken to influence another government. Like Allison, Halperin argues that any decision that is taken emerges from a process of pulling and hauling between individuals and groups within the government, and is basically a compromise between different positions on what will work to influence that government. Officials in the government toward which the action is directed, says Halperin, will also view the action according to their own interests and the internal debate within their own government and society. The other government's response will be influenced as well by the internal pulling and hauling. Halperin therefore draws the conclusion that when we explain the behavior of two nations in relation to each other, we should focus on the motives, interests, and sources of power of the various participants in the bargaining process which led to the decisions. In explaining the response, he says, we should do the same.[38]

Political Fragmentation and the Likelihood of Agreement

Besides the fact that political fragmentation within government results in a process of bargaining among policy-makers on different policy options, it also influences the likelihood of agreement between competing policy-makers on a final policy choice. Hagan suggests that the likelihood to build a coalition of supporters for a proposed policy depends on three aspects of political fragmentation: level of fragmentation, presence of a predominant leadership, and polarization over foreign policy issues.[39] To capture the level of political fragmentation within a government Hagan distinguishes between three basic types of government with respect to the internal political division.

The first type is a government dominated by a single cohesive party or group. Power is spread within a collective leadership, while bureaucratic and personal conflicts are not constant and vary from issue to issue. It makes consensus building on foreign policy issues possible. A second type is a government controlled by a single party or group that is internally divided by factions. A single group controls the government but there are established political factions who have substantive differences on policy issues, and compete continuously for control over policy. The conflicting policy positions hinder agreement, but debates remain under control because of a shared interest of all the factions to keep their party's or ruling group's control on the government. The third type is a government ruled by a coalition of autonomous political groups. Here power is widely spread over separate political parties or groups who have ongoing clear-cut policy differences and compete openly for political power. The building of consensus among coalition members is difficult because any group within the government can block policy proposals by threatening to withdraw from the coalition. Reaching an agreement is even more complicated when a coalition is composed of two or more groups of comparable political strength and there is an absence of one decisive authority.[40]

This brings us to the second characteristic of political fragmentation that influences the likelihood of agreement between competing policy-makers on a final policy choice: presence of a predominant leadership. A predominant leadership exists, says Hagan, when an individual leader or ruling group controls all power within a government. This may be the case as a result of constitutional arrangements, personal charisma of the leader, or when a ruling group controls a vital power base of the government, such as votes in parliament, military force, or legitimizing ideology. A predominant leader or ruling group may allow policy debates among officials but nobody can directly challenge the leadership, which makes consensus building easy. As Hagan argues, since no other participant in the decision-making process can overrule the leadership, the range of policy options to be considered is limited by the preferences of the predominant leadership. Moreover, a predominant leadership with clear policy preferences simply imposes its first choice on other participants in the decision-making process.[41] The third feature of political fragmentation that affects the likelihood of building a coalition of supporters for a proposed policy is the extent of polarization over foreign policy issues. Such a polarization exists when there are sharp divisions among key decision-makers about foreign policy orientations. As Hagan explains, this intensifies debates on the fundamental problems facing a nation, and increases differences on how to deal with these problems. Such basic differences over the nation's foreign policy, also constraints the ability of decision-makers to reach an agreement on specific foreign policy issues.[42]

FOREIGN POLICY IS POLITICS

To complete the discussion of the various effects of domestic politics on foreign policy, I turn now to the question of how the drive for political survival and the incentive for consensus building influence the content of foreign policy choices made by political leaders and other key decision-makers in the ruling group. I will begin with the inner circle of foreign policy-making to examine how the existence of opposition and the need to bargain with one another affects policy choices, and move then to the broader domestic environment to look at the effects that the electoral vulnerability and the closely related pressure of public opinion may have on the content of foreign policy.

The Effects of Opposition and Bargaining

From the discussion so far it is obvious that the ruling leadership has to act in response to opposition outside or within the ruling group. The ruling policy-makers respond to the existence of such opposition in different ways, with diverse effects on foreign policy. As Hagan explains, leaders may try to accommodate organized opposition with restraint in foreign policy. This results in foreign policy statements that do not commit the state, foreign policy initiatives that are less risky, and decisions that are reversible. The guiding principle is to avoid controversial foreign policy actions that may provoke increased opposition and trigger debates over the leadership's policies. But a ruling leadership may also try to mobilize support for its policies by an appeal to nationalism and taking advantage of the rally around the flag effect or using the strategy of bashing the foreigners. The rally around the flag effect refers to the phenomenon of increased support for a leader during an international crisis and the first stages of a war, while the strategy of bashing the foreigners describes the phenomenon of blaming outsiders for policy failures and the attempt to divert the hostility derived from frustrations over internal policies into hostility toward outsiders. The effect on foreign policy is a tendency toward aggressive and confrontational foreign policy behavior. It leads to belligerent statements and highly visible and forceful actions. However,

Hagan reminds us, leaders may also try to insulate a foreign policy issue from domestic politics. This is for example the case in crisis situations, where the ruling leadership wants to conduct an assertive foreign policy and protect its policy choices from domestic pressures.[43]

The effects of the existence of strong opposition on foreign policy are also significant during international negotiations. Any successful agreement, argues Putnam, must gain the necessary majority among the constituents of each of the parties to the accord, when simply voted up or down. The ability to gain such a majority depends on concrete ratification procedures, as it is clear that ratification is more difficult under the requirement of a two-thirds vote instead of a simple majority, but it is also determined by the power, preferences, and possible coalitions among major domestic actors. For example, constituents who face low costs from no-agreement, which often represents the status quo, will offer less support for a proposed agreement, while others may face high costs from no-agreement and offer more support. Putnam therefore suggests that the positions taken by a leader or a ruling leadership at the negotiation table are affected by the prospects of the requirement to secure a majority in parliament for ratifying international treaties, as well as the need to gain the endorsement and cooperation of important interest groups and societal organizations.[44] In a joint study several international relations scholars have demonstrated that the need to gain the necessary domestic majority to ensure ratification for an international agreement indeed influences the process as well as the outcomes of international negotiations. They found, for example, that the relative autonomy of international leaders decreases continuously and substantially during international negotiations, since the more clearly international options become defined, the more leaders are constrained by mobilized interest groups.[45]

The way the internal bargaining among participants in the foreign policy-making process may influence policy outcomes is closely related to the nature of the decision-making entity in which the bargaining takes place. As the foreign policy literature suggests, different decision-making dynamics and diverse decision rules structure the bargaining process in small groups, and settings in which each individual participates in the bargaining in his or her own right.[46] Building upon this literature, a number of foreign policy scholars, in a collaborative research effort, have indicated how the structure and process in a decision unit composed of a single group or a coalition of autonomous actors can affect foreign policy outcomes.[47]

In a single group all individual members interact directly with one another to reach a decision collectively. They can form or change their position on an issue without outside consultation. As Charles Hermann, Janice Gross Stein, and Stephen Walker argue, group members can deal with internal disagreement or conflict over the preferred course of action in three different ways: they can avoid it, they can resolve it, or they can accept it. A group which is committed to avoiding internal conflict, they say, usually suppresses disagreements and is very likely to select the primary option considered by group members. Only when the group norms permit disagreement and encourage consideration of each other's proposals, the group may choose an alternative that represent the preference of all members but involves some shift from initial preferences. They further argue that a group which has a tendency to resolve group conflict recognizes that substantive disagreement among group members and the need to bridge these differences is part of the policy-making process. Since all group members must agree to any proposal, two outcomes are possible. If they are unable to bridge their differences then stalemate results. A compromise instead of deadlock becomes more likely if one or more group members assume a broker role and persuade some group members to change their first choice or discover a solution that satisfies everyone. However, group members may also recognize that achieving agreements that are acceptable to everyone is impossible and that they have to operate with a majority-voting rule, which settles disagreement by the acceptance of solutions that are satisfactory to a majority of the group members while others remain opposed. Only when a minority includes respected members who advocate intensely their preferences, the group may still agree on a choice that does not represent the initial preferences of all the members or simply deadlocks.[48]

The ability to reach an agreement on a policy choice is more complicated when the decision-making entity is formed by a coalition of politically autonomous actors. All participants are bound to specific positions taken elsewhere and must consult with their constituents before taking a decision or changing his or her initial position. In circumstances where a government or any other decision-making body is composed of such independent individuals or groups every actor needs the support of other participants for a policy initiative. However, as Hagan, Philip Everts, Haruhiro Fukui, and John Stempel demonstrate in separate case studies, the possibility of reaching an agreement among autonomous actors depends on the rules of decision-making that guide the interaction among the actors engaged in the decision-making process. Decision-making in a multiparty coalition cabinet with established decision rules that require unanimous agreement among participants is constrained by the ability of each actor to veto a decision, which means that a deadlock is the most likely outcome. On the other hand, decision-making bodies governed by established decision rules that require some kind of majority can avoid a deadlock by making compromises among participants with relatively close preferences and reach an agreement with a minimum wining coalition. As they further illustrate, in decision-making situations where accepted decision rules are almost absent, which is typical for a revolutionary coalition in an authoritarian regime or a less institutionalized political system, deadlock is also the most likely outcome.[49]

The Effects of Electoral Vulnerability and Public Opinion

Moving from the inner circle of foreign policy-making to the broader domestic environment brings us to the effects that the electoral vulnerability of the political leadership, and the closely related pressure of public opinion, may have on the content of foreign policy. Since there is some debate among international relations scholars about the relationship between public opinion and national security policy, in particular over the extent to which the choice of voters is determined by foreign policy issues, I will follow in this matter the view of Bernard Cohen who has suggested that "public opinion as a political force has bearing on foreign policy to the extent that foreign policy makers perceive in the environment outside of their political orbit some encouragements or limitations that facilitate or modify preferred behavior."[50] Russett, for example, clearly argues that leaders usually make their policy choices within some range of acceptable options. Their maneuvering space, he says, is limited to the range of alternative policies that a majority of the public is prepared to tolerate.[51] The domestic political consequences of becoming involved in a real war, for example, motivates leaders to avoid the use of force. As Russett points out: "all great power governments that have lost major wars in the past century have been overthrown from within if not by their external enemies. But even leaders who conduct and win costly wars are likely to be 'punished' by their longsuffering electorates."[52] He recalls the loss of Winston Churchill in the first British elections after the Second World War, and reminds us that the former American presidents, Harry Truman, Lyndon Johnson, and Richard Nixon, saw their popularity damaged by the American involvement in the Korean War and the Vietnam War. Leaders therefore prefer to carry out a conflict with an adversary by means of threats, the employment of economic sanctions, and the limited use of force, instead of taking provocative actions that may result in a crisis which can escalate and lead to military commitment. Faced with a public demand to do something about an international situation they prefer to use the instrument of economic sanctions, even though it is known that economic sanctions rarely succeed in realizing the objectives for which they are employed.[53]

However, Russett also provides evidence for the fact that in many instances various kinds of security policies are likely to be politically acceptable for achieving a general goal like peace and security. Russett gives the example of the Vietnam War where majorities could be found in favor of bombing North Vietnam and for sending more American troops to South Vietnam, but also in support of negotiations and even for allowing Viet Cong participation in the South Vietnamese government. It gave American presidents different options to end the war, varying from military actions to a negotiated settlement. This mix of toughness and conciliation applies, according to Russett, to many other issues in the field of foreign and security policies. He therefore argues that public opinion sets a broad range of political options within which leaders can choose, and within which creative national security leaders may operate, although the incentive to get public approval will help to shape the kind of decision finally made. Since a majority of the population is not extremely hawkish, nor extremely dovish, a leader is rewarded for choosing policies that are within this centrist mainstream.[54]

Nonetheless, the actual selection process may lead to a final decision that is acceptable from a domestic political standpoint but is less preferable from a foreign policy perspective. As Bueno de Mesquita and David Lalman have argued, many leaders and ruling groups are faced with the dilemma that on the one hand they want to meet the desires of domestic constituencies on whom they depend for their continuation in office as much as possible, but on the other hand they must be aware of the costs they will suffer if their responsiveness to domestic pressures leads to foreign policy disasters.[55] This is demonstrated by the experience of the American involvement in the Vietnam War. Daniel Ellsberg, for example, rejected already in the early 1970s the quagmire theory as an explanation for the escalation of the American involvement in the Vietnam War. The quagmire theory saw the policy-making regarding Vietnam as a step-by-step process, each new step always promising the success the former step had also promised, but failed to deliver. Ellsberg claimed that successive American presidents deliberately adopted policies that were considered at the time of decision as inadequate to win the war and were believed to restore, at best, a violent stalemate.[56]

To explain this phenomenon Ellsberg argued that successive American presidents were actually guided in their policy choices by two rules. The first rule stated: do not lose the rest of Vietnam to Communist control before the next elections. The second rule asserted: do not commit American ground troops to a land war in Asia. Ignoring the first rule or breaking the second rule, he said, exposed the president to the political risks of loss of electoral support, loss of Congress, and loss of reputation. To resolve this dilemma the second rule was extended to a list of military measures that were not taken unless it was essential to satisfy the first rule. The military actions were ranked according to their relative disruption of normal life, their impact on American casualties, and their risk of war with China and Russia. According to Ellsberg, no president was ready to solve the Vietnam problem by either taking much riskier measures to win or to get out of Vietnam. Each president rather preferred to make choices that were simply oriented toward the short-term consideration of buying a stalemate. However, every setback in the American policy led to escalating decisions, since the desire to regain a stalemate was reinforced by a tendency to escalate if and as necessary to avoid defeat. Hence, the consequences of applying the two rules to policy choices in Vietnam, Ellsberg said, set at work a mechanism that he called a stalemate machine. It resulted in a pattern of decisions that were purposefully dedicated to preserving a stalemate, at ever increasing levels of violence.[57]

4

A SECOND CUT

CHOOSING STALEMATE

Building on the findings discussed in the former chapter I examine in this chapter the way domestic political conditions explain the Jewish acceptance and the Palestinian rejection of a partitioned Palestine in 1947, as well as the willingness of Israel and the PLO in 1993 to recognize each other's existence and to sign the Oslo accords that implied the acceptance of a two-state solution. As I have indicated in chapter 3 the conception of these choices as an outcome of a domestic political process means that the leadership's drive for political survival and the need to secure internal support for a policy are critical for explaining these decisions, and requires consideration of the domestic political context and the institutional setting in which these choices were made.

To capture the impact of the need of the Israeli and Palestinian leadership to maintain and enhance the political base for staying in power on the choices they have made, I will look at the leadership's response to opposition from other political parties that competed for control of the government and opposition from groups within the ruling party or ruling group who wanted to change the existing policies. I will consider as well the effects of the electoral vulnerability of the political leadership and the pressure posed by Israeli and Palestinian public opinion and organized societal and interest groups. I will also examine whether the ruling Israeli and Palestinian leadership tried to accommodate the opposition by avoiding controversial decisions and less risky actions, or if it tried to mobilize support for their policies by an appeal to nationalism and taking advantage of rally around the flag effect or using the strategy of bashing the foreigners. To explore the influence of the need of the Israeli and Palestinian leadership to build domestic support for their policies on the content of their decisions, I will look at the internal bargaining process. I will examine whether they were sensitive to the requirement to achieve sufficient consensus in support of their policies and decisions, and if the internal bargaining dynamics and decision rules enabled the participants in the decision-making process to reach an agreement on a policy choice in the form of a compromise, or if it resulted in a deadlock.

But before I turn to examine these questions I have to clarify one important point. In the literature that I discussed in chapter 3 the authors usually refer to a national government as the actor that responds to a foreign policy problem and makes the foreign policy decision. However in the first issue, the problem of partition, neither the Jewish community nor the Palestine Arab community were a state and therefore lacked, as per definition, a government. As I will explain later, the two communities developed nonetheless decision-making bodies that resembled a national government, although the level of institutional development in the two communities was very different. After the establishment of the Jewish state, Israel had a full-blown government. The Palestinians missed for a while an organization that resembles a government. But with the founding of the PLO and the creation of an executive committee the Palestinians had in fact a decision-making body that had all the characteristics of a government and could be seen as an authoritative decision unit as defined by Margaret Hermann.[1] The creation of the Palestinian Authority as a result of the Oslo Accords constituted finally a real Palestinian government.

ACCEPTANCE AND REJECTION
OF PARTITION

The Jewish and Palestinian communities in Palestine took opposite positions on the issue of partition. Although the whole Jewish community did not endorse the idea of partition the ruling leadership of the Jewish community approved the UN partition plan, which suggested the partition of Palestine in a Jewish and an Arab state. The Palestinian Arabs community, for their part, shared a consensual rejection of partition. The Jewish leadership was successful in overcoming opposition toward partition within and outside the ruling leadership, and was able to create a consensus for the establishment of a Jewish state only in part of Palestine. But the Palestinian Arab leadership was unable to bridge the structural division within its political elite in order to cope effectively with the political and military consequences of their all or nothing policy, and lost the opportunity to establish the Arab state called for by the UN partition plan.

The Jewish Internal Divisions

The crucial decisions in favor of partition and the establishment of the state of Israel were made in the Jewish Agency Executive (JAE). This elected executive body was the predominant decision-making institution of both the world Zionist movement and the Jewish community in Palestine until the establishment of the state of Israel in 1948. In fact, the JAE acted and functioned under the leadership of Ben-Gurion as a quasi-government. It derived its leading role from the official status it had under the terms of the British Mandate in which the Jewish Agency was recognized as the official representative body of the Zionist movement and entitled to cooperate with the British mandatory government in the establishment of a national home for the Jewish people in Palestine. The decision in favor of partition was not a unanimous decision. Ben-Gurion managed to secure a majority within the JAE in support of the idea of partition, so that he could present a clear position of the Jewish Agency during the visit of UNSCOP to Palestine. But the vote in favor of the so-called viable state formula, which in fact meant partition, was merely won by a tight majority. All the three coalition parties that made up the JAE were actually split down the middle, and in order to get a majority Ben-Gurion had to declare that the Zionist movement had the right to the whole of western Palestine. As Joseph Heller notes, this was a maneuver to soften the decision for those who found it hard to agree to partition.[2]

The Jewish community in Palestine was even more divided on the issue of partition than the JAE, as not all the conflicting views on the issue of partition were represented in the JAE. There was first of all a bitter political gap between the two main political movements within the Jewish community: the socialists and the revisionists. For the revisionist movement, which was in opposition outside the JAE and had no influence on the decision-making process in the Zionist movement, any territorial compromise was out of the question. They remained faithful to the revisionist ideology of their charismatic leader Zeev Jabotinski who died in 1940 but whose ideas still dominated the revisionist movement. One of his core principles was the Jewish right to statehood and political sovereignty over the whole land of Israel (Eretz-Israel), which included both banks of the river Jordan. Menachem Begin, the dogmatic leader of the revisionist underground military organization—the Irgun Zvai Leumi (IZL)—considered therefore the territorial integrity of the future state of Israel within the historical borders of the land of Israel as sacred and consequently non-negotiable. Begin also rejected partition because he did not believe that the British government would withdraw from Palestine, given its strategic interests in the country. For that reason he considered the UNSCOP plan not as the end of the struggle against the British authorities but as the beginning of a new confrontation, as Begin strongly believed that Jewish independence would be achieved only by the pressure of guerrilla activities, which he saw as a war of libera-tion. Begin and other revisionist leaders considered the acceptance of the UNSCOP partition plan by the JAE a complete surrender, and demanded the immediate establishment of a Jewish state. To put morale pressure on the JAE the revisionists presented a warning that if the JAE will not proclaim the establishment of a Jewish state immediately, the IZL will start a national revolt.[3]

In comparison with the clear-cut position of the revisionists the socialist movement was much more divided on the issue of partition. The largest group within the socialist movement was the Mapai party, which represented mainstream socialists and was led by Ben-Gurion. The Mapai party was also divided internally between moderates and activists. The moderates, who formed the major group in the party, followed a gradualist and pragmatic approach toward Jewish state-hood. They supported in principle a strategy that was based on the use of diplomacy rather than force and wanted to clash with the British authorities only on immigration and settlement. The activists by con-trast favored a continuous struggle against the British. The party was nevertheless able to agree on a pragmatic middle course that satisfied both moderates and activists and created broad support in the party for a limited active struggle against the British that was focused on the establishment of new settlements and illegal immigration. On the issue of partition the Mapai party also followed a pragmatic line that was advocated by the moderates. They argued that since the goal of the Zionist enterprise was to build a Jewish state in which Jews form a majority, partition was the only reasonable option because it offered a territory with a Jewish majority. Reaching a demographic Jewish supremacy in a state that will comprise the whole of Palestine was in their view unrealistic, given the already existing Arab majority in Palestine and the high birth rate of the local Arab population.[4]

However, two factions within the socialist movement did not share the pragmatic political course of the mainstream socialists. One faction formed a radical left wing opposition; the other faction represented an

activist right wing opposition. Both factions opposed partition, but
for completely different reasons. The radical left wing was a Marxist
oriented party that differed strongly with Mapai on the solution of the
Palestine problem and therefore operated as an independent party
under the name Hashomer Hatzair. In the many debates that were
conducted within the Jewish community in the past about the option
of partition, it always opposed partition on pure ideological grounds.
As its leaders preached a class-oriented integration between Jews and
Arabs, partition was at odds with their strong ambition to achieve a
one state solution, a binational state in which Jews and Arabs share the
same territory. Binationalism was for this radical left party a sacred
principle. The consequence of this position was that it opposed the
idea of an independent Jewish state in a part of Palestine. It advocated an independent Jewish state within a binational framework that
could be achieved only through a political agreement between the
Jews and the Palestinian Arabs and would be based on political equality. The party maintained its traditional opposition to partition also
toward the UNSCOP partition plan. But although the party leadership rejected the UNSCOP plan they understood that they have to
adapt the party's binational ideology to the concrete reality in order
to avoid political isolation. Such an adjustment was also justified by
the need to bring to Palestine the displaced survivors of the Holocaust,
which created a completely different situation. The solution was the
acceptance of partition as a transition phase toward a binational state.
This more flexible position enabled the party to secure further
cooperation with the other socialist parties.[5]

   The most serious opposition to partition within the socialist
movement was formed by the activist right wing within the socialist
movement, which separated from Mapai in 1944 and formed an independent political party called Achdut Haavoda. Its leaders combined
social radicalism with political and military activism, and were dedicated to an ethos of settling and conquering the whole of Palestine.
The most important aim was to create a Jewish majority in Palestine,
and for that purpose they advocated a very activist policy of illegal
immigration and continued settlement. The party was ready to play a
vanguard role in the struggle for a socialist Jewish state in the undivided land of Israel. It believed in the logic of force and demanded a
powerful response to the Arab aggression against Jews, arguing that
the Jewish state could be realized only by imposing its will on the
Arabs. Given their commitment to an undivided Palestine they ruled
out any form of partition and were unwilling to compromise for pragmatic reasons or under the pressure of Arab violence. The willingness

of the JAE to consider partition was condemned as betrayal. But their opposition toward partition was not only a matter of principle. They disputed also the small minimalist size of the proposed Jewish state that included a very large Arab minority, namely 49 percent of the population, and advocated for security reasons a larger territory even if this meant the transfer of the local Arab population.[6]

Although Achdut Haavoda did not participate in the decision-making of the JAE it had great influence as it formed the ideological home for many of the young field commanders of the underground military elite units, named Palmach that formed the backbone of the clandestine military organization of the Jewish community, the Hagana. These native borne sons of the Zionist pioneers formed the elite of the youth of the Jewish society in Palestine. As Shlomo Ben-Ami rightly says, they were possessed by a sense of native ownership of the land they were born into and were confident that they will triumph in the inescapable war between Jews and Arabs over the possession of Palestine.[7] To prepare themselves for the decisive struggle with the Arabs they developed a military strategy based on military initiative and offensive tactics, lived in collective agricultural settlements (kibbutzim) where they combined the life of a warrior with that of a farmer and from where they carried out reprisals and collective punishments against Arab villages. These young military commanders formed a powerful pressure group that opposed partition. The military commander of the Palmach, Yigal Allon, made no secret of his views when he expressed his opinion on the UN partition plan saying that: "the borders of partition cannot be for us the final borders . . . the partition plan is a compromise plan that is unjust to the Jews. . . . We are entitled to decide our borders according to our defence needs."[8]

The powerful influence of this group of young military leaders became evident during the war of 1948. Allon and other field commanders, like Moshe Dayan and Yitzhak Rabin, fulfilled a key role in defining the strategic objectives of the war and in leading the military operations. From the very beginning they advocated military actions that were aimed at conquering Arab areas beyond the partition lines so that Jewish settlements that were not included in the proposed Jewish state could be linked to the state of Israel. These operations were also planned to change the demographic balance in the areas that came under control of the state of Israel by encouraging and forcing a massive expulsion of the Arab population from the cities and villages that were located in the newborn state and areas that came under control of Jewish forces.[9] As Shlomo Ben-Ami observes, "The borders of the Jewish state were defined by the logic of military operations. It was not Cabinet decisions that determined the borders of the new state, but military operations that were almost invariably proposed or initiated by the military commanders themselves."[10]

Building a Domestic Consensus

In spite of the internal divisions within the Jewish community in Palestine regarding the issue of partition, almost all the political parties of the Jewish community accepted the UN resolution on partition. This general agreement was the result of the effort of Ben-Gurion to build the broadest possible domestic political consensus in the Jewish community for a political strategy that aimed at the immediate establishment of a Jewish state and was based on two components: an active resistance against the British and a readiness to accept partition. This approach was not a simple change of tactics but a strategic turnabout: from the use of diplomacy to the use of force, and from a claim for a Jewish state in an undivided Palestine to the acceptance of partition. To ensure a broad domestic consensus for this new policy Ben-Gurion had to win the support of his own party, overcome the opposition in the socialist movement, and to isolate the opponents in the revisionist camp.

To gain the support of his own party, Ben-Gurion had to bridge the considerable differences of opinion within the party between moderates and activists. The ideological differences between the two groups deepened after the end of the Second World War when it became evident that the new British Labor government, which was expected to be sympathetic to the Jewish cause after the Holocaust, had no intention of changing the severe restrictions on Jewish immigration and settlement imposed by former British governments. While the moderates still believed in the power of diplomacy and rejected any military actions that would lead to a confrontation with the British authorities, the activists came to the conclusion that diplomacy alone does not work and advocated armed resistance to the British. In an attempt to create a common denominator between moderates and activists in his party Ben-Gurion coined the phrase: neither Massada nor Vichy, by which he meant that the Jewish community must neither place itself in an impossible situation nor compromise its principles. This guiding principle helped him to call for a flexible policy that combined the use of force with diplomacy and subordinated the military struggle to political considerations. It satisfied both moderates and activists and created broad support in the party for a limited active struggle against the British and focused the confrontation on illegal immigration and the establishment of new settlements.[11] Ben-Gurion followed a similar tactic with respect to the issue of partition. To avoid a debate over partition that may lead to polarization between moderates and activists, he used the slogan of a viable Jewish state without a demarcation of its borders, saying that this formula would be the basis for negotiations about a future state. The Mapai leadership by a large majority approved this rather vague formula, indicating that they were prepared to accept a territorial compromise.[12]

Winning the support of his own party was an important step toward the building of a broad domestic consensus, because Mapai was the largest political party in the Jewish community and the Zionist movement and dominated the JAE. But Ben-Gurion wanted to build a strong consensus in favor of partition also within the JAE where he formed a coalition with the right-center liberal party and the national-religious parties who controlled the JAE together with the Mapai. The national-religious parties could form a serious obstacle, but the formula of a viable Jewish state without a demarcation of its borders was effective in the JAE as well. Giving up his opposition to partition the representative of the national-religious parties who demanded in the past a Jewish state on both sides of the river Jordan he now said: "I love the Land of Israel, and I love the people of Israel too. But the people takes precedence over the land. If the people is annihilated, there is no hope that we could live under any regime, including Britain's . . . even with the Messiah's appearance Nablus would not belong to the Jews. We can only hope that we shall get a state in part of the Land of Israel."[13] The right-center liberal party, which was also split between radicals and moderates, did not give its unanimous support to partition. But this was not a stumbling block for Ben-Gurion to present to UNSCOP a broad Jewish consensus over the readiness to accept a territorial compromise, when the UN inquiry commission visited Palestine in 1947. Just before its arrival, a majority of JAE members voted in favor of the establishment of a viable independent Jewish state in Palestine, that is, for partition.[14]

Ben-Gurion was also successful in bringing the two other socialist factions within the socialist movement into the domestic consensus, using the rally around the flag effect. Members of both factions were deeply involved in the illegal immigration struggle and were placed in the forefront of the military preparation for the war with the Palestinian Arabs and the neighboring Arab states. As the war of 1948 began Ben-Gurion invited the leaders of the two factions to join the provisional emergency government and take full responsibility for the conduct of the war. The leadership of the two factions, that in the meantime decided to unite and form a new radical socialist party named Mapam, could not refuse this opportunity to influence the decision-making over the course of the war and accepted Ben-Gurion's invitation.[15]

Ben-Gurion left only the revisionists outside the domestic consensus, but this was done deliberately. He wanted to isolate the revisionist party and in particular its underground organization that did not recognize the authority of the JAE and used terror tactics, which he condemned as being a danger to the Jewish unity of policy and action. After the establishment of the state of Israel, as the leadership of the revisionists and the IZL were ready to accept the authority of the provisional government but at the same time refused to give up its struggle for the whole of Palestine, Ben-Gurion turned down all the attempts made by the revisionist party to join the provisional government or get involved in the official decision-making. His determination to isolate the revisionists and end the existence of the IZL as an independent military organization culminated in the *Altalena* affair, which occurred in June 1948 and is named after the ship that carried weapons intended for IZL units. To demonstrate his firm decision to subordinate the IZL to the authority of the government of the newborn state, Ben-Gurion ordered the preventing of the unloading of the ship by the use of force, which resulted in the sinking of the *Altalena* just off the coast of Tel Aviv.[16] The isolation of the revisionist party and the former IZL that reemerged in 1948 as a legal opposition party named Herurt under the leadership of the former IZL leader Begin, continued in fact as long as Ben-Gurion served as prime minister.

The Palestinian Domestic Political Structure

The Palestinain Arabs were less divided on the issue of partition than the Jewish community. Their unanimous rejection of the UN partition plan was a consequent continuation of the position that the Palestinian Arabs took on every occasion in the past regarding partition: an unequivocal rejection of every proposal to divide the country between the two communities. When it came to the national rights, all Palestinians denied any Jewish claim and demanded an Arab government over the whole of Palestine. In such an independent Palestinian Arab state there was room for a small Jewish community composed in principle only of Jews who lived in Palestine before the British arrival. But in spite of this consensus, in practice the Palestinian

Arabs could not organize themselves into one unified nationalist front with a cohesive and centralized leadership. The main reason for this incapability lies in the domestic political structure of the Palestinian Arab community and their failure to form self-governing institutions.

The first important characteristic of the Palestinian Arab community was its regional oligarchic structure. It was a society in which political loyalties were based on family and clan relations as well as links to a town or village rather than to a vague Palestinian territorial entity. In fact, until the British occupation of Palestine in the First World War Palestine did not exist as a single administrative unit. Under Ottoman rule, the northern areas of Palestine were part of the Ottoman province of Beirut, while the center and most of the south formed the separate district of Jerusalem which was placed under the direct authority of Istanbul. The political and economic power was concentrated in the hands of a small and deeply divided elite, composed of a number of competing notable families that dominated Palestinian politics. This basically urban elite did not create strong links with the population, which lived mainly in villages in the countryside. The villages were politically self-centered and largely uninvolved in national affairs. The notable urban families that owned much of the land on which the villagers lived represented their interests.[17]

The second significant characteristic of the Palestinian Arab community was the internal division within the political elite. The split was less along ideological lines than along family lines and local relationships. The notable families were in fact divided into two major camps. The first camp was dominated and led by the Al-Husayni family that controlled the Supreme Muslim Council (SMC), the Arab Executive, and its successor the Arab Higher Committee (AHC). Those who opposed them formed the other camp and were led by the Nashashibis. The two camps also established in the 1930s political parties in which membership was, once again, based on family loyalties and local connections. The bitter struggle between the two parties was more about power and economic benefits than about ideological differences, as both parties opposed Zionism, wanted to end the British rule, and demanded Arab statehood in all Palestine.[18]

The governmental system set up by the British to rule over Palestine did not change these fundamental features of Palestinian politics. Under the British Mandate regime, the British high commissioner was the only source of authority. The Palestinian Arabs composed a vast majority of the population, but were not allowed to form any autonomous self-governing institutions to assist the British authorities in running the country. Contrary to the Jewish community and the

Arabs in the neighboring countries, the Palestinian Arabs had no executive body, an elected representative council, or any other institutional framework that could help them to develop their statehood and express their nationhood. The only institution the British authorities created was the SMC, headed by a *mufti* who was appointed by the British high commissioner. But the SMC was basically a religious institution that managed the Muslim properties and Islamic courts, maintained the mosques, and appointed religious officials. The first nominated *mufti*, Amin al-Husayni, who was in principle a religious leader, was nonetheless quite successful in using the SMC as a power base for his nationalist activities. At one point the British authorities were willing to create an Arab Agency, but the Palestine Arabs rejected the British proposal because its members would have been appointed by the British high commissioner rather than elected by the Palestinian Arab population. The Palestinian Arabs themselves founded in the early 1920s the Palestine Arab Congress that elected an Arab Executive, which represented the different groups within the Palestine Arab elite. It functioned several years as the de-facto representative body of the Palestine Arabs, but was ineffective and almost ignored by the British authorities. Another effort to create a central countrywide executive body was made at the beginning of the Arab Revolt in 1936. The leaders of different political parties joined forces and constituted the AHC to coordinate the struggle against the British authorities. However, political differences among its members prevented it from functioning properly, so that the local National Committees instead of the AHC actually organized the struggle. It was further paralyzed during the rebellion by the arrest or the forced exile of its members. The Arab League revived the AHC in 1946 but it never became an influential decision-making body, as the Arab League itself took the important decisions regarding the Palestine problem.[19]

The Pressure Toward Radicalism

Despite the consensus among the Palestinian Arabs about the goal of an independent Arab state in the whole of Palestine, they were divided about the desired strategy for achieving that goal. While the division among the political elite was mainly about tactics, the gap between the urban elite and the rural population as well as the poor inhabitants in the cities was deep-seated. It was in the rural areas where the expansion of the Zionist enterprise had the most impact on the local Arab population. As a result of the Zionist purchase of land from the big Arab landowners, local notables as well as absentee landlords, many Arab tenants lost their land and became hired workers for peasants who still owned their land or were forced to move from the villages to the poor neighborhoods in the cities where unemployment was widespread. No wonder that the resistance to the Zionist movement and the British rule, which was closely associated with the growth of the Zionist enterprise, was great in the rural regions and the poor neighborhoods. It was in these areas, where local leaders and popular preachers could exert a strong influence by an appeal to nationalist and religious sentiments, recruit guerrilla fighters, and initiate military actions against the British that culminated in the Arab Revolt in 1936.[20]

The initial response of the urban Arab elite to the rebellion of the lower classes within the Palestinian Arab community against the British was hesitant. The AHC, that represented essentially the urban Arab elite and had close relations with the British authorities, tried to control the rebellion by calling for a general strike and organizing nationwide demonstrations. But as the local rural leaders intensified their pressure on the British in 1937 with a bold guerrilla war against the British army, the leader of the AHC Al-Husayni adjusted to the pressure from below and adopted a more radical and aggressive policy in order to secure his political leadership of the nationalist movement. Al-Husayni surrendered to the demands of the militant local leaders and young commanders of the rebels who insisted on complete and unconditional independence. He rejected the British White Paper in 1939, in which the British government proposed the establishment of a unitary independent state after a transitional period of ten years coupled with a strict limitation on Jewish immigration and land sales to Jews. However, the price for this radical policy was the breakdown of the fragile coalition within the AHC, as other members of the AHC favored acceptance of the White Paper. Most of the Palestinian Arab leadership, in particular the rival Nashashibi camp, welcomed the British recognition of the existence of an Arab national majority with a right to independence and statehood, and were therefore ready to take a more positive attitude toward the White Paper.[21]

A prominent analyst of the Palestinian failure to deal with the problem of partition and its consequences in 1947 and 1948, like Khalidi, traces the roots of that failure to the devastating effects of the Arab Revolt on their national leadership, social cohesion, and military capabilities. As he argues: "Factors such as the poor political calculations, and the disorganization, confusion and leaderless chaos on the

Palestinian side, all of which contributed measurably to the debacle, need to be factored into the Palestinian historical narrative. So too does the fact that Palestinians, still suffering acutely from the after-effects of the defeat of the 1936–39 revolt, and deprived of a central para-state mechanism, a unified leadership, and representative institutions, in consequence never had a chance of retaining control of their country."[22]

THE MUTUAL ACCEPTANCE OF A TWO-STATE SOLUTION

The Oslo accords between Israel and the PLO were one of the great watersheds in the history of the Israeli-Palestinian conflict. It marked an important turning point in the Israeli approach to the Palestinian problem and the closely related issue of the future of the West Bank and Gaza Strip. It was also the beginning of a new stage in the realization of Palestinian statehood. However, the two main features of the Oslo agreements, the joint recognition of each other's existence and the mutual acceptance of the principle of a two-state solution, exposed sharp divisions in the Israeli as well as the Palestinian society between supporters and opponents of the Oslo accords. The Israeli population was divided between two almost equal camps that adopted two opposite positions. One half of Israeli society, led by the Labor party, supported a policy of reconciliation with the PLO. It also accepted the principle of a territorial compromise, which implied withdrawal from large parts of the West Bank and the Gaza Strip and the transfer of government in the evacuated territories to a Palestinian Authority under the leadership of Arafat. The other half of the Israeli population, led by the Likud Party, rejected the transfer of any part of the West Bank and Gaza Strip to the Palestinians and considered recognition of the PLO illegitimate. The Palestinians were also split over the Oslo agreements. While the PLO and its supporters in the occupied territories saw the Oslo accords as the beginning of a process that would end Israeli occupation and lead to a Palestinian state, the Hamas rejected any territorial compromise or any other settlement that implied a recognition of Israel. After a brief description of the deep divisions among Israelis and Palestinians on the recognition of each other's existence and the principle of a two-state solution, I will analyze how the ruling leadership on both sides dealt with the absence of broad domestic support for the Oslo accords, given the leadership's drive for political survival.

Labor's Pragmatism

The Oslo accords were the fulfillment of a promise that Prime Minister Rabin made to the Israeli public in his election campaign in 1992. If he would be elected as prime minister, he told the Israeli electorate, he would reach an agreement with the Palestinians over Palestinian self-rule in the occupied territories within nine months of being elected.[23] However, during that election campaign there was not yet any indication that Rabin would recognize a year later the PLO and would accept the principle of a two-state solution in order to end the Israeli-Palestinian conflict. In the elections campaign Rabin still remained within the traditional views of the Labor party regarding the Palestinian issue, as formulated in the Labor party's electoral platform. The Labor party was in favor of bilateral talks with the Palestinians, but these talks had to be held with Palestinians from the West Bank and the Gaza Strip, not directly with the PLO. In return for peace the Labor party was ready to accept a permanent solution to the Palestinian problem that was based on a territorial compromise, but it excluded a return to the 1949 armistice lines. It was willing to give up territories on the West Bank and the Gaza Strip that have a dense Palestinian population, but it rejected the possibility that those territories would form an independent Palestinian state, as it favored the establishment of a Palestinian-Jordanian entity.[24]

The political platform did not reflect a political consensus but rather a common denominator among the different views that were represented within the Labor party on the Palestinian issue and the future of the territories that Israel has occupied during the war of 1967. As a result of the need to maneuver between the party's moderate mainstream and the more extreme right wing faction, the Labor party was quite ambiguous in its approach toward the future of the occupied territories and in particular the West Bank and the Gaza Strip. The party's mainstream advocated withdrawal from almost all the territories and their separation from Israel in order to preserve Israel as a Jewish state. They did not want to take a formal stand on the future of the West Bank and the Gaza Strip since they saw the conquest of the new territories, which they called the Administered Territories, as temporary and serving mainly as a bargaining chip in negotiations over a peace settlement with the Arab neighbors. However the price for withdrawal was a permanent peace treaty based on agreed and secured borders. The right wing factions wanted to keep the territories, since they gave Israel the strategic territorial depth it missed under the 1949 ceasefire borders. They supported an expansionist policy that would establish strong ties with the territories and create new facts, which could not be ignored in a final political settlement. Short after the 1967 war the readiness to trade peace for territory has been the predominant view in the Labor party. But as it became clear that the Arabs adopted a policy that rejected peace with Israel, excluded its recognition, and ruled out any negotiations with the Jewish state, the dovish group lost ground to the hawkish group. Keeping the territorial status quo until a final peace settlement was possible remained Labor's formal line. But the political preferences of the hawkish group, which encouraged controlled Jewish settlement in strategic points in the occupied territories including the West Bank and the Gaza Strip and building an infrastructure that supported the settlers, dictated more and more the actual policies of Labor during its long stay in power.[25]

While Labor lacked a general agreement about continued control and presence of Israel in the West Bank and the Gaza Strip, hawks and doves alike, opposed the establishment of an independent Palestinian state and banned the PLO from negotiations on the future of the West Bank and the Gaza Strip. In an attempt to find an alternative for a Palestinian state and to avoid negotiations with the PLO, Labor leaders advocated the so-called Jordanian option. It implied that since the West Bank was before June 1967 part of Jordan, the heavily populated areas on the West Bank that were proposed for Palestinian self-government would be handed over to Jordan rather than the Palestinians. Consequently, not the Palestinians but the Jordanian King Hussein was the rightful negotiation partner. Labor leaders tried to convince moderate Palestinian leaders in the occupied territories to accept this so-called Jordanian option, and held, several times, secret talks with King Hussein in an attempt to find a formula for his cooperation. However, the Jordanian option could never become a real basis for a political settlement, as neither the Palestinians, nor Hussein, were ready to consider a territorial compromise that would leave some parts of the West Bank in Israel's hands.[26] By the time the Labor party assumed power in 1992, the Labor leadership already realized that the Jordanian option was dead and that the only negotiating partner on the future of the occupied territories were the Palestinians.

Such bilateral talks were in fact already going on between Israeli and Palestinian representatives from the occupied territories that participated under the cover of a joint Jordanian-Palestinian delegation in the Madrid peace process, which was launched in October 1991. But these talks deadlocked soon after they were started as a result of the uncompromising stands of the former Likud government and the Palestinians. In order to force a breakthrough in these negotiations, as the Labor leadership has promised during the elections campaign, it was ready to implement a full-fledged autonomy in the occupied territories. To demonstrate its goodwill it was even prepared to retreat from Gaza, where the Palestinians could then start to exercise self-rule. However, the Labor leadership knew that the local Palestinian representatives received their instructions from the PLO and missed the authority to accept any offer that did not meet the demand to end the occupation in all the Palestinian territories. It began therefore to accept the idea that not the local Palestinian leaders but the PLO leadership was the key for an agreement on the "Gaza-first" option, and that it therefore must talk directly to the PLO. Hence, although Labor still excluded the PLO from participation in the official negotiations that took place within the framework of the Madrid peace process, it began to move toward acceptance of the PLO as a negotiation partner, not by desire but by necessity. In July 1993, for example, when the Labor members of parliament discussed the question of direct negotiations with the PLO, which were already going on without their knowledge, all of them were essentially in favor of such talks.[27]

Likud's Ideological Rigidity

Whereas the Labor party moved cautiously toward an important change in its traditional ambiguous stand on the future of the West Bank and Gaza Strip and a drastic alteration of its attitude to the PLO, its most serious political rival, the Likud party, held on to a rigid and dogmatic position on those issues. The West Bank and Gaza Strip were for the Likud party an integral part of the land of Israel and therefore nonnegotiable and the PLO was a terrorist organization with whom no dialogue could be held. Since the East Bank of the river Jordan was in the ideological perception of many Likud leaders an integral part of the biblical land of Israel, they felt that Israel already made a major concession to the Palestinians by accepting the existence of Jordan. As far as the Likud party was concerned Jordan was in fact a Palestinian state so that there was no need for another Palestinian state on the West Bank. When the Likud party emerged in 1977 as the winner of the elections, after thirty years of opposition, the Likud leadership declared that the West Bank, which they called Samaria and Judea, are an undeniable part of Israel. In order to demonstrate Israel's intention to stay in the West Bank the new Likud government made the building of new Jewish settlements the cornerstone of its policy. These new settlements were built not only on strategic sites but also in densely populated Arab areas and clearly had the aim to make it very hard for a future Israeli government that was ready to accept a territorial compromise to implement a forced evacuation of the settlements.[28]

During Likud's fifteen years stay in government its leaders refused to make any concessions that could imply eventual Israeli withdrawal from the West Bank and the Gaza Strip, and did not agree to abolish the building of new settlements. The Likud government managed to conclude with Egypt a separate peace by giving up the Sinai, without making concrete concessions on the Palestinian question and the future status of the West Bank and Gaza Strip. In the Camp David accords the Likud government promised full autonomy to the inhabitants of these territories, but it did not spell out what this meant in practice. When the actual talks between Egypt and Israel began in 1979 about the modalities of a Palestinian autonomy, no progress could be made on the establishment of Palestinian self-rule and the negotiations deadlocked. The Likud government emphasized throughout the autonomy negotiations that it would always oppose a territorial compromise and any form of self-rule that may lead to the creation of a sovereign and independent Palestinian state. It was willing to offer the Palestinian inhabitants of the West Bank and Gaza Strip only a functional autonomy that allowed them to regulate their own internal affairs while Israel kept the sovereignty over the occupied territories. Moreover, it insisted on the application of an autonomy only to persons and not to the land, which gave the Jews the right to settle anywhere in the West Bank and Gaza Strip.[29] The unsuccessful autonomy talks between Egypt and Israel came to a definite end as a result of the Lebanon war.

One of the major objectives that the ruling Likud leadership wanted to achieve when it went to war in Lebanon in 1982 was to create conditions that would improve the prospects for consolidating Israel's indefinite control of the West Bank. The Likud government believed that liquidating the PLO's territorial base in Lebanon would deal the PLO a heavy blow from which it would not recover for years. Although the Likud leadership realized that driving the PLO out of Lebanon and destroying the PLO's independent infrastructure in that country would not destroy Palestinian nationalism, it thought that the elimination of the PLO power base in Lebanon would weaken the PLO influence in the West Bank and Gaza Strip. It assumed that this would allow moderate Palestinian leaders in the occupied territories to come forward and accept the autonomy scheme offered to them by Israel. Besides this undeclared goal, the Likud leaders had another hidden ambition in mind when they started the Lebanon war. They hoped that the collapse of the PLO state within a state in Lebanon would initiate a process that would result in the overthrow of King Hussein's rule in Jordan and the transformation of that country into a Palestinian state.[30] However, none of these two undeclared goals were realized. Crushing the PLO stronghold in Lebanon did not reduce the resistance of the Palestinians to the autonomy plans or remove King Hussein from his rule in Jordan. On the contrary, it triggered a process within the occupied territories that led to the outbreak of the first *intifada*, a popular revolt against Israel's rule that lasted until the signing of the Oslo accords.

The war in Lebanon was the first war in Israel's history that was not supported by a national consensus. It aroused great controversy because many Israelis considered it to be a war of choice that was not imposed on Israel by its Arab enemies. It led in two subsequent elections—in 1984 and 1988—to a decline in Likud's power, but since both Likud and Labor lost seats in parliament, neither party was able by itself to form a stable coalition with the smaller parties. The two parties were forced to form twice a national unity government, as the Labor-Likud coalition governments were called. Staying in government enabled the Likud leaders to continue their firm settlement policy, and to undermine every attempt of Labor to initiate negotiations on the future of the West Bank and the Gaza Strip. In the Likud's view such negotiation would start a dynamic that would lead inevitably to territorial concessions, which they refused to do.[31] Paradoxically, after Labor's departure from the national unity government in 1990, the Likud leaders were forced to submit to American pressure and to participate in the international peace conference that the United States organized in Madrid in October 1991. However, as the Likud prime minister admitted later, he had no intention of giving up his government's plans to consolidate and build new settlements. In Shamir's own words: "I would have carried on autonomy talks for ten years and meanwhile we would have reached half a million [Jewish] people in Judea and Samaria."[32]

Labor's Controversial Breakthrough

The Labor government that decided in September 1993 to recognize the PLO and sign the Oslo agreement that would lead to the creation of a Palestinian entity alongside Israel in large parts of the West Bank and Gaza Strip was a very vulnerable government. The forming of the new government by the Labor leader Rabin was only possible thanks to a blocking coalition of 61 seats out of the 120 seats in parliament that Labor controlled together with the leftist Meretz bloc and two Arab parties. To be less dependent on the two Arab parties Rabin invited the religious Shas party to participate in his government, which it did for the duration of one year, but even then it provided the governing coalition just a tight majority in parliament.[33] Since the two Arab parties did not join the coalition government, Rabin ruled in fact most of the time a minority government. This source of political instability was a major weakness of his government.

Despite this restraint Rabin's government was politically very ambitious. It was determined to cut the spending and investments in existing settlements in the occupied territories, and to stop the building of new settlements. Rabin's government also committed itself to begin a peace process that would inevitably lead to a withdrawal of Israeli forces from the occupied territories. Furthermore, the new government had resolved to find a political solution to the popular revolt in the occupied territories against Israeli rule, the so-called first *intifada* that broke out in December 1987. After several years in which Rabin thought that the uprising could be repressed by an iron fist policy, he began to accept that the *intifada* could not be solved by military means and that it required a political solution that addressed the root of the matter: the occupation. He believed that the establishment of full autonomy could offer such a political solution.[34]

However, as it became clear to Rabin that the PLO was able to block any interim arrangement on autonomy, which was not linked to a final agreement that met the Palestinian demand for statehood, he sought to break the stalemate by negotiating directly with the PLO. Moreover, in order to reach an agreement with the Palestinians as he promised his voters, Rabin was ready to make far-reaching concessions, which were a drastic departure from all the previous Israeli positions. While Israel always refused to deal with the PLO and insisted on negotiations only with Palestinian inhabitants of the occupied territories, the Labor-led government was now ready to recognize the PLO as the representative of the Palestinian people and a legitimate negotiating partner with whom it was prepared to conclude a deal directly. For the first time an Israeli government was also willing to withdraw Israeli forces from the occupied territories, to begin with the Gaza Strip and the Jericho area but with the prospect of moving further away from Palestinian cities in the West Bank soon thereafter. What's more, for the first time an Israeli government was ready to transfer the territorial jurisdiction over parts of the occupied territories to the

Palestinians, in addition to the functional authority. But what made this territorial concession even more radical was the willingness to transfer the sovereignty over the evacuated areas to a Palestinian authority and to allow the PLO chairman Arafat to enter these territories with an armed force to establish itself as the local power.[35]

The Vigorous Opposition

During the negotiations with the PLO, which were conducted in a secret location near Oslo, Rabin managed to minimize domestic interference. By keeping the recognition of the PLO and the Oslo agreement undisclosed until they were a fait accompli, he was able to neutralize the opposition of the Likud and other opponents on the right, and prevent a debate with critics in his own party. But the moment the Oslo accords were made public it provoked a strong and fierce resistance from the opposition parties and extra parliamentary pressure groups that refused to accept a retreat from any part of the occupied territories. The Likud party, which led the opposition in parliament, accused the government of betrayal of Israel's security and national interests. The Likud and the other rightist parties considered the recognition of the PLO and the transfer of Gaza and the Jericho area to the PLO as an act of treachery and blamed the government for abandoning the settlers in the occupied territories to the mercy of Palestinian terrorists. The Likud totally rejected the Oslo accords and promised to cancel it once they returned to power. However, the Likud and the other rightist parties had a minority in parliament and were unable to mobilize a blocking majority to prevent the ratification of the Oslo accords. From the 120 parliament members only a minimal majority of 61 members voted in favor of the Oslo accords. But since this majority included the votes of two Arab parties, the Likud disputed the legitimacy of the Oslo accords on the grounds that a Jewish majority in parliament did not approve it. It demanded a referendum or new elections that would truly reflect the will of the Jewish population.[36] All in all, it was not the Likud that became the dominant actor in the political struggle against the Oslo accords.

The most forceful opposition to the Oslo accords came from the extra parliamentary group Gush Emunim (Bloc of the Faithful) that was closely related to the National-Religious Party (NRP). Gush Emunim was a militant nationalist-religious settlement movement that opposed the retreat from any part of the occupied territories. It was created in 1974 as a grassroots movement with the purpose of settlement in all parts of the biblical land of Israel. Its leaders and members were devoted disciples of Zionist orthodox rabbis who declared the sanctity of the entire land of Israel west of the river Jordan and maintained that the holiness of the land of Israel derived from a divine promise that the Jewish people inherited from their Fathers. Since this entire land was definitely Jewish, no part of it could be handed to others. Furthermore, to preserve this legacy Jews had to inherit the land physically through the act of settlement. This deep religious belief was the driving force behind a militant settlement campaign intended to impose the building of new settlements throughout the West Bank. Under the motto: every Jew is entitled to live anywhere in his ancestral homeland, the leaders of Gush Emunim challenged Labor governments before 1977, by the building of illegal settlements in the heart of the densely Arab populated areas near Nablus and Hebron. After Likud's coming to power in 1977 Gush Emunim was a natural partner of the Likud government, with whom it shared an ideological commitment to holding on to the West Bank. The Likud did not adopt Gush Emunim's call for annexation, but it helped to realize a massive settlement program throughout the West Bank that had the aim to make a de-facto annexation of the occupied territories permanent.[37]

By the time the Oslo accords were signed in 1993, Gush Emunim was already a powerful extra parliamentary aggressive political actor, whose impact was felt throughout the Israeli political system. Some of their leaders were members of parliament through the NRP, where they formed an active coalition in support of a dynamic settlement policy with parliament members of the Likud and other parties on the right. Gush Emunim members formed also the hard core of Yesha, an acronym for the Council of Jewish settlements in Judea, Samaria, and Gaza, that was established in 1980 to represent the Jewish settlers in the occupied territories. It functioned from the beginning not only as a local representative body but also as an influential lobby and pressure group on behalf of the settlers. Crucial for Gush Emunim's campaign against the Oslo accords was also the support of a number of prominent and influential rabbis, who used their moral authority to struggle against the legitimacy of Rabin's government and the Oslo accords. Many of them lived in the occupied territories and were organized in the Rabbinical Council of Judea and Samaria.

The rabbis questioned the legality of a government that relies on the Arabs for its majority, and issued several Jewish religious rulings that prohibited the removal of Jewish settlements and the evacuation of military bases, which they considered to be settlements as well. They called upon Israeli soldiers to disobey orders to evacuate settlements and military bases, as no Jew was allowed to take part in any act aiding in the evacuation of a settlement or a military compound. Some of these rabbis even issued rulings that Jews should give their lives in the struggle against the destruction of Jewish settlements. Following a series of Palestinian suicide bombings in Israel and the killing of soldiers, settlers, and other Israeli civilians in the occupied territories, Rabin himself became more and more the target of their attacks. They linked the evacuation of Israeli soldiers from Gaza and Jericho and the formation of a large Palestinian police force to the escalation of Palestinian terrorism and blamed the architects of the Oslo accords, Rabin and Peres, for it. Although none of them authorized the killing of Rabin, a number of them allowed their students to believe that Rabin qualified for a death sentence.[38]

The Missing Peace Coalition

Rabin did not face opposition to the Oslo accords within his government. His longtime political rival within the Labor party, Peres, served as foreign minister in his government and was in fact the driving force behind the secret Oslo back channel. During the secret negotiations they worked together in close harmony to make the Oslo accords a Middle East reality. The other ministers who were actually excluded from the decision-making were surprised but approved the Oslo accords unanimously, in spite of the reservations made by some officials who were also left out. One coalition party, Meretz, also supported the recognition of the PLO and the Oslo agreement entirely. However, within the other coalition party, Labor, some hawkish parliament members felt misled by the secretive method in which the Oslo accords were negotiated. The Labor hawks had also doubts about the unconditional recognition of the PLO and the creation of a Palestinian armed police in Gaza and the West Bank. They shared the criticism of Ehud Barak, at that time the chief of staff of the Israeli army, who was kept in the dark during the negotiations and felt hurt for not being consulted on the security consequences of the Oslo accords. As many of them were former high ranking military and closely associated with Rabin, the chief of staff during the June war, who led the hawkish group in the party before he became prime minister, this hawkish group kept their misgivings behind close doors. As long as the peace process was moving forward the hawks closed ranks with the doves in the party behind the Labor-led government and accepted the Oslo accords. But when the terrorist attacks began in 1994 and escalated further in 1995 they expressed their reservations in public and backed the leading military who claimed that the Oslo accords were full of security problems that could have been prevented if the military experts would have participated in the secret Oslo negotiations.[39]

However, the real cause for the adoption of a more critical attitude toward Rabin was not the Oslo agreement but the future of the Golan Heights. After the signing of the Oslo accords Rabin concluded a peace treaty with Jordan in October 1994, and resumed the dialogue with Syria on a peace settlement that was started as part of the Madrid peace conference. Between November 1994 and June 1995 negotiations were conducted in Washington between the Israeli and Syrian chiefs of staff on concrete security arrangements that Israel required as a crucial precondition for any withdrawal from the Golan Heights. Rabin made no secret of his wish to make peace with Syria and his readiness to pay the price of a substantial territorial retreat. The hawkish group in the party opposed such a withdrawal for security reasons, and was afraid that Rabin would surprise them again with a fait accompli. To avoid such an accomplished fact, a core group of five Labor parliament members proposed a bill that required a special majority for any withdrawal from the Golan Heights. Such an evacuation could not be approved by a simple majority in parliament but needed, according to the proposed bill, a majority of at least 70 parliament members or the approval of at least fifty percent of the votes in a national referendum. Since the proposed bill could easily be passed in parliament with the help of the opposition, the Labor party took a decision that forbade the five rebels to submit such a bill. The rebellious Labor parliament members considered the establishment of a separate party, but postponed their departure for a while.[40]

To accommodate the rebels the ruling Labor leadership offered the rebels a compromise, which allowed them to present the bill but did not allow voting for it. When a small rightist party submitted its own version of the same bill, the Labor leadership even gave the disobedient parliamentarians permission to support the bill. The proposed bill failed, nonetheless, to receive a majority in parliament thanks to the votes of some members of a small opposition party who were not willing to support the bill. The insubordinate Labor parliament members almost brought about a collapse of the whole peace process when two of them voted in October 1995 against the interim agreement between Israel and the PLO that extended the Palestinian self-rule to Arab cities and some other rural areas in the West Bank. The interim agreement was approved by only a minimal majority of 61 votes.[41] The split in the Labor faction in parliament became definite as the rebellious

Labor members decided to establish a new party called the Third Way. This meant that the already unstable peace coalition eroded further since the Labor-led government lost the blocking majority it had in parliament together with its coalition partner Meretz and the two Arab parties. It became completely dependent on the votes of Shas members, who sometimes voted with the government and sometimes against it. In fact, the government missed a stable majority to ratify a probable peace treaty with Syria or to approve agreements with the PLO that involved additional territorial concessions.

The eroding parliamentary support for the continuation of the Oslo peace process and the resistance against a probable peace with Syria caused Rabin to face a significant challenge to his stay in office. However, Rabin believed that his political survival depended on his ability to attract broad support for the continuation of the peace process from the public, rather than parliamentary backing. New elections also meant the introduction of a new electoral system in which the next prime minister would be elected directly by the voters and would be given the first opportunity to form a government. In other words, not the largest party in parliament but the directly elected prime minister would be able to form a government regardless of the number of seats his party had in parliament. With this electoral change in mind Rabin's main concern was to attract direct support from the Israeli public. In the 1992 elections Labor anticipated the direct election for the prime minister by placing Rabin at the center of Labor's election campaign, presenting him as a leader who was better qualified than his Likud rival to bring peace and security and lead the country in negotiations with the Arabs. It motivated floating voters of the Likud to switch to labor in the 1992 elections, allowing Rabin to take office. The Oslo accords demonstrated that Rabin was indeed able to deliver an autonomy arrangement with the Palestinians as he had promised in the elections campaign. It already brought him support from a majority of the Israeli public. One poll, taken in August 1993, showed that 53 percent of the Israeli public supported the Oslo accords while 45 percent opposed it. Another poll even indicated that 65 percent approved the Oslo accords and only 13 percent were very much against it.[42] Rabin expected that the support for the Oslo agreement would increase after the implementation of the "Gaza and Jericho first" plan, as the Israeli public was eager to get rid of Gaza that has become a breeding ground for hatred and violence against Israel. He also assumed that the public would understand that to make the deal attractive for Arafat, he had to give him and the PLO a foothold not only in Gaza but also in Jericho.

But Rabin was unable to broaden the public support for the peace process. As a result of successive terrorist suicide attacks on Israeli civilians, carried out by Hamas and the Islamic Jihad, the public felt less rather than more secure by the peace process. It made further implementation of the Oslo accords even more controversial. Although Rabin began to face a significant challenge to his position, he had no intention of stopping the implementation of the Oslo accords or his search for peace with Syria. As he knew that a person and not a party would win the next elections, he stuck to his image as peacemaker. He attended the Nobel Peace Prize ceremony although a majority of the population thought that the ceremony should be delayed until real peace was achieved and Labor parliament members asked him to stay home. Rabin persisted with his peace policy and tried to rally public support for the cause of peace by calling the terror acts attacks on peace, the casualties of terrorism the victims of peace, and making a distinction between the PLO and the organizations that committed the terrorist acts, which he branded as the enemies of peace who kill Israelis in order to kill the peace. Despite the heavy criticism from the opposition leaders and the settlers, which became more and more personal, Rabin was determined to move ahead with the peace process. He called upon his Labor party to stay on course regardless of the decline in the polls for both the party and himself, arguing that the same polls also indicate that a majority of the Israeli public was still in favor of the peace process, as 51 percent of the public supported the interim agreement with the PLO, in the face of the mounting terror attacks.[43] At the time of his assassination, in November 1995, Rabin attracted the largest crowd ever to gather in favor of the peace process. However, neither Rabin, nor his successor Peres, was able to collect the peace dividend from the Oslo accord, which they hoped would help them to maintain and enhance the political base for staying in office.

Rabin's successor, Peres, was more sensitive to the domestic costs of the controversial peace policy of the government. With the next elections, scheduled for May 1996, in mind, Peres postponed further progress in the Oslo peace process until after the elections. He refused to sanction a secret unauthorized draft agreement reached between Israeli and Palestinian officials, the so-called Beilin-Abu Mazen plan, about the final status of the occupied territories. He also stalled the peace negotiations with Syria, which were gaining momentum shortly before Rabin's murder. Moreover, to show the Israeli electorate that he was determined to fight terrorism and to bring peace and security, he authorized the murder of a Hamas leader who was portrayed as being responsible for the organization of a number of the terror attacks, and started a heavy bombardment campaign against Hizbollah guerilla positions in southern Lebanon from where they fired rockets across the border on Israeli villages. However, Peres was unable to turn the tide of decreasing popular support for the peace process, as the Hamas took revenge by a series of terrorist attacks that provoked mass demonstrations against the government and the peace process. As Ben-Ami observes, the Israeli public could not stomach a policy whereby the victims of terrorist attacks were buried in the morning and negotiations were resumed in the afternoon.[44] Paradoxically, Labor was the largest winner in the 1996 elections but the Likud formed the new government as its new leader, Benjamin Netanyahu, won the direct election for prime minister (by a margin of 1 percent). Labor was still seen as better able to bring true peace, but the Likud was perceived as more likely to know how to fight terror and handle the tradeoff between returning land for peace.[45] The new coalition government of nationalist and religious parties, and headed by a Likud prime minister who was a declared opponent of the Oslo accords, adopted a policy that had to undo the agreements with the Palestinians or to preserve, at least, a stalemate. It made negotiations on further implementation of the Oslo accords conditional on Arafat's ability to suppress the terror carried out by Hamas and Islamic Jihad, a requirement that he was unable to fulfill.

PLO's Internal Politics

When Arafat took the decision to sign the Oslo accords in 1993, he had to deal with two different domestic environments. The first one was the domestic environment of the state-in-exile; the second one was the domestic environment of the state-in-the-making in the occupied territories. The first domestic environment, in which Arafat operated as a head of state leading a de-facto government in exile, was decisive for the approval of the Oslo accords. The second domestic environment became more important as Arafat moved inside the occupied territories and established the Palestinian Authority, which became the government of the state in formation. While the two domestic environments had a different institutional setting, Arafat had to build support for his policies in both environments and deal with an opposition that was more significant in the second environment.

The first domestic environment in which Arafat had to secure his political survival was the PLO, a loosely structured umbrella organization housing different Palestinian guerrilla groups. Although the

PLO declared the establishment of an independent Palestinian state that belonged to Palestinians throughout the world in November 1988, it remained the essential institutional setting for internal Palestinian politics. The new state caused no immediate institutional changes, as it controlled neither territory nor population. The only institutional change was to make Arafat, besides chairman of the PLO, president of the state of Palestine. The Palestinian National Council (PNC) and the PLO ruling executive committee, chaired by Arafat, continued to be the two central political bodies that governed the PLO. The executive committee has always been the highest executive authority in charge of directing the PLO's day-to-day affairs. However, its political survival depended on the PNC, which was according to the PLO constitution the supreme authority in determining PLO policy. It elected the executive committee, it could amend the PLO's charter by a two-thirds majority vote, and it could adopt resolutions and set the general direction of the PLO policy. The PNC was a sort of Palestinian parliament-in-exile, and although the PLO's constitution stipulated that PNC members had to be elected by the Palestinian people, in practice this was never done. Membership of the PNC, as well as membership of the executive committee, was actually the result of negotiations between leaders of all major PLO factions prior to each PNC session. The seats in the PNC were usually distributed between guerrilla groups, representatives of Palestinian mass organizations like student organizations and trade unions, and independent representatives of different Palestinian communities that were generally closely linked to one or another of the guerilla groups. When the PNC was not in session a central council, elected by the PNC, linked the PNC and the executive committee.[46]

The PNC has always been comprised of various groups with competing ideologies. Fatah, Arafat's own guerilla group, constituted PLO's mainstream and formed the major center of power and authority within the PLO. It enjoyed a broad base of support among the Palestinians and had more members and resources than all the other PLO groups combined. Through its superior resources and its ability to form coalitions with other groups it dominated the PLO executive committee and the PNC and, in fact, shaped the PLO's strategy and tactics. Fatah had different factions but its core leadership was a cohesive and stable group, which contributed to its influence and staying in power. Its ideology emphasized self-reliance and independence, and a strategy of armed struggle that appealed to many young Palestinians. Fatah had some rival guerrilla groups within the PLO with conflicting views on the best strategy to advance Palestinian goals. The most important challengers were the Popular Front for the Liberation of Palestine (PFLP) and the Democratic Front for the Liberation of Palestine (DFLP). Both groups viewed the Palestinian struggle in Marxist terms, and took an uncompromising position on Israel. But the two groups differed on the tactics to regain Palestine. While the PFLP was willing to use any tactic including terrorism against Israeli civilians inside and outside Israel, the DFLP opposed terrorism and was critical about operations outside Israel and the occupied territories.[47]

Control of Opposition

By the time Arafat decided to reach an agreement with Israel on the Oslo accords, he had complete control of the PLO. Although the PLO principles emphasized collective leadership and joint decision-making, Arafat did not behave as primus inter pares and demonstrated clearly a preference for unilateral decisions. In the years that Arafat stayed in Lebanon (1970–1982) he consolidated his position as political leader of Fatah and head of the PLO, and reduced the Fatah-dominated PNC to a forum of discussion with the other guerrilla groups.

In 1974, for example, the PNC approved a resolution in which it decided to establish a "fighting national authority" on any Palestinian soil evacuated by Israel. As Sayigh observes, it implied readiness to put off the total liberation of Palestine, if not abandon it altogether. It was the beginning of a diplomatic strategy aimed at placing Palestinian statehood on the international agenda and establishing the PLO as a legitimate negotiating partner on the future of the occupied territories. The PFLP and other guerrilla groups rejected this moderation in the traditional PLO position, but Arafat was assured of the support of a coalition between Fatah and independent representatives in the PNC. Arafat demonstrated disregard for proper consultation and consensus politics once again in 1977, when the United States was planning a Middle East peace conference in Geneva and called on the Palestinians to renounce their aim of destroying Israel in order to gain a seat at the eventual peace talks. Arafat announced without any consultation with the PNC that the PLO sought a Palestinian state and was willing to attend the Geneva peace conference. This fell far short of recognition of Israel, but it signaled willingness to enter into indirect negotiations with the Jewish state. To accommodate opponents to this further moderation Arafat remained within the PLO consensus and refused to accept UN Security Council resolution 242 as basis for negotiations, unless the wording was changed so that it would deal with the Palestinian issue as one of self-determination and not only as a refugee problem. When this unilateral decision triggered opposition within the PLO, led by the PFLP and the DFLP, who demanded a formation of a committee that included the leaders of all the guerrilla groups to supervise PLO decision-making, Arafat ended the internal dissent by demonstrating his determination to resort to military means in order to maintain political control.[48]

After the Israeli destruction of the PLO military and political infra-structure in Lebanon in 1982, followed by the forced evacuation of the Palestinian guerrilla groups from the country, Arafat further concentrated the control over PLO decision-making in his own hands. Arafat's room for political maneuver increased as many leaders of rival guerrilla groups that could possibly challenge his decisions lost their power base in Lebanon and moved to exile in Syria. He survived a Syrian-backed revolt in Fatah and the disintegration of the PLO on grounds of ideological differences. Arafat's major concern was not the opposition to his diplomatic strategy from within the PLO, but the potential emergence of an alternative leadership in the occupied terri-tories, where a popular uprising was taking place since December 1987. This challenge became manifest when the United States in the wake of the Gulf War began in 1991 to organize a Middle East peace conference and conducted preparatory talks with Palestinian public figures from the West Bank and Gaza. Many of them were PLO affil-iated activists who pressed the PLO leadership to take a moderate position in order to secure Palestinian participation in the proposed peace conference. To prevent a situation in which the United States and Israel might turn to these local public figures as a negotiating partner in the coming peace conference, Arafat took a flexible position and broke two taboos. He authorized, by means of a PNC resolution, the participation of representatives from the occupied territories in the opening session of the peace conference in Madrid in October 1991 as members of a joint Palestinian-Jordanian delegation, and allowed them to negotiate directly with Israel in the bilateral track that start in December in Washington. However, when the actual bilateral negotiation began the PLO leadership became deeply involved in the actual negotiations. Although the delegation members were PLO affiliated activists they received personal instructions from Arafat and were supervised by a PLO negotiations follow-up commit-tee comprised of PLO officials. As it became clear to the Israeli lead-ers that if they wanted a deal they have to do it directly with Arafat and started direct talks with the PLO leadership through the secret back channel in Oslo, Arafat frustrated any attempt to reach a settlement negotiated through the bilateral track in Washington. From the moment that the Oslo accords were made public they provoked strong opposition within the PLO. Arafat did not present the Oslo accords in the PNC, as he expected that the opposition would frustrate endorsement. Instead, Arafat sought ratification by Fatah's central committee, his home base, and PLO's executive committee. Arafat faced strong resistance in both bodies, but after a long debate Fatah's central committee and the PLO executive committee finally approved the Oslo accords. Arafat secured a majority in favor of the Oslo accords thanks to the resignation and self-imposed absence, in protest, of five members of the executive committee. Only nine of the original 18 members of the executive committee voted in favor of the Oslo accords.[49]

A New Political Setting

The Oslo accords radically changed the domestic environment in which Arafat had to operate in order to survive politically, moving the major institutional setting from the PLO to the Palestinian Authority (PA) and shifting the political constituency from the Palestinian diaspora to the occupied territories. Arafat still considered himself the leader of the Palestinians everywhere. He remained the chairman of the PLO and the PNC and the PLO executive committee continued to exist as a decision-making body that represented all Palestinians. But as the institutional setting of the new established Palestinian Authority (PA) was taking shape, Arafat had to adjust to the new political environment in the occupied territories. The interim agreement on the West Bank and the Gaza Strip that implemented further the Oslo accords, established a Palestinian Legislative Council (PLC) and created the post of president of the PA. The population of the West Bank and the Gaza Strip would elect both the PLC and the president. Arafat assumed immediately the leadership of the PA after his arrival in Gaza in July 1994, but also remained leader of the PLO. As Brown argues, Arafat used his dual position as president of both the PA and the PLO to outmaneuver critics. To PLO dissidents he presented himself as president of an embryonic state, and to PA rivals he emphasized that his position in the PLO made him a representative of Palestinians everywhere. All orders and decrees from Arafat cited both positions, says Brown, which allowed him to slide back and forth between the two roles.[50]

Two powerful groups that dominated the internal politics of the West Bank and Gaza before his arrival challenged Arafat's authority as head of the PA. The first group formed a potential threat and comprised the local activists from within PLO's own ranks. The second group posed itself as a political alternative and consisted mainly of Hamas, an Islamic nationalist movement that was deeply rooted in the Palestinian society in the Gaza Strip and the West Bank. Khalil Shikaki has called the first group the "young guard" in the Palestinian nationalist movement. It was composed of the new political and populist leadership in the occupied territories and the commanders of Fatah's semi-militias who were purely local residents. They were authentic young leaders who initiated and led the uprising in the occupied territories during the first *intifada* from 1987 to 1993, and have earned their leadership status thanks to the reputation that they have built during the uprising and their stay in Israeli prisons. Shikaki distinguished this young guard from the old guard, the established nationalist leadership that came with Arafat from the PLO headquarters in Tunis. The relationship between the young guard and the old guard were uneasy from the moment the Oslo accords were signed. Some members of the young guard who participated in the bilateral negotiations in Washington felt frustrated by the secret deal that the old guard made with Israel in Oslo, while they were negotiating in Washington. Moreover, they were supervised by members of the old guard and were instructed to demand from Israel more than the Oslo accords finally delivered. Arafat expressed his misgivings about these young leaders by suggesting that they had private political ambitions and were used by the United States as "a Trojan Horse." When the secret Oslo deal was made public a prominent member of the young guard, Faisal al-Husaini, called briefly for the establishment of a Palestinian government of national salvation.[51]

Members of the young guard felt further marginalized when the PA was established in 1994. Arafat did almost no effort to integrate the local young PLO leadership into the PA, and relied almost completely on associates from the old guard who spent most of their life outside the Palestinian territories and now dominated the PA. Arafat also introduced a political style, characterized by a lack of democracy, which made it impossible for the young guard members to enter the PA political system. The young leaders wanted therefore to open the PA by means of transparency, accountability, and a stronger role for the legislature and other public institutions. The young guard shared with the old PLO establishment that surrounded Arafat the objective of an independent Palestinian state coexisting with Israel, but the young guard was more radical in its policy for achieving that goal. While the old guard wanted to continue its effort for reaching a negotiated settlement and were critical of violence against Israel, the young leaders favored violent actions to increase the pressure on Israel to withdraw from the occupied territories. For that reason they also favored a coalition with the Hamas and opposed any crackdown on Hamas activists by the PA security forces. As the young guard lacked formal authority, it recognized Arafat's leadership and had no intention of replacing him. Arafat remained for them important as a symbol of the Palestinian national movement, but they demanded from him support for their policies. Arafat, for his part, saw himself as head of both the old and the new groups. As Shikaki explains, since Arafat's political survival depended on the support of both sides, he tried to ensure his ability to survive by balancing the interests of both groups. One day he supported the effort of the old guard to find a formula for further negotiations with Israel, and the next day he supported violent acts of the young guard.[52]

That Arafat managed to survive politically was evident already during the first elections for the PA's legislative council, when Fatah, headed by Arafat, won 77 percent of the PLC seats. In the simultaneously held election for the president of the PA, Arafat received more than 70 percent of the vote. However, many of the opponents of the Oslo accords among the Palestinians did not participate officially in the elections or cast blank ballots.[53] The Islamic fundamentalist movement Hamas, for example, which presented the main challenge to Arafat's authority, boycotted the elections. Hamas began to form a threat to the traditional political hegemony of the PLO in the occupied territories already during the *intifada*. Its active participation in the uprising led to competition between Fatah and Hamas, but a potential power struggle between the two groups was avoided by the practical need to cooperate in the day-to-day struggle against the Israeli authorities. It led actually to a tacit alliance between the armed wings of the Fatah and the Hamas. When the PLO leadership signed the Oslo accords, the Hamas leadership rejected the Oslo accords on the grounds that it recognized the existence of Israel and included a commitment to end the armed struggle against Israel. This contradicted the ultimate goal of Hamas: to liberate Palestine through armed struggle and to establish a Palestinian Islamic state on the whole territory of Palestine that would replace Israel. But the Hamas leadership also recognized that if it wanted to present itself as a political alternative to the PLO leadership and compete for political influence among the Palestinian population in the West Bank and the Gaza Strip, it had to follow in practice a more flexible policy. They therefore differentiated between the long-term goal of an Islamic state that would replace Israel, and the short-term objective of the establishment of an independent Palestinian state in the West Bank and the Gaza Strip. This was a temporary step toward the realization of the ultimate goal. But the Hamas leaders declared that they would continue their armed struggle against Israel to end the occupation.[54]

The unwillingness of the Hamas to give up the military operations against Israel made a confrontation between the PA leadership and Hamas inescapable, since Israel made the implementation of the Oslo accords conditional on the actions of the PA's ability to prevent Hamas from committing violence against the Israeli military and civilians. This led to cycles of short arrests and releases of Hamas leaders and activists. But Arafat had no intention to take forceful measures against Hamas, as he knew that Palestinian public still supported the use of violence in order to end the occupation. Moreover, Arafat realized that the use of arms to enforce his authority would result in a civil war. In search for a working formula, Arafat started a dialogue with Hamas and once again carried out a balancing act. He reached in 1995 a mutual understanding in which Hamas promised to stop military operations against Israel from PA-controlled areas.[55] In other words, Hamas could continue its violence as long as it was not initiated from PA areas. Hence, in spite of the rivalry between the PA leadership and Hamas and the tension between the two, Arafat treated Hamas as a legitimate opposition and preferred to adopt a policy of restraint instead of collision.

5

A Third Lens

Underlying Rules of World Politics

In this chapter I look at international relations from the perspective of the international structure. I concentrate on theoretical approaches that limit their analysis to the level of the international system and conceive the choices of leaders and the actions of states as resulting from the characteristics and the nature of the international system. A theory is considered systemic, says Alexander Wendt, when it emphasizes the causal powers of the structure of the international system in explaining state behavior. It is distinguished from theories of state behavior that emphasize factors like decision-makers' psychology and domestic politics.[1] As I will illustrate in this chapter, international relations scholars who focus on systemic explanations share some basic views about certain aspects of the international system, such as the key role of states and the existence of anarchy. However, they differ on the consequences that the anarchical environment in which states are embedded has for the behavior of states, in particular whether they encourage conflict or cooperation.

In addressing the issue of how the international system acts to determine the behavior of states, I will discuss three competing schools of thought. I simply present the exchange of arguments between international relations scholars, as I have no intention of determining which one best explains the influence of anarchy on the behavior of states or provides better insight into the actual issues which I will deal with in the next chapter. I will begin with the realist perspective, which is the most familiar systemic approach to international politics. As Stephen Walt and Randall Schweller rightly argue, realism is not a single theory but rather a tradition that covers a range of complementary and to some extent even competing theories, presented under labels like: classic realism, neorealism, offensive realism, or defensive realism. However, all these different brands of realism are derived from a set of core assumptions and basic propositions about international relations, which form the common ground from where a range of scholars associated with these different strands of realism, have developed their ideas about world politics.[2] I will then move to various theories grouped under the label of neoliberal institutionalism, which form the main challenge to the realist tradition. They accept the realist views that the anarchical structure of the international system influence states to be preoccupied with their security and power, and does not promote their willingness to cooperate. But they argue that realists give too much weight to conflict and believe that the creation of international institutions affect the way states perceive a mutual interest in cooperation. I will end this chapter with a discussion of some other systemic international relations theories, positioned within the constructivist approach to the international system. These theories do not close the eyes to the anarchical structure of the international system but they lay much more emphasis on the social interactions among states in the international system, that create, in their view, different incentives for the choice between conflict and cooperation.

THE CENTRALITY OF STATES

Before I begin my discussion of the different systemic approaches it is important to stress that scholars working within all the three different schools of thought share the state centric assumption. Human beings, proposes the prominent realist Robert Gilpin, confront one another not as individuals but as members of competing groups. They organize themselves into political groups and are loyal to groups that inevitably conflict with one another. Throughout history, he says, such conflict groups have varied from tribes and city-states to empires and kingdoms, but in the modern world the principal conflict groups are the territorial nation-states. Individuals have transferred their loyalty from earlier types of political entities to the state, explains Gilpin, because it has been more efficient in fulfilling the primary functions of protecting the property rights and personal security of its people vis-à-vis the citizens and actions of other states.[3]

For Kenneth Waltz, the preeminent neorealist scholar, states are also the primary actors in international politics. In his view they are the major building blocks whose interactions shape the structure of the international political system.[4] Waltz and other realists don't deny the existence of other non-state actors in the international system, like international organizations and multinational corporations. But states are considered to be the most important actors in international affairs and they will long remain so, because they set the rules within which states, along with non-state actors, function. Despite the fact that states may choose to interfere little in the affairs of non-state actors, when a critical situation comes, states remake the rules by which other actors operate.[5]

Other scholars who disagree with some of the realist assumptions, as I will discuss later in this chapter, share the basic realist belief that states are the dominant actors in world politics. Prominent neoliberal institutionalist theorists like Rober Keohane and Joseph Nye have drawn attention in the early 1970s to the importance of transnational relations in world politics. However, they accepted later that states have been and remained the most important actors in world affairs, and have qualified the significance of non-state actors. Keohane has admitted that subsequent research persuades him that non-state actors continue to be subordinate to states, although states may act in nontraditional ways due to changing systemic constraints. Also Nye has recognized that states are more important than the non-state groups. States are the major actors in international politics, he says, although they do not have the stage to themselves.[6]

A major constructivist theorist like Wendt also considers states to be at the center of the international system. According to Wendt the international regulation of violence is one of the most fundamental problems of order in world politics. But when it comes to the regulation of violence internationally it is states one ultimately has to control, because the state is a structure of political authority with a monopoly on the legitimate use of organized violence. He does not rule out that non-state actors have important, even decisive, effects on the frequency and manner in which states engage in organized violence. But as Wendt emphasizes, states are still the primary means through which the effects of other actors on the regulation of violence are channeled into the world system. Moreover, system change ultimately happens through states.[7]

THE EFFECTS OF ANARCHY

For almost every international relations scholar anarchy is the fundamental fact of international relations. Realist scholars, in particular, start with the basic assumption about the anarchic nature of the international political system in which states operate. They believe that the international system consists of independent states, which have to exist in a world order characterized by political anarchy. It means that the states have no central authority above them and that there is no system wide authority to which they can appeal for protection.[8] Waltz, for example, says that the prominent feature of international politics is the lack of order and formal organization; it is politics in the absence of government. As Waltz further emphasizes, all states are sovereign political entities in the sense that they develop their own strategies, chart their own courses, and make their own decisions about how they will cope with their internal and external problems. Each state is the equal of all the others; none is entitled to command and none is required to obey.[9]

The Quest for Security and Power

Theories emerging from the realist tradition build further on the anarchical nature of the international system. Waltz has made the assumption that the most important goal of states is to ensure their survival the cornerstone of his neorealist version of realism. He argues that as each state in an anarchic system can decide for itself whether or not to use force to advance its policies and no appeal can be made to a higher body with the authority and the ability to avoid the use of force, states have to provide for their own security. Waltz suggests that all states must be prepared either to counter force with force, or pay the cost of weakness and live at the mercy of militarily more powerful states. Hence, to survive in a dangerous world where the security of states is not assured, states must rely on the military means they can generate alone or together with other states, and the defense arrangements they can make for themselves. Self-help, says Waltz, is necessarily the principle of action in an anarchic order. This does not mean that anarchy results always in violence and conflict. But under the conditions of anarchy, with no central authority to prevent conflict and the possibility for each state to make its own judgment about the use of force, the possibility of conflict that may lead to war is always in the background.[10]

John Mearsheimer, the outspoken neorealist scholar associated with offensive realism, accepts to a large extent the ideas of Waltz about the implications of anarchy for the behavior of states. Yet, Mearsheimer argues that if states want to survive in an anarchical international environment they must maximize their power. He maintains that the need to maximize power is rooted in the fact that in an anarchical international system with no central authority that can protect them from each other states always fear each other and have to anticipate danger. States are potentially dangerous to each other, as they always possess some offensive military capability that gives them the possibility to hurt or destroy each other. This leaves little room for trust because states can never be certain about the intentions of other states, as no state can be sure that another state will not have offensive intentions to go along with its offensive capabilities. Mearsheimer contends that to guarantee their survival, states, and in particular great powers, seek to maximize their relative power over other states. The more military power they gain at the expense of potential rivals, the more secure they are. The ideal outcome is to end up as the hegemonic state in the system.[11]

The crucial importance that Mearsheimer ascribes to power maximization is in line with the traditional realist perspective, which views power as the ultimate goal of states. Hans Morgenthau, the distinguished classic realist scholar, has summarized the core assumption about the essential role of power in international relations in one statement: "statesmen think and act in terms of interest defined as power."[12] International politics is, in Morgenthau's view, a struggle for power. Whatever the essential aims of international politics, power is always the immediate aim; and whenever statesmen strive to realize their goal by means of international politics, they do so by striving for power. Moreover, all nations must ultimately seek the maximum power available to them. Morgenthau claims that humans are driven by a lust for power and maintains that it is an undeniable fact that the struggle for power is universal in time and space and that throughout history states have met each other in contests for power.[13] One of the most famous illustrations of this logic of power politics is the statement made by the Athenian leaders in their well-known debate with the rulers of Melos, during the Peloponnesian War in 416 BC, in which the Athenians demand the Melians to surrender: "you know as well as we do that right, as the world goes, is only in question between equals in power, while the strong do what they can and the weak suffer what they must."[14]

Waltz attributes as well great significance to power. He argues that in view of the fact that all states are similar sovereign states, the only method to distinguish between states is by the way in which power is distributed across the states in the system. The system wide distribution of capabilities (or power resources) among states makes it possible to measure the number of great powers and to define the polar structure of the international political system, that is, to describe it as being a bipolar or a multipolar system. Waltz expects that in addition to the demands imposed on the behavior of states by anarchy, the polarity of the system also determines how states, in particular the great powers, will behave. But for Waltz, in contrast to Morgenthau and Mearsheimer, power is not an end in itself. As mentioned earlier, Waltz believes that the major goal that the anarchic system encourages states to seek is security. Increased power may or may not serve that end. Moreover, what matters is not the absolute power of states but their relative power, since placement in the international system is determined by the capabilities that a state has in relation to other states. Waltz therefore claims that the first concern of states is to preserve their relative power position in the system, and not to maximize their power. He emphasizes that in a self-help system, competing states, in particular great powers, are not stimulated to increase their power but are motivated to create balances of power, because none of the great powers wants another great power to emerge as the hegemonic leader of the system.[15]

Other scholars within the realist tradition, known as defensive realists, also dispute the belief that security-seeking states are driven by power maximization. They argue that states can increase their security by moving from a focus on the assessment of power alone to a focus on the evaluation of the effective defensive capabilities that a state possesses to protect itself, such as military technology and geography. States that seek only security and are satisfied with the status quo, say defensive realists, don't need offensive military capabilities and can eliminate insecurity by the deployment of adequate military defensive capabilities.[16] Changing an offensive posture into a defensive posture helps states escape the effects of the security dilemma. It refers to a situation in which the attempt by one state to increase its own security has the effect of decreasing the security of other states and causes them to take countermeasures that, in turn, threaten the first state. As Charles Glazer claims, maximizing relative power is not always the best way to increase security as it overlooks the security dilemma: "a state that increases its relative power might nevertheless decrease its security because its increased relative power could make its adversary less secure, which could in turn increase the value its adversary places on expansion."[17] Glazer therefore suggests to consider not just power but also to assess how much and what types of military capability a state can produce with its power. He proposes a shift from a balance of power theory to a military capabilities theory, and a distinction between offensive capabilities and defensive capabilities. In his view states should care most about the military capabilities that are necessary for deterrence and defense, not about relative capabilities or a balance in capabilities.[18]

Defensive realists also believe that the change from offensive to defensive strategies encourages international cooperation. As Jervis argues, when states become less hostile and more benign as a result of the employment of defensive strategies that do not threaten others, the likelihood and the ability to reach various forms of cooperation between states with common interests increases, especially among status quo powers that are satisfied with mutual security.[19] In this respect they differ from mainstream realist thinkers who recognize the importance of cooperation but hold a less optimistic view about the possibilities for international cooperation.

The Constraints on International Cooperation

For the hard core of realist thinkers, cooperation is difficult to achieve. Anarchy restrains the willingness of states to cooperate, and international institutions are unable to reduce these constraining effects.[20] Neorealist scholars like Waltz, Joseph Grieco, and Mearsheimer, are very clear about the limits that the anarchic structure of the international system set on the cooperation between states, even when they gain from such cooperation.

In a condition of anarchy, states Waltz, relative gain is more important than absolute gain. Because the international system is a self-help system in which states feel insecure and worry about their survival, considerations of security constrain cooperation and subordinate economic gain to political interest. A decision to reduce the barriers to trade between states or cooperation in the form of a full division of labor among states provides advantages in the long run and in absolute terms for all countries. However, such cooperation would benefit some countries more than others and is therefore constrained by the worry of states about a division of possible gains that may favor others more than themselves. Waltz says that every state faced with the possibility of cooperating for mutual gain through a division of labor, has to consider how an expected gain will be divided. They have to ask not whether both will gain but who will gain more, even if the absolute gains for both states are large. Since no state can be certain about the intentions and future actions of other states, an unequal division of gain that increases the power resources of one state could always be used in the future to damage or destroy the other. Waltz claims further that cooperation in the form of a division of labor is also hindered by the concern of states about the maintenance of their autonomy as a result of specialization through a division of labor, which makes a state more dependent on others to supply the materials and goods it does not produce. In a self-help system, where states have to take care of themselves, states don't want to place themselves in situations of increased dependence.[21]

Building on Waltz and other realist theorists, Grieco and Mearsheimer argue that states face two major barriers to international cooperation under anarchy: a concern about cheating and a worry about relative gains. A major hinderance for states to enter into cooperative agreements, says Mearsheimer, is the anxiety that the other will cheat on the agreement. Grieco considers uncertainty about the compliance of partners in a joint arrangement with their promises and the absence of a centralized authority to enforce such promises, to be a great obstacle for cooperation. However, Grieco and Mearsheimer stress that even if states have solved the problem of cheating through various measures that ensure compliance, they still worry about the problem of relative gains. Each side considers not only its own gain, but also whether it does better compared to the other state in any agreement. The concern about relative gains, suggest Grieco, arises not from a desire to maximize gains but from the danger that relative gains may prove advantageous to potential adversaries. He maintains that states will refuse to join cooperative arrangements if they believe that their partners are achieving relatively greater gains, because friendly partners in the present could become a powerful opponent at some point in the future. Driven by an interest in survival, the fundamental goal of states in any relationship is to prevent others from increasing their relative capabilities.[22]

Although Grieco claims that states must solve the cheating as well as the relative gains problem in order to achieve cooperation, he does not exclude the possibility of cooperation among states through international institutionalized arrangements. This is for example the case in situations where the institutional arrangements are in fact a binding mechanism that helps weaker states control a stronger state. Grieco proposes a binding thesis, which says that: "if states share a common interest and undertake negotiations on rules constituting a collaborative arrangement, then the weaker but still influential partners will seek to ensure that the rules so constructed will provide for effective voice opportunities for them and will thereby prevent or at least ameliorate their domination by stronger partners."[23] The binding thesis explains, according to Grieco, the willingness of the state members of the European Union (EU) in 1991 to establish a European Monetary Union (EMU), in which France and other European countries choose to cooperate in the monetary field with a stronger partner like Germany. The move toward EMU is motivated, in his view, by concerns of France and other European countries about German monetary power in the 1970s and 1980s, and their wish to reduce German domination of European monetary affairs. The centralized institutional structure of the EMU, he says, ensured greater symmetry in voice opportunities for the EU member states and helped France and other EU member states regain effective control over monetary policies.[24]

Mearsheimer also recognizes that states sometimes operate through international institutions. States form alliances, such as NATO, in which they cooperate against a common enemy. Even rival states cooperate through arms control agreements, which reflect the distribution of power and satisfy concerns about cheating. But Mearsheimer argues that international institutions matter little, and are in essence a place for exercising power politics. As he states: "The most powerful states in the system create and shape institutions so that they can maintain their share of world power, or even increase it."[25] Mearsheimer maintains that NATO, for example, was essentially an American tool for managing a balance of power system in Europe during the cold war. NATO as such—that is, NATO as an institution—did not prevent a war in Europe. He claims that NATO was simply a manifestation of the bipolar distribution of power in Europe, and it was that balance of power that maintained stability on the continent.[26]

THE IMPACT OF INTERNATIONAL INSTITUTIONS

A large group of international relations scholars, in particular neoliberal institutionalists who represent the mainstream approach to the study of international institutions, accept the basic diagnosis of the international system as being anarchical, but they differ with realist scholars about the effects of anarchy on the preferences of states. Scholars, who work within the neoliberal institutional school of thought, dispute the neorealist pessimistic views on the prospects for international cooperation under anarchy and the influence of international organizations. They do not deny that the international system is first and foremost anarchical, in the sense that it lacks a common government. Nor do they reject the crucial role of states in world affairs and the view that states behave on their conception of their own self-interests. But they believe that the centrality of anarchy to world politics has been overemphasized at the expense of another significant feature of international relations: a high degree of cooperation among states through various institutional arrangements. They emphasize the widespread existence of international organizations, the proliferation of international regimes, and the large number of multilateral frameworks that institutionalize cooperation among states, as well as the broadening and deepening of regional integration. Neoliberal institutionalism, says a leading neoliberal institutional thinker like Keohane, pays much more attention to the study of the roles of institutions and the emergence of international rules as well as the obedience to them by states. It emphasizes the role of international institutions in changing conceptions of self-interest and demonstrates that states can cooperate under some conditions on the basis of complementary interests, and that institutions, broadly defined, affect the patterns of cooperation that emerge.[27]

In thinking about international institutions neoliberal institutionalists have moved beyond the traditional focus on formal international organizations. As Beth Simmons and Lisa Martin say, most scholars have come to regard international institutions as a sets of rules meant to govern international behavior.[28] Keohane, for instance, offers a broad definition of international institutions. He defines international institutions as: "persistent and connected sets of rules (formal and informal) that prescribe behavioral roles, constrain activity and shape expectations."[29] For neoliberal institutionalists international institutions may therefore take various forms. The most familiar type of international institutions is the numerous universal, regional, and technical intergovernmental and nongovernmental organizations with explicit functional tasks and clear decision-making rules. International institutions include as well the large number of international regimes that consist of sets of explicit and implicit principles, norms, rules, and decision-making procedures that regulate the behavior of states in specific issue areas. But international institutions comprise also conventions with implicit rules and understandings that enable actors to understand one another and coordinate their behavior.[30] An international institution such as the convention of sovereign statehood is, in Keohane's view, as fundamental to world politics as is the distribution of power resources among states.[31]

The Willingness to Cooperate

Neoliberal institutional scholars do not claim that international cooperation under anarchy is easy to achieve or to maintain. In an international environment where cheating is widespread and trust is uncommon cooperation is not automatic, in particular between independent states that are motivated by their own conception of self-interest. It is obvious that states must at least have some mutual interests, that is, they must gain from their cooperation. The greater the conflict of interests between states the lesser the likelihood that they will cooperate.[32] To understand the success and failure of attempts to cooperate, neoliberal institutionalists rely heavily on rational choice analysis and game theory. They expect states to behave as rational egoists who act only to further their own interests. As Keohane clarifies, states have consistent ordered preferences and they calculate costs and benefits of alternative courses of action in order to maximize their utility in view of those preferences. Being egoists, their utility functions are independent of one another so that states do not gain or lose utility simply because of the gains or losses of others.[33] This means that states are more interested in their absolute gain and are less concerned about their relative gain.

Many neoliberal institutionalists use a game called Prisoner's Dilemma in order to illustrate how mutuality of interests is perceived and preferences are determined. The Prisoner Dilemma is a game played by two people who have to make a choice between cooperative and uncooperative behavior. The payoff structure creates for both players an incentive not to cooperate because each player finds himself in a disadvantageous position if only one side decides to cooperate. The dilemma is that the choice not to cooperate is not the optimal outcome and that both players do better if they choose to cooperate. The players can overcome the dilemma and move from mutual uncooperative behavior to mutual cooperation if one side makes a short-term sacrifice and cooperates in order to assure the other side of its good intentions. That way he creates an incentive for the other side to cooperate as well, so that both players could achieve the most desired optimal outcome of mutual cooperation in the future. The two players can reinforce cooperation in the future if they use a Tit-for-Tat strategy, which means cooperating after the opponent cooperated and defecting after defection. Such a strategy is even more successful when coupled with being a bit forgiving, that is, punishing once, and then trying again to cooperate.[34]

Thus, cooperation can emerge among egoists under conditions of anarchy. As Axelrod and Keohane argue, expectations about the future encourage cooperation and the use of strategies based on reciprocity, like Tit-for-Tat, help to maintain cooperation. However, such a result requires that these egoists expect to continue to interact with each other for the indefinite future and that these expectations of future interactions be given sufficient weight in their calculations. This shadow of the future is also affected, according to Axelrod and

Keohane, by the reliability of information about actions of the other side. Uncertainty, they say, reduces the confidence with which expectations are held about the future and may therefore hinder the development of cooperation through reciprocity.[35]

The Significance of International Regimes

Neoliberal institutionalists believe that international regimes, in particular, enable governments to achieve their interests through limited collective action. International regimes are arrangements in the form of sets of implicit or explicit principles, norms, rules and decision-making procedures that are designed to regulate international behavior within specific issue areas. According to Keohane, international regimes serve state objectives by facilitating the making and keeping of mutually beneficial agreements among governments on matters of substantive significance. They help to make the expectations of governments consistent with one another in a way that would otherwise be difficult or impossible to achieve. International regimes, says Keohane, make it possible for states to reduce transaction costs, which are the costs related to negotiations and enforcement of agreements. Regimes, for example, make it easier for states to reach agreements by providing a framework of rules, norms, and procedures for negotiations and the use of negotiation strategies such as issue linkage or side payments that may improve the readiness to cooperate by dissatisfied states. Arrangements within regimes make it also feasible to monitor each other's compliance with the commitments made, and to implement the norm of reciprocity by sanctioning retaliation for those who violate rules. In addition, international regimes help to improve the quality of information that reduces mutual uncertainty.[36]

Hence, neoliberal institutionalists think that institutions such as international regimes enable states to solve the problem of cheating, which is in the neorealist perspective an important obstacle for cooperation. They are therefore quite optimistic about the willingness of states to enter into interstate cooperation that constitute international regimes, and argue that the existence of regimes is fully consistent with the realist view of international politics. Arthur Stein, for example, claims that: "the same forces of autonomously calculated self-interest that lie at the root of the anarchic international system also provide the foundation for international regimes as a form of international order."[37] He suggests that it is the self-interest of sovereign states in a condition of anarchy that leads them to move from independent decision-making to joint decision-making in international regimes. When national governments are faced with dilemmas of common interests or common aversions, jointly reached outcomes are in both cases preferable to decisions made independently.[38] Keohane recognizes that cooperation will never be perfect and that the possibility that the interests of states in relative gains will make cooperation more difficult, but he maintains that even if the costs of interstate cooperation remain substantial, states will create international institutions, such as regimes, as long as the institutions enable states to achieve valued objectives that are unachievable through unilateral or bilateral means.[39]

In one of the first theoretical assessments of the West European integration process written in the 1950s, Ernst Haas, the eminent thinker on regional integration theory, argued in a very similar way. He pointed out, that progress toward integration has to be based on agreements between the member-states through an accommodation of individual interests, and that a shift of loyalty will take place from the nation-states to a higher supranational authority only if more satisfaction is expected from the new supranational institution than from the existing institutions of the nation-states.[40] As I have discussed elsewhere, egoistic self-interest is indeed the basic rationale for the willingness of the member states of the European Union to transfer power and sovereignty to a new center of authority, and to surrender voluntarily their right to make independent decisions in a large number of policy areas with the ultimate aim of building a community beyond the nation-state. Driven by self-interest a large number of member states were even willing to replace a traditional symbol of sovereignty like a national currency by a single European currency. But as I have emphasized, self-interest also conditions the willingness of the member-states to pool and mix their national sovereignty with the powers of the Union. This bounded voluntarism explains why foreign policy in the European Union is only loosely integrated, compared to other policy areas.[41]

CHALLENGING THE PRIMACY OF ANARCHY

While neorealists and neoliberal institutionalists share the core assumption of international anarchy and disagree essentially on the implications that this may have for the behavior of states, other international relations theorists have questioned the primacy of anarchy. Scholars associated with the international society tradition have emphasized already in the 1960s and 1970s the role that norms and international law play in international politics. They maintained that since states hold shared norms and rules, the international system does not operate only according to the logic of anarchy. It functions more or less as a society of sovereign states, or to use Hedley Bull's label "an anarchical society."[42] More recently adherents of the theoretical approach called constructivism developed this argument further. In their view anarchy is not simply a given, as neorealists and neoliberal institutionalists claim, but is socially constructed by the interaction among states. It is this practice that determines the character of anarchy, whether it is conflictual or cooperative. As the prominent social constructivist Alexander Wendt has phrased it: "anarchy is what states make of it."[43]

The Notion of International Society

Hedly Bull, a leading scholar within the international society tradition, does not dispute the anarchical nature of the international system, as it is obvious that sovereign states are not subject to a common government. But he rejects the idea that states can form together any form of society only by subordinating themselves to a common authority. Bull and other scholars within the international society approach argue that states in the contemporary international system actually form a society of states. By making an important distinction between a system of states and a society of states, they distinguish between anarchy in which states operate in the absence of rules and anarchy in which states operate in accordance with rules and form an international society.[44] As Bull and Adam Watson clarify, a group of states form an international system when the behavior of each state is a necessary factor in the calculations of the others, whereas an international society exists when a group of states, aware of certain common interests and common values, form a society in the sense that they conceive themselves to be bound by a common set of rules and institutions in their dealings with one another, and recognize their common interest in maintaining these arrangements.[45]

Hence, anarchy does not mean that the relations between states are not constrained by some norms and rules, which once formulated regulate their interaction. According to Bull, states respect the basic rules of coexistence in international society such as mutual respect for sovereignty, the rule that agreements should be kept, and rules limiting resort to violence. Most states also participate in the work of international organizations, agree to the forms and procedures of international law and recognize the system of diplomatic representation. However, Bull does not close his eyes to the limits that the conditions of anarchy impose on the existence of a society of states. He acknowledges that the absence of a supreme government makes each state a judge of his own cause and as a result the enforcement of law is uncertain. He also recognizes that since sovereign states can consider war as one of the courses of action, the possibility of war and conflict exists at all times. Because the current international system contains elements of a society of states and elements of anarchy he prefers to use the term anarchical society.[46] This raises the question of how order is then maintained in such a society. The answer that Bull gives is that order is preserved in the first place by a sense of common interests in some elementary goals like the preservation of the society of states itself and keeping the independence or sovereignty of individual states. But order is not kept simply by a sense of shared interests. Order is maintained by rules that dictate patterns of behavior that are consistent with these goals. These rules may have the status of international law, moral principles, customs, or operating procedures. With the absence of a supreme government, international institutions, like diplomacy and international law, help to make these rules effective.[47]

Andrew Hurrell has approached the issue of international society and the question of why international rules are followed from a more legal point of view. He argues that self-interest is only part of the explanation for the fact that rules are created and obeyed. Because states follow rules even when a state's self-interest suggests otherwise, there must be some notion of binding that explains such compliance. Hurrell emphasizes the importance of the legal sense of community and gives a key role to international law. An essential element in decision-making, he says, is the legitimacy of rules that derive from the common sense of being part of a legal community. The power of legitimacy applies to powerful as well as weak states. Powerful states have usually a decisive influence over the content and application of international legal rules and therefore benefit from the rules that maintain stability and sustain the existing political order. For weak states a legal international order provides some protection as it includes legal conventions of sovereignty that determines legal recognition as well as restraints on intervention and the use of force. Hurrell claims that once an international legal order exists, it represents the idea of being bound and voluntarily accepting a sense of obligation, which is based on the existence of shared interests, shared values, and shared expectations.[48]

Anarchy is a Social Construction

The idea that the behavior of states under anarchy is affected not only by state interests but also by international norms and rules that are constructed through social interaction, is a central claim made by a number of international relations theorists who work within the theoretical approach called constructivism. They start from two basic principles. First, that the key structures in the states system are determined primarily by shared ideas rather than material forces. Second, that the basic character of states—referred to as state identity—and interests are in important parts constructed by these shared ideas through social interaction rather than given to the system exogenously by human nature or domestic politics.[49]

The influential constructivist theorist Wendt argues that the structure of the international system is a function of the relationships among states. It is only through the interaction of states that the structure of the international system is produced, reproduced, and sometimes transformed. Wendt maintains further that the character of the international system is determined by the beliefs and expectations that states have about each other. States, he says, act differently toward enemies than they do toward friends because enemies are threatening and friends are not. If states threaten each other's security in their first encounter, then competitive dynamics may follow, giving rise to egoistic conceptions of self. But if states bring a friendly attitude to their first encounter, then different dynamics of identity formation may develop. Wendt believes that anarchic structures explain little by itself. The distribution of power, he says, may always affect states' calculations, but how it does so depends on the intersubjective understandings that constitute their conceptions of self and other. During the cold war, for instance, British missiles had a different significance for the United States than did Soviet missiles. What matters is the identities and interests that states bring to their interactions. Anarchy of friends is different from one of enemies, or as Wendt states: anarchy is what states make of it.[50]

Wendt claims that anarchy can take different forms. He clusters anarchic systems in three ideal types: Hobbesian, Lockean, and Kantian. In all three possible forms of anarchy actors have different shared ideas about the use of violence between self and other, based on different representations of self and other. In the Hobbesian form of anarchy, Wendt maintains, states see each other as enemies. The other is seen as an actor that does not recognize the right of the self to exist as an autonomous entity, and therefore will not freely limits its violence toward the self. The logic of Hobbesian anarchy is therefore a war of all against all in which actors operate on the principle of kill or be killed. This is a self-help system in which survival depends only on military power, and where actors cannot count on each other for help or even to observe basic self-restraint. The Hobbesian anarchic structure generates, according to Wendt, tendencies toward endemic and unlimited warfare; the concentration of power as a result of the elimination of states that have not adapted for warfare or are too weak militarily to compete; and the inclination of powerful states to avoid elimination by balancing each other's power.[51]

Although Hobbesian anarchy, says Wendt, has characterized important parts of international history, since the emergence of the modern states system after the peace of Westphalia in 1648 that established the state as a legal entity having the special status of sovereignty, the Hobbesian anarchical logic of kill or be killed has been replaced by the Lockean anarchical logic of live and let live. As Wendt explains, in the Westphalian system, states recognize each other's sovereignty and therefore see each other as rivals rather than enemies. States expect each other to act as if they recognize their sovereignty as a right. Wendt further argues that sovereignty becomes a right only when other states recognize it and are ready to restrain themselves. In other words, sovereignty is not only a property of individual states but becomes a norm shared by many states and formalized in international law. Even with the absence of centralized enforcement, says Wendt, almost all states in the contemporary international system keep this rule almost all of the time. Not only a powerful state but also a weak state that does not have the capability to defend its sovereignty can expect that other states will respect its sovereignty. Moreover, if the existence of weak states is at stake, other states tend to act collectively to restore the status quo. Hence, the Lockean anarchical logic suggests, according to Wendt, a world in which the weak are protected by the restraint of the strong, not a survival of the fittest. Nonetheless, under Lockean anarchy warfare is not excluded. It is accepted that rivals sometimes use violence against each other to settle disputes. But such violent behavior is exercised within certain limits.[52]

While the Lockean form of anarchy has dominated world politics, according to Wendt, in the last three centuries, he argues that a third form of anarchy, which he calls Kantian anarchy, has emerged in Western Europe and the North Atlantic region after the Second World War. In a Kantian anarchical structure, says Wendt, states regard each other as friends rather than enemies or rivals. Friendship exists, he maintains, when states expect each other to observe two rules: the rule of nonviolence and the rule of mutual aid. The first rule requires states to settle disputes without war or the threat of war, the second rule demands states to fight as a team if the security of any one is threatened by a third party. The two rules generate, according to Wendt, tendencies toward a pluralistic security community and a collective security system. A pluralistic security community is a system of states in which conflicts are settled through negotiation, arbitration, or the courts, and the use of violence as a means to handle conflicts is considered illegitimate. A collective security system is based on the principle that all members of the system agree to oppose together a threat to the security of any one of them, even if they are not individually threatened.[53]

Hence, despite the continuing anarchical structure of the international system, Wendt argues that states sometimes have made something new of anarchy. States have changed the anarchical structure of the international system from a Hobbesian world where the principal rule was kill or be killed, to a Lockean world where war is constrained by the established rule of sovereignty, and they are transforming it again in some parts of the international system into a Kantian world where the prevailing rule is collective security. Each type of anarchy has different degrees of internalized norms and rules with respect to conflict and cooperation, based on ideas about the other that each state takes into account in its interaction. A structural change in international politics happens, Wendt maintains, when actors redefine who they are and what they want. Actors can engage in critical self-reflection and choices designed to transform their identities and interests, and as a result transform a competitive security system into a cooperative one. This is exactly how the cold war ended, says Wendt. Mikhail Gorbachev's policy of new thinking started with the breakdown of the shared Leninist belief about the inherent conflict of interest between capitalist and socialist states followed by a critical examination of old ideas about self and other. As competitive security systems are sustained by foreign policy practices that create insecurity and distrust, Gorbachev had to change the practice of interaction with other states, so that they learn that the Soviet Union can be trusted and should not be viewed as a threat to their security. He did this by withdrawing from eastern Europe and implementing asymmetric cuts in nuclear and conventional forces. These significant unilateral peace initiatives and important self-binding commitments, which were rewarded by the United States and other western countries, created new forms of interactions that provided a firm basis for the transformation of competitive identities and interests into new cooperative identities and interests.[54]

Norm and Rule Driven Behavior

Other constructivists have provided as well a more social view of the environment in which states and other actors operate. They have drawn attention to the rule driven behavior of states in specific issue areas, arguing that socially constructed norms that set standards for the appropriate behavior of states influence the ways in which actors define their interests and act. In various empirical studies they have demonstrated how the broad acceptance of certain international norms, which may change over time through the behavior of states, matter as causes of national security policy.[55] Martha Finnemore, for instance, does not deny that power and interests are important. But she maintains that in order to understand what interests states pursue in humanitarian interventions, realist and liberal theories do not provide good explanations for the simple reason that states do not gain geostrategic, political, or economic advantages by their intervention. A constructivist approach that explains how international norms form the interests of states—that in turn shape the actions of states—is more helpful, as it emphasizes the normative context in which such interventions happen. Finnemore claims that the social nature of international politics creates normative understandings among actors that shape behavior and outcomes. She stresses that although norms do not determine action they create permissive conditions for action. What is more, since norms are socially constructed and evolve with changes in social interaction, new or changed norms may change state interests and enable new or different international behavior.[56]

Finnemore has examined the effects of changing humanitarian norms on patterns of military intervention over the past 150 years. She has illustrated how the changing pattern of humanitarian interventions throughout that period correspond with changes in normative understandings about which human beings merit military protection and the way in which interventions to protect those people should be realized. During the nineteenth century almost all the military interventions by countries like Russia, Britain, and France in the Balkan where aimed at the protection of Christians from the Ottoman Turks. As Finnemore explains religion was important in both motivating humanitarian action and defining who is human. Saving Christians was central to the justification for intervening, since the European powers clearly considered the massacre of Christians a human disaster. The mass murder of non-Christians or the mass killing of Christians of a different kind, such as the intense massacre against Armenians, did not provoke intervention. Finnemore argues that since 1945 a larger set of interconnected international norms has been developed to justify humanitarian military interventions. In the first place, the recognition of human equality and the universal right to self-determination, has qualified all human beings as deserving humanitarian protection by foreign governments. Secondly, to make military humanitarian interventions legitimate, intervening states cannot justify their actions simply with humanitarian claims. As military interventions are in conflict with the universal rule of sovereignty, intervening states must seek authorization for their actions from the United Nations or some other international organization. Moreover, military humanitarian interventions must be multilateral for political and normative reasons. These requirements, says Finnemore, have been constituted socially through state practice and the development of shared norms by which states act.[57]

Nina Tannenwald's analysis of the normative prohibition against the use of nuclear weapons is another example of how norms matter in international politics and how they shape the security policies of states. Tannenwald argues that an explanation of why these weapons have remained unused after 1945 based on rational deterrence theory, cannot account for the nonuse of all kinds of nuclear weapons in situations where they offered a clear military advantage and when there was no fear of retaliation. She maintains that such an explanation has to take into account the development of a global norm that has stigmatized nuclear weapons as unacceptable weapons of mass destruction. Tannenwald has examined American decision-making on the use of nuclear weapons during the Second World War, the Korean War, the Vietnam War, and the Gulf War to demonstrate a significant role for a normative element in the United States restraint with regard to the use of nuclear weapons. In 1945 nuclear weapons were new and no nuclear taboo existed on their use to end the war against Japan. Nuclear bombs were simply seen by political and military decision-makers as a new effective weapon for carrying out a wartime bombing strategy that had raised to a large extent the brutal bombings of civilians in European and Japanese cities. But during the Korean War a normative stigma against nuclear weapons was beginning to emerge. Decision-makers considered seriously the use of tactical nuclear weapons, but the political and moral concerns rather than a fear of retaliation formed an obstacle for their deployment. While the military were divided on the usefulness of atomic weapons in the war, the politicians already ruled out the use of such weapons. They were concerned about the harmful effects that the disproportionate destruction and killing of civilians will have on the support of foreign governments and world opinion for the United States.[58]

In the Vietnam War and the Gulf War, claims Tannenwald, a nonuse norm already operated as a strong normative prohibition. Even though American presidents wanted to win the war in Vietnam, none of them considered seriously the use of nuclear options. The military were willing to employ a few small tactical nuclear weapons against strategic targets in North Vietnam in an attempt to save American human losses and to bring the war to an end. But for the American leaders and policy-makers the use of such weapons was unthinkable. They feared not only the massive furious domestic and international protests the use of nuclear weapons would cause, most of them also opposed using nuclear weapons on moral grounds. The nonuse of tactical nuclear weapons was already taken for granted in the Gulf War in 1991. Although small tactical nuclear weapons could have been used against massed Iraqi troops and underground Iraqi targets, there was hardly any consideration of the use of such weapons by American military and political decision-makers. As Tannenwald illustrates, all policy-makers saw the use of nuclear weapons contrary to the personal conviction about the illegitimacy of nuclear use and conceptions of the appropriate behavior of civilized nations. In other words, nuclear weapons were taboo and therefore unusable. The effect of the nuclear taboo on policy-making is even more evident when one realizes that in the Vietnam War and the Gulf War American decision-makers did not resist the employment of other highly destructive conventional weapons, which were as destructive as nuclear weapons but politically and morally more acceptable.[59]

In this connection it is useful to mention that constructivists usually make a distinction between regulative norms and rules and constitutive norms and rules. Regulative norms and rules regulate an actor's behavior by specifying standards of appropriate behavior. Traffic rules, for example, require actors to behave in a certain way in specific situations. World trade is regulated by a number of international trade rules, such as the most-favored-nation principle. It ensures equal treatment of imports from different origins by stipulating that every trade advantage a member of the World Trade Organization gives to any country should be extended to all other members. Constitutive norms and rules have in essence an enabling function as they create or define forms of behavior. In a play of chess, for example, the underlying rules of the game create the possibility of playing chess as they enable actors to respond to each other moves by defining the acceptable behavior in a particular situation and specify what counts as checkmate. In international relations the norms and rules of sovereignty have constitutive effects on the behavior of states in the sense that shared knowledge about what counts as a violation of sovereignty makes possible the very idea of a sovereign state.[60]

Tannenwald argues that the nuclear nonuse norm has regulative effects as well as constitutive effects. The nuclear taboo helps to define a category of unacceptable weapons of mass destruction, distinguished from conventional weapons that are seen as legitimate and useable. If anarchy and self-help are what states make of it then the existence of prohibitive norms like the nuclear taboo, constrains the practice of self-help in the international state system by delegitimizing certain kinds of weapons. But the nuclear taboo, maintains Tannenwald, also defines what it means to be a civilized member of the international community. National leaders are forced to use other weapons in war or else risk being placed outside the boundaries of civilized international society. As Tannenwald states, society not anarchy is the source of constraining and permissive effects.[61]

6

A THIRD CUT

CONFLICTING INTERNATIONAL PRESSURES

In this chapter I focus on how the three competing theories that emphasize the causal powers of the structure of the international system in explaining state behavior, provide an explanation for the way the Israelis and the Palestinians dealt with the two central issues under consideration: The UN partition plan and the signing of the Oslo accords. As I have discussed in chapter 5 the three contending theories agree on the anarchical nature of the international system but differ on the implications that this has for state behavior. Realists would argue that the Israeli and Palestinian handling of these issues were first and foremost determined by the main goal of ensuring national survival and the principle of self-help. Neoliberal institutionalists would emphasize the decisive role of international institutions in changing the Israeli and Palestinian conceptions of self-interest and promoting mutual cooperation. Constructivists would maintain that the choices that the Israelis and Palestinians have made in each issue were influenced by the beliefs and expectations that they had about each other as a result of their interactions, and point out that since these ideas are affected by practice they may change over time.

THE PREVAILING LOGIC OF HOBBESIAN ANARCHY

The UN decision to divide Palestine between its Arab and Jewish inhabitants was based on the Lockean anarchical logic of live and let live. The international community expected the territorial compromise would help Jews and Arabs to reconcile their conflicting claims to an independent state in Palestine, and would make possible a peaceful coexistence in two separate states. But, it is evident that within the two communities the logic of Hobbesian anarchy, in which actors operate according to the principle of kill or be killed, dominated the policy-making.

The prevailing Hobbessian logic was in the first place a result of the way the two communities perceived each other. From the first encounter the Jews and Arabs in Palestine came to see each other as enemies. The Palestinian Arab enmity was the collective reaction of the native Arab population to the irresistible drive of the Zionist settlers to possess the land, the increased size of their population, and the consolidation of their political institutions. The Palestinian Arabs clearly perceived the Jewish ambitions as a threat to their natural rights in Palestine. Faced with a British authority that in the early days of its rule over Palestine collaborated with the Zionist enterprise and facilitated the Jews to take over little by little large areas in Palestine, the Palestinians felt that they had to fight for their lands and rights. The clear outcome of this growing hostility was the Arab riots in 1929 and the outbreak of the Arab revolt in 1936.[1] The basic Jewish hostility toward the local Arabs developed as a response to these events. The Jewish settlers were at first almost indifferent to the existence of the local Arab population, but the Arab riots made the Jewish community aware of the basic enmity of the Palestine Arabs toward the Jews. This realization was reinforced by the Arab revolt, which was seen as the beginning of a violent movement against the Zionist presence in Palestine that would not disappear. From that moment it was clearly:them or us.[2]

National Survival and Self-help

As it became obvious to the Jewish community and the Palestine Arabs that the conflict would be decided by the logic of force and that the countdown for an Arab-Jewish military confrontation had begun, the conflict between the two communities became a matter of national survival. To ensure its survival the Jewish community considered self-help to be the main rule of conduct. The experience of the Holocaust was decisive for the Jewish conception of the international environment as anarchical with no central authority to which they can appeal for protection. The Jewish leaders remembered the conspiracy of silence, as the dismissal of news about the Nazi genocide against the Jews during the Second World War was characterized. They knew that in case of a total war with the Arabs, the Jewish community could not rely for survival on anyone else but themselves. They did not expect help from the UN or any other major external power, and realized that to survive the Jewish community in Palestine was completely dependent on its own power resources. The Arab determination to resist any form of Jewish statehood by the use of force made the war in the view of the Jewish community a zero-sum game. As a loss of the war would mean destruction, the Jews were ready to fight. They believed that they stood with their back to the sea and could not retreat to another country, the way the Palestinian Arabs could move away to neighboring Arab countries.[3]

For the Jewish community, however, the main source of concern was not the poorly equipped local Arab gangs, but the lack of sufficient weapons to triumph against the invading Arab armies and in particular the British-trained Arab Legion of Transjordan. Their leaders started to make strategic plans and accumulate military capabilities to cope with a joint Arab attack as early as 1946. They anticipated a total war in which regular and irregular Arab forces would invade Palestine in an attempt to destroy the Jewish community and certainly with the objective to prevent the establishment of a Jewish state. In such a situation the Jewish leaders regarded the UN partition resolution as dead. They approved the plans of the Jewish military commanders that were aimed not only at resisting and destroying the Arab military forces, but had also the intention to wipe out the Arab villages lying inside or directly near the borders of the Jewish state and to expel its hostile Arab population to Arab areas across the border.[4] At the eve of the declaration of independence they generated an impressive military force by a very effective transformation of the Jewish underground from illegal paramilitary militias into a regular army with a central command. The new Israeli army was able to enlarge its manpower by well-organized enlistment and training systems at home and the recruitment of newly arrived immigrants and volunteers from abroad. As a matter of fact, in terms of combat troops it outnumbered the Arab forces in the decisive last stage of the war. It also succeeded in improving the inferior weaponry at its disposal, by bringing into the country great quantities of armaments in spite of a UN supervised embargo.[5]

To survive, the Palestinian Arabs accumulated power as well. But although the Arab population was twice as big as the Jewish, the Palestinian Arabs were less successful in building a military capacity within Palestine. The main source of their weakness was the lack of a unified national military organization. Their military forces consisted in fact of a number of large bands and many separate small local militias in Palestinian towns and villages. To increase their relative power capabilities the Palestinian Arabs had to mobilize military help from outside Palestine. The Arab League decided already in 1946 that a Jewish-Arab confrontation in Palestine would involve not only the two communities but the Arab states as well. At a secret meeting, held in Bludan in Lebanon, it established a special Palestine committee that was given the task to prepare the Arab states for their war in Palestine. This committee made concrete military plans to conquer Palestine by an armed force of 100,000 men from the independent Arab states.[6] During the first period of the war the Palestine Arabs indeed relied heavily on the military help of the irregular Arab Liberation Army, which was formed by the Arab League and comprised largely Syrian volunteers. In the second and decisive phase of the war they were completely dependent on the military force of the regular Arab armies that invaded Palestine. However, the number of Arab irregular and regular combatants never reached the ambitious amount of troops planned before the war. What was even more crucial for the fate of the Palestine Arabs was that not all the Arab leaders sent their troops into Palestine with the objective of preventing the establishment of a Jewish state or helping the Palestinian Arabs create their own state. Some leaders had a rather different aim, namely, to satisfy their own territorial ambitions regarding Palestine. King Abdullah of Transjordan, for instance, used his very well trained and equipped Arab Legion only to get control of major Arab areas in Palestine with the clear intention of incorporating this territory into Transjordan.[7]

The Jewish community made also an effort to mobilize support abroad. The Jewish leaders learned quickly after the Second World War that they could not count any more on British help for the Zionist objectives in Palestine. The British government hindered Jewish immigration from Europe to Palestine and refused to adopt the recommendation of a combined Anglo-American Committee of Inquiry to let 100,000 displaced Jewish survivors of the Holocaust into Palestine. The British navy tried to stop the illegal Jewish immigration campaign by capturing the ships that brought Jewish immigrants into Palestine in spite of the British ban and expelled the illegal immigrants to internment camps in Cyprus. In an attempt to break the backbone of the Jewish military underground the British army and police forces initiated also huge actions against the Jewish community, including organized arrests of major Jewish leaders and activists and massive search of illegal weapons in possession of the Jewish underground.[8]

But winning the diplomatic backing of the two new superpowers, the United States and the Soviet Union, compensated the loss of British support. The American support was the result of an effective lobby campaign of the American-Jewish leaders, domestic political considerations of the American president, Harry Truman, and his sympathetic attitude toward the Zionist cause. Shortly after the war he already called for the immigration on humanitarian grounds of 100,000 survivors of the Holocaust from the displaced persons camps in Europe to Palestine. He also opted for the creation of a Jewish state in a part of Palestine, supported the partition plan of UNSCOP, and secured an American vote in favor of the partition resolution in the UN. Shortly after the state of Israel declared its independence, the president recognized the new state against the advice of the American State Department. The policy-makers at the State Department advocated a more cautious position, as they were more sensitive than the president to the American interests in the Arab world. They considered in particular the strategic importance of maintaining friendly relations with the Arab states to ensure the undisturbed flow of Arabian oil and to protect the interests of American oil companies. In their disagreement with the president, the State Department policy-makers had two successes. They managed to receive Truman's approval for the abortive American plan for a trusteeship regime over Palestine, as well as the imposition of an American arms embargo on both sides.[9]

The Soviet Union was, in the decisive years of the international debate on partition and the creation of the state of Israel, even more helpful than the United States. Although the leaders of the Jewish community were much more oriented toward the west they could count, nonetheless, on the diplomatic support, and to their surprise also indirect military assistance, from the Soviet Union. The helpful attitude of the Soviet Union for the Jewish cause in Palestine was motivated by geostrategic reasons. The Soviet Union wanted the British to leave Palestine and expected that the new Jewish state would have at least a neutral foreign policy orientation. This implied a weakening of western power in the region and benefited the Soviet Union in the global competition between east and west. To put pressure on the British authorities in Palestine, the Soviet Union allowed the illegal immigration of Jews to Palestine from countries in eastern Europe that were under Soviet influence. In the UN, where the major diplomatic battles took place, the Soviet Union continuously defended the Jewish position. During the UN debate on partition it took an unequivocal stand in favor of the proposed partition plan. The Soviet Union also resisted the attempt of the United States to postpone the creation of a Jewish state by replacing the British Mandate with a UN trusteeship. It opposed as well the proposal of the

UN mediator Count Folke Bernadotte to keep certain parts of Palestine under British control after the end of the British rule over Palestine. Like the United States, the Soviet Union recognized the state of Israel immediately after the declaration of independence. But contrary to the United States, it offered Israel indirect military help during the war in 1948 by sanctioning the shipment of weapons from Czechoslovakia to the newborn state. These weapons were crucial for improving the military balance in favor of Israel.[10]

The Failure of International Institutions

The involvement of the UN with the issue of partition stemmed from the decision of the British government in February 1947 to submit the problem of the future of Palestine to the judgment of the UN. After several decades of unsuccessful attempts of the British government to create a common ground between the conflicting national aspirations of the Jewish and Palestine Arab communities it was now for the UN to decide on the future government of Palestine. As the successor of the League of Nations, which entrusted the administration of Palestine to Britain at the San Remo Conference in 1920, the UN was indeed the natural international forum to debate and decide the issue. As the UN had to take a decision before the withdrawal of the British forces from Palestine on May 15, 1948, it assigned the task of finding a solution to the problem to UNSCOP.

However, the UN commission, like the previous British commissions of inquiry, failed to produce a solution that would have the approval of both communities or create any incentive for a willingness to cooperate in finding a common solution. The Jewish community was ready to accept the solution suggested by a majority of the UNSCOP members, partition into two sovereign Arab and Jewish states linked by an economic union. It was seen as a recognition by the international community of the right of the Jewish people to establish their independent state. But the Palestinian Arabs were not ready even to think about a solution recommended by a minority of the UNSCOP members, a single federal government for all of Palestine with two constituent states that enjoyed a significant amount of autonomy. The Palestinian Arabs in fact boycotted the UN commission, arguing that the UN had no morale right to give away half of the territory of Palestine to a Jewish minority. The only option they were ready to consider was a unitary sovereign state with a government that reflects the real composition of the population, which was for the most part Arab. For the Palestinian Arabs and the Arab states it had to be all or nothing. When the UN General Assembly adopted, in spite of their opposition, the partition plan as recommended by the majority of the UN commission by a two-thirds majority vote, they felt not bound by the UN resolution. The Palestinian Arabs regarded the UN resolution as immoral and a threat to their national survival. They thought that they could make their own judgment about the use of force to advance their goal of preventing partition, and made no secret of their determination to fight. As the general secretary of the Arab League said after the voting: "The partition line will be nothing but a line of fire and blood."[11] Reviewing the UN vote in favor of partition Avi Shlaim draws the conclusion that it provided not just international legitimacy for creating Jewish and Arab states but, unintentionally, the start for a brutal war between the two communities in Palestine.[12]

Although the UN resolution presented a detailed scheme for the implementation of the partition plan, the UN failed to take concrete measures for the realization of partition in case of a civil war. The General Assembly and the Security Council, the two main decision-making bodies of the UN, were unable to decide on any effective intervention to end the war. The UN considered very briefly organizing an international police force to enforce partition. But the United States was unwilling to commit American troops and opposed the participation of the Soviet Union in such a force. It preferred to postpone further implementation of the UN resolution, and submitted a proposal that would bring Palestine under a UN trusteeship. The UN partition commission that was supposed to carry out the UN resolution on partition was in fact unable to do its work. The British authorities that technically still ruled the country and had military units in Palestine did little to stop the fighting and simply left the country in the midst of the civil war. All the Security Council did to stop the fighting and solve the conflict over partition was to appoint in May 1948 a special mediator for Palestine, the Swedish Count Folke Bernadotte. He managed to achieve the agreement of the two parties for a ceasefire that lasted for a short period. But the Israelis and the Arabs rejected his proposals for a political settlement, as it implied fundamental revisions of the original partition plan. His murder in Jerusalem by Jewish extremists ended his mission. The belligerent countries ignored almost all the successive calls of the Security Council for a ceasefire until January 1949, when Israel and the Arab states were ready to start armistice negotiations under the auspices of the UN. Bernadotte's successor, the American diplomat Ralph Bunch, helped the parties bridge their disagreements and sign separate armistice agreements. Yet the armistice accords between Israel and her neighbors Egypt, Jordan, Lebanon, and Syria, which were not peace agreements but detailed ceasefire agreements, meant the definitive failure of the UN to implement the resolution on partition. Israel considered from now on the ceasefire lines as the de-facto borders of the state of Israel, while Transjordan got hold of a large part of Palestine and had no intention of establishing on that territory an independent Palestinian state.[13]

The armistice agreements had the purpose of serving as a first step toward peace treaties between Israel and the Arab states. The UN assigned the task of reaching that goal, as well as solving the problem of the Palestinian Arabs population who were displaced from their homes during the war, to a special UN commission, the Palestine Conciliation Commission (UNPCC). It organized indirect talks between Arab and Israeli delegations in Lausanne from April until September 1949. But the conference was a complete failure. The Israelis and the Arabs felt that they would not gain from cooperation, and the UNPCC mediators were unable to change the Israeli and Arab conception of self-interest. Israel did not want to revise the new territorial and demographic status quo created by the war. It insisted that the ceasefire lines should be the permanent borders with only small adjustments, and it refused to allow the return of a large number of Palestinian refugees to their previous homes. The Arabs, on their part, wanted to restore the situation that existed before the war. They demanded that Israel retreat from the ceasefire lines to the territory that was allocated to her in the UN partition plan, and to take back all the refugees who wanted to return to their original homes and compensate those who choose not to exercise their right of return.[14]

The Deepening of Israeli-Palestinian Hostility

The outcome of the war of 1948 had enormous consequences for the future Jewish-Palestinian relationship. While the Jewish community established its own independent state with borders beyond the territory allocated to it by the UN partition plan, the Palestinian Arabs were unable to establish their own Palestinian Arab state in the remaining areas of the country, which became known as the West Bank and the Gaza Strip. The de-facto partition of Palestine between Israel and Jordan and the later annexation of the West Bank by Jordan, as well as the placing of the Gaza Strip under Egyptian control, sealed the fate of an independent Palestinian Arab state. But the war ended for the Palestinian Arabs not only in a political disaster, it also created a humanitarian catastrophe. By the time the war was over more than half of the native Palestinian Arab population of the country was displaced. They fled or were expelled from areas that became the Jewish state and had to resettle in the West Bank, the Gaza Strip, and neighboring Arab countries like Jordan, Syria, and Lebanon. Many of them ended in refugee camps and became dependent on international assistance provided by the UN Relief and Works Agency (UNRWA), that was created in 1949 to guarantee basic economic and social help for Palestinian refugees in need.[15] No wonder that the war of 1948 is named in Israel the War of Independence, while the Palestinian Arabs call it *al- Nakba*, meaning the disaster.

The loss of Palestine and the military defeat made the hostility of the Palestinian Arabs toward the Jewish state stronger and more intense. It triggered a wave of massive infiltrations of Palestinian refugees and organized bands of Palestinian Arabs from the West Bank and Gaza into Israel that posed a day-to-day danger to the security of the border settlements. To cope with the infiltration problem, the Israeli army started to carry out military retaliatory actions against Arab border villages and military installations along the West Bank and Gaza borders. The retaliatory raids were meant to demonstrate to the Arabs that no attack on Israeli civilians would go unpunished and to motivate the Arab leaders of the neighboring countries to stop the terrorist infiltrations.[16]

However, the reprisals did not stop the infiltrations but created a vicious circle of violence. As the Israelis and Palestinians believed that they have to live by the sword the Israeli-Palestinians relationship continued to be dominated by the logic of Hobbesian anarchy, of kill or be killed. This reality was clearly expressed by Moshe Dayan, at that time the chief of staff of the Israeli army, during the funeral of an Israeli border settler who was killed by Palestinians:

> Let us not today cast blame on the murderers. What can we say against their terrible hatred for us? For eight years now, they have sat in the refugee camps of Gaza, and have watched how, before their very eyes, we have turned their lands and villages, where they and their forefathers previously dwelled into our home. . . . Beyond the border surges a sea of hatred and revenge; revenge that looks toward the day when the calm will blunt our alertness, the day when we shall listen to the envoys of malign hypocrisy who call upon us to lay down our arms. . . . We are a generation of settlements, and without the steel helmet and the gun's

muzzle we will not be able to plant a tree or build a house. Let us not
fear to look squarely at the hatred that consumes and fills the lives
of . . . Arabs who live around us. . . . That is the fate of our generation.
This is our choice—to be ready and armed, tough and harsh—or to let
the sword fall from our hands and our lives be cut short.[17]

MOVING TOWARD A LOCKEAN
ANARCHICAL LOGIC

The significance of the Oslo accords lies in the two core goals it tried
to achieve: to end the long history of mutual denial by two national
movements that did not recognize each other's right to exist; and to
establish a two-state vision that would reconcile the mutual claim of
two people to the same territory. After several decades of mutual rejection and enmity, the handshake of Rabin and Arafat at the signing
ceremony of the Oslo accords symbolized a beginning of a cautious
movement from the logic of Hobbesian anarchy, in which actors operate
according to the principle of kill or be killed, toward a Lockean
anarchical logic, in which relations are dominated by an attitude of
live and let live. Although a final peace settlement has proved difficult
to achieve, as Dennis Ross concludes, mutual recognition of Israelis
and Palestinians proved to be irreversible: "There has been no return
to the mutual rejection and denial of the past. Moreover, a new
consensus emerged among Israelis and Palestinians and internationally
as well on the essential requirement for peace: two states, Israel and
Palestine, coexisting and living in secure and recognized borders."[18]

The Asymmetry in Power

The issue of national survival played no role in Israel's decision to
reach agreement on the Oslo accord. Israel was a strong and prosperous country. The swift military victory of Israel against the Arab countries in the 1967 June War and its ability to transform an initial
military setback to a military victory in the 1973 October War, made
the Israeli leaders believe that they could impose their will and their
strategic priorities on its Arab environment. The willingness of Egypt
to live in peace with Israel without a settlement of the Palestinian
problem convinced the Israeli leaders that being the most powerful
state in the region they could use its military power to create a
regional order that fitted Israel's interests. In this regional order was
no room for a Palestinian state or quasi-state. This notion was the

rationale for the Israeli invasion in Lebanon in 1982. The formal goal of the war was to destruct the PLO military strength and their entire infrastructure throughout Lebanon, which became the base from where the PLO continued its armed struggle against Israel. But the undeclared goal of the war was to eliminate the influence of the PLO in the occupied territories. From the Israeli point of view, the PLO frustrated their effort to impose a limited autonomy in the West Bank and the Gaza Strip as a final solution for the Palestinian problem. Israel was indeed successful in achieving its military goal. Under massive Israeli military pressure the PLO forces were overpowered and driven out of Lebanon. But the disintegration of the PLO as a result of its expulsion from Lebanon did not accomplish the political goal of undermining the PLO influence in the occupied territories, or convincing the local Palestinian leadership to accept the Israeli proposals for Palestinian autonomy. On the contrary, in spite of the imbalance in power the Palestinians in the occupied territories were firmly determined to ensure their national survival and started in 1987 an uprising against Israel to end the occupation.

The Palestinian uprising created a new reality. It taught the Israeli leaders the limits of hard power, while the Palestinians discovered the usefulness of soft power. The *intifada* developed into a complete confrontation between Palestinian residents of the West Bank and the Gaza Strip, and Israeli soldiers and settlers. The Palestinians attacked Israeli with rocks, knives, homemade firebombs, and guns. But the Israeli army was unable to use its overwhelming military power to put an end to the uprising and restore law and order. The general punitive measures no longer produced effective results and the political and military leaders were reluctant to use arms or other severe punitive measures against civilians for political, moral, and legal reasons. It strengthened Palestinian resolve to continue the uprising and to realize a separation between Israel and the occupied territories. While the Israeli leaders and public learned the paradox of power, the local Palestinians leaders and residents were successful in putting the Israeli occupation on the top of the international political agenda. As Gazit explains, television screens throughout the world presented the Israeli military occupation in the most ugly light with Israel's armed soldiers trying in vain to deal with Palestinian kids throwing stones at them and making fools out of them. The pictures and headlines spread and imprinted the desired messages on people's consciousness, presenting the Palestinian problem to the whole world and gained the Palestinians a great deal of world sympathy. The Palestinian *intifada* forced all sides to reconsider their fixed positions toward the ongoing Israeli occupation and offer new approaches to solve the Palestinian problem.[19]

However, when a Middle East peace conference was organized at Madrid in the aftermath of the Gulf War, the effect of the *intifada* was less helpful. The Palestinians in general and the PLO in particular lost much of the empathy they have gained, by the explicit support of the Palestinians and the PLO leadership for Iraq and its leader Saddam Hussein after the Iraqi invasion of Kuwait. The PLO lacked, in fact, any leverage to influence the emerging Middle East peace process. The modest power of the PLO was demonstrated already at the opening of the peace conference by the unwillingness of the co-organizers, the United States and the Soviet Union, to accept the PLO demand for participation on equal footing with the other parties. By contrast, they accepted the Israeli requirement to deny the PLO a seat at the conference table and to allow Palestinian representation only through inhabitants of the occupied territories as part of a joint Jordanian-Palestinian delegation. The PLO leadership managed nevertheless to exercise indirect influence via the Palestinian representation and to make it clear to Israel that if they want a deal it could be done only directly with the PLO. But when it was criticized for its readiness to accept indirect representation in a joint delegation with Jordan, a PLO leader explained that there was actually no other choice: the PLO had either to join the peace process or exit history.[20]

The imbalance of power between Israel and the PLO became even more evident during the direct negotiations between Israel and the PLO at Oslo. Israel was able to exert much more leverage than the PLO, as Arafat was much keener to reach an agreement than Rabin. The Labor government wanted to reach an agreement that would end the *intifada* at the lowest possible price but not at any price. The *intifada* did undermine the sense of personal security of many Israelis, but it did not present a threat to Israel's existence or its control of the occupied territories. Besides the recognition of the PLO, Rabin made actually only one additional concession. He agreed to hand over the control over Gaza and some parts of the West Bank to the PLO. But Rabin conceived even this concession as a relative gain. From his point of view such a withdrawal improved rather than deteriorated Israel's security, since the transfer of power in Gaza from Israel to the PLO would also shift the responsibility of dealing with Hamas from Israel to the PLO. Rabin expected that Arafat would use his new power base in the occupied territories to reduce the power of Hamas.

Arafat in contrast to Rabin negotiated from weakness. The PLO was without a territorial base after its expulsion from Lebanon, and it lost the financial support of many Arab countries that was vital for its functioning as a result of its political support for Iraq during the Gulf War. Hamas challenged the PLO authority in the occupied territories, and the realization of the independent Palestinian state it had declared in 1988 was only a remote possibility at that moment. Since a failure to reach agreement would have put at risk the whole existence of the PLO, Arafat was desperate to reach an agreement even at the price of some painful concessions. Arafat actually abandoned in the negotiations at Oslo some key demands on which he made any settlement conditional in the past. The Oslo accords gave the PLO in the Oslo accords only a territorial foothold in Gaza and Jericho with the right to establish Palestinian self-rule in these areas. It also contained an Israeli commitment to further withdrawal from the West Bank and the Gaza Strip, but although the two parties realized that Palestinian self-rule might lead to Palestinian statehood it did not mentioned a guarantee to establish a Palestinian state. The Oslo accords included only an Israeli promise to negotiate further on a final settlement without any indication to how the two parties would settle the issues of Palestinian statehood, the definite borders, the future of the Jewish settlements in the occupied territories, the problem of the refugees and the sensitive issue of Jerusalem in the final-status negotiations. But although the Israeli government made no prior pledge for the final solution of these issues, the PLO leadership believed that the Oslo accords offered it some absolute gains. Arafat saw the foothold that he obtained in Gaza and Jericho as a territorial base from where he could build further a Palestinian state, as the prospect of additional Israeli withdrawals could advance mutual separation. Moreover, the recognition by Israel and the specific conditions for further negotiations gave him a more powerful position in future negotiations. If the terms of the Palestinians for a settlement were not accepted, said Arafat, they could return to violence but this time this would be done with 30,000 Palestinian soldiers at their disposal and while they control a territory of their own.[21]

As Robert Rothstein has argued, in the light of the asymmetries in power between Israel and the Palestinians, Arafat's "peace of the brave" appears to be a "peace of the desperate." But as he has further emphasized, Arafat did not come away from Oslo empty-handed. He hoped that a new bargaining game had been established, in which the PLO was recognized by Israel as a legitimate negotiating partner, and the PLO acquired access to the White House and the American administration in Washington. It generated hopes, says Rothstein, that Arafat could induce the American government to persuade Israel to do what it would not otherwise be willing to do.[22] Thus, the willingness of Israel and the PLO to cooperate and to produce the Oslo accords was clearly motivated by their own conception of self-interest and the expectations that Israel and the PLO had about their respective absolute gains from such cooperation.

Shaping a Two-State Solution

An important factor in changing the conception of self-interest were also two explicit ground rules that the international community had developed since the June War of 1967 for Middle East peacemaking: the principle of land for peace and the principle of Palestinian self-determination. These basic rules set out the conditions for an Israeli-Palestinian settlement. They were rooted in international conventions such as the inadmissibility of the acquisition of territory by war, the right of every state to live in peace and security, and the right of a people to form its own state. The gradual acceptance of these ground rules by Israel and the PLO was reinforced by the immense political leverage the United States could exert to implement these rules. It was the combination of these ground rules and American diplomatic pressure that pushed Israel and the PLO gradually toward a two-state solution.

The first ground rule was the land for peace principle. Israel had to return the occupied territories, in exchange for a peace settlement. In other words, Israel was not allowed to hold the occupied territories indefinitely, but at the same time it was not forced to withdraw from the occupied territories in return for less than a peace agreement. This basic rule was established in the aftermath of the June War of 1967 and was laid down in UN Security Council resolution 242, which formulated the framework for a negotiated peace settlement in the Middle East. Resolution 242 emphasized the inadmissibility of the acquisition of territory by war and therefore called for withdrawal of Israeli armed forces from territories occupied in the June War. But resolution 242 also stressed the need to work for just and lasting peace in which every state in the area can live in security. This required termination of all claims of belligerency and acknowledgment of the sovereignty, territorial integrity, and political independence of every state in the area and their right to live in peace within secure and recognized boundaries free from threats or acts of force.[23]

The principle of land for peace formed the basis for the peace treaty between Egypt and Israel in 1979. Israel withdrew all its troops and settlements from the entire occupied Sinai in return for a peace treaty with Egypt. The Camp David accords that Egypt and Israel signed in 1978, as a first step toward the final peace treaty, contained a separate part on a framework for a peace settlement regarding the West Bank and Gaza Strip. Israel agreed to hold negotiations with a joint Jordanian-Palestinian delegation on the final status of the West Bank and Gaza Strip based on all the provisions and principles of resolution 242. This implied that Israel accepted the application of the land for peace principle also to the West Bank and the Gaza Strip. However, Israel made it clear that the negotiations, but not necessarily the results of the negotiations, would be based on resolution 242.[24] Successive Israeli governments interpreted the land for peace principle in terms of withdrawal for security and tried to find a formula that would allow Israel to maintain control of all or at least some parts of the West Bank. While the Likud governments sought a solution in diverse autonomy plans, the Labor governments searched for various options that offered Israel and Jordan joint control of these areas or permitted Israel to keep control of some strategic parts. However, King Hussein always refused to settle for less than a full return of all the occupied West Bank to Jordan. The issue became further complicated after the decision of the Arab leaders during their Rabat summit in 1974 to recognize the right of the Palestinians to establish an independent state on any part of the occupied territories that Israel evacuated under PLO leadership, which was recognized to be the sole legitimate representative of the Palestinian people. This decision excluded Jordan as the key party in effecting a future political solution to the occupied West Bank and Gaza Strip. Since Israel adopted a policy of refusal to deal with the PLO, the occupied West Bank and Gaza Strip remained in Israeli hands.

After the Rabat summit Israel began an intensive settlement policy in order to create facts on the ground that would prevent the establishment of a Palestinian state. But, with the exception of Arab East Jerusalem that was annexed immediately after the June War, Israeli governments carefully refrained from annexing the West Bank and the Gaza Strip, as the ultimate measure against the emergence of a Palestinian state. The Labor and the Likud government had different arguments for their reluctance, but they shared the knowledge that any attempt to annex parts of the occupied territories would be considered to be an intolerable violation of resolution 242. It would bring Israel in conflict with the entire international community and lead in particular to an unbearable tension with the United States, on which Israel was dependent for its diplomatic support as well as military and economic aid. To avoid a serious clash with the

United States, successive Israeli governments choose a policy of building settlements in places from which Israel had no intention to withdraw instead of annexation. But the Americans never sanctioned this creeping annexation policy. They always insisted that any territorial change in the status of the occupied territories could only be the outcome of a negotiated settlement. President Ronald Reagan, who launched his own plan for a diplomatic settlement of the Israeli-Palestinian conflict in 1982, clearly stated that he opposed Israeli annexation and emphasized that the withdrawal provisions of resolution 242 should apply to the West Bank and the Gaza Strip. Referring to the land for peace principle he added that the extent of Israeli withdrawal from occupied territories should be influenced by the extent and the nature of the peace and security arrangements offered in return.[25]

Before the start of the Madrid peace conference the American foreign minister James Baker, made no secret of his opposition to the building of settlements in the occupied territories, which he and President George Bush saw as a major obstacle to peace. Addressing an important pro-Israeli American-Jewish organization in May 1989 he said:"For Israel, now is the time to lay aside, once and for all, the unrealistic vision of a greater Israel. Israeli interests in the West Bank and Gaza—security and otherwise—can be accommodated in a settlement based on resolution 242. Forswear annexation. Stop settlement activity. Allow schools to reopen. Reach out to the Palestinians as neighbors who deserve political rights."[26] Bush went even one step further. When Israel requested in 1989 an American loan guarantee to build housing for Jewish immigrants from the Soviet Union, Bush required a letter from the Israeli prime minister, Shamir, assuring him that Israel had no plans to build housing for Russian Jews in the occupied territories, which in Bush's view included East Jerusalem. Bush used this stick again in 1991 when Israel asked for another loan guarantee for the same purpose. This time Bush and Baker insisted on a dollar-for-dollar reduction from the loan guarantee for every dollar spent on settlement activity. Since the Likud government rejected this condition the loan guarantee was postponed.[27] This was not the first time that U.S. policy-makers considered concrete measures to demonstrate their disapproval of the Israeli settlements policy. President Jimmy Carter was advised already in 1978 to reduce aid to Israel by a certain amount for each settlement that Israel continued to build, when Israel turned down his demand to freeze the building of new settlements, as the United States had no intention of subsidizing illegal settlements.[28]

The Likud government that led Israel during the Madrid peace conference, which was convened on the basis of resolution 242 and 338, had no intention of making any territorial concessions in exchange for peace or surrender the claim on the West Bank. A change in the Israeli attitude came only after the change of guard in Israeli politics, when Labor defeated Likud in the 1992 elections. Guided by the land for peace principle and being more sensitive to American pressure, the new Labor government adopted a more flexible position. The gradual withdrawal of Israeli forces from significant parts of the occupied territories as a consequence of the Oslo accords as well as the subsequent Cairo agreement and interim agreement on the West Bank and Gaza Strip, was an important Israeli step toward the implementation of the land for peace principle. Although the interim agreement resulted only in a partial withdrawal of Israel from densely populated Arab areas in the West Bank, Israel promised to hold further negotiations over a permanent settlement that would lead to the implementation of resolutions 242 and 338. In the meanwhile the West Bank was divided into three areas. A first area that consisted of the main Arab cities came under full control of the Palestinian authority, a second area that included the Jewish settlements remained under Israeli control, and a third area came under a mixed form of authority. In the spirit of the Reagan plan, the extent of further Israeli withdrawal from occupied territories was dependent on the ability of the Palestinian authority to deliver security for withdrawal. It is this failure that led to the return of the Likud party to power in the 1996 elections, and caused a stalemate in the further implementation of the Oslo accords.

The second ground rule for Middle East peacemaking was the Palestinian right to self-determination. This basic rule began to take shape in the process of Middle East peacemaking under the presidency of Carter, who was the first American president to recognize that the Palestinian problem was more than a refugee problem. While resolution 242 treated the Palestinian problem as a refugee problem, Carter made several public statements at the beginning of his presidency in 1977 in which he said that the Palestinian problem had a political as well as a humanitarian dimension. He also used for the first time the notion of a Palestinian homeland. Carter clearly had the ambition of dealing with the Palestinian issue as part of a comprehensive Middle East peace settlement that he wanted to achieve at a Middle East peace conference in Geneva. One of the principles on which the participants in the conference had to agree on before the conference started, concerned the Palestinian right to participate in determining their own future status. Carter was also prepared to accept Palestinian and even PLO participation in a joint Arab delegation, if the PLO would accept resolution 242 as the basis of negotiations.[29] The peace conference did not take place as a result of Egypt's decision to negotiate separately with Israel, but the Palestinian issue did not disappear from Carter's agenda for Middle East peacemaking. It came back in the Camp David accords that were reached between Egypt and Israel in 1978 with the help of Carter, who led the negotiations and was actually the architect of the Camp David accords. The essential part of the Camp David accords was an agreement on a framework for peace in the Middle East, which included two parts. The first part dealt exclusively with the West Bank and the Gaza Strip, and specified a number of arrangements that were aimed at the resolution of the Palestinian problem in all its aspects. It proposed an interim regime for the West Bank and Gaza Strip that would offer the Palestinians self-government, with a clear commitment to a second phase negotiations toward the end of the transitional period to resolve the issues of borders, sovereignty, and Palestinian rights in accordance with resolution 242.[30]

During the negotiations at Camp David Israel managed to water down the proposal but the final text of the Camp David accords nevertheless contained a reference to two general principles for a resolution of the Palestinian problem: the legitimate rights of the Palestinian people and their right to choose their own form of government. It also spelled out some practical measures in order to start with a concrete implementation of these principles: self-government for the Palestinians in the West Bank and Gaza Strip for a transitional period of five years; a self-governing authority to replace the existing military government to be elected by the inhabitants of these areas; withdrawal of the Israeli military government and its civilian administration as soon as the self-governing authority was established; withdrawal of Israeli armed forces and redeployment of the remaining Israeli forces into specified security locations; and establishment of a local police force. Moreover, after the beginning of the transitional period negotiations had to take place to determine the final status of the West Bank and Gaza Strip, based on all the provisions and principles of resolution 242, and conducted by representatives of Israel, Jordan, and elected representatives of the inhabitants of the west Bank and the Gaza Strip.[31] Although none of these ideas was given real content in the abortive negotiation on Palestinian autonomy after the signing of the Camp David accords and a separate Egyptian-Israeli peace treaty, these ideas formed a firm foundation for future plans aimed at a negotiated settlement of the Palestinian issue. As Itamar Rabinovich argues, the core of the Oslo agreement was based on the model created by the Camp David accords. Palestinian self-rule was to be established in West Bank and Gaza Strip for a transitional period of five years; at the end of the second year negotiations would begin over final-status issues; and Israeli forces would be redeployed in several stages.[32]

While Carter recognized that the Palestinian problem had to be solved by self-determination for the Palestinians, this did not imply an independent Palestinian state under the leadership of the PLO. Carter never mentioned in his plans for Palestinian self-determination any explicit or implicit role for the PLO. In indirect contacts with the PLO Carter had always insisted that the PLO had to renounce its aim of destroying Israel in order to gain a place at eventual peace talks.[33] His successor, President Ronald Reagan was even more explicit. On the day that the PLO completed its evacuation from Beirut he presented a plan for a settlement of the Israeli-Palestinian conflict, in which he sought a solution to the Palestinian right to self-determination not by the forming of an independent Palestinian state, led by the PLO, but in Palestinian self-government in the West Bank and Gaza Strip in association with Jordan.[34] For the PLO there was actually no role in such a settlement since the PLO remained for American-policy makers an illegitimate participant in a negotiated settlement of the Palestinian problem, as long as it did not accept the principles of resolution 242 and 338 as a basis for a peace settlement, recognized Israel's right to exist, and renounced terrorism. These conditions reflected in the American view the basic rules of coexistence in international relations. The Americans had promised Israel not to recognize or negotiate with the PLO unless the PLO recognized and accepted resolutions 242 and 338.[35]

However, the United States told the PLO that if it wanted to be involved in Middle East peacemaking, it had to meet the American conditions. Arafat responded by the proclamation of a Palestinian independent state at a Palestinian National Council meeting. At this occasion the PNC endorsed resolutions 242 and 338, as well as UN General Assembly's resolution 181 regarding the partition of Palestine. It demonstrated a commitment of the PLO to the coexistence of Israel and a Palestinian state. But for the United States this was not enough. Quandt has described how Arafat was pushed by Foreign minister George Shultz to make several public declarations in which he finally and without making any reservations declared in December 1988 that the PLO accepted resolutions 242 and 338 as a the basis for negotiations with Israel, recognized the right of Israel to exist in peace and security, and renounced terrorism.[36] It paved the way for bringing the Palestinians on equal footing into Middle East peacemaking, and removed an important obstacle for Israel to deal with the PLO as a full party to a negotiated settlement.

A Marginal Role for the International Community

From the discussion so far it is evident that the American pressure on Israel and the PLO was decisive in the progress that the two parties made toward a two-state solution. The entire international community adopted the formula of two states for two nations as a way of dealing with the difficult Palestinian problem. But the two other key actors in the international community, the Soviet Union and the European Union (EU), missed the leverage to implement this solution. The Soviet Union was guided in its policy toward Middle East peacemaking primarily by one overall objective: to prevent a *Pax Americana*. Although the Israeli-Palestinian conflict did not rank high on the list of foreign policy priorities of the Soviet Union, it wanted, nevertheless, to be a party to any Middle East peace settlement. But the lack of diplomatic relations between Israel and the Soviet Union from 1967 to 1989 and the Israeli perception of the Soviet Union as pro-Arab and in particular pro-Palestinian, made it impossible for the Soviet Union to fulfill any active mediating role in the search for a political settlement to the Israeli-Palestinian conflict. The only way the Soviet Union could prevent an American mediated settlement of the conflict was the convening of an international peace conference. The Soviet Union therefore always pressed the United States to agree to a Middle East peace conference appealing to the need for superpower cooperation in the resolution of regional conflicts, and bringing into play its ability to generate support from radical Arab regimes for a peace conference and moderate their positions. Because of the absence of relations between the United States and the PLO, the Soviet Union also had the advantage that it was the only superpower that could deal with the PLO.[37]

There was some new thinking about a settlement of the Israeli-Palestinian conflict in Mikhail Gorbachev's new thinking in Soviet foreign policy. He maintained the traditional Soviet position that referred to resolutions 242 and 338, the need for Israeli withdrawal, and self-determination for the Palestinians without any concrete description of the form of Palestinian self-determination. As Galia

Golan says, the Soviet Union did not rule out but it did not explicitly demand the creation of an independent Palestinian state. In 1988 Gorbachev even tried to persuade the PLO leadership to abstain from the proclamation of an independent Palestinian state, as he believed that this step would complicate negotiations with Israel on a settlement of the Palestinian issue. Gorbachev also took a more active role than his predecessors by demanding from Arafat the acceptance of resolution 242 and the recognition of Israel in order to make a breakthrough in the Middle East peace process. While the Soviet Union recognized the PLO as representative of the Palestinians it did not insist on PLO participation in an eventual peace conference, and like the United States it was resolute about the need to accept resolution 242 and to recognize Israel as basis for participation.[38]

The EU had always desired an active mediating role in Middle East peacemaking, but until the Madrid peace conference the EU played a marginal role in Middle East peacemaking. The reason for the inability of the EU to fulfill a significant function in the peace process has been simply the fact that the United States wished no interference of EU member states, in particular France, in its Middle East peace diplomacy, and that the EU was an unacceptable mediator to Israel. The United States could do without the EU, as the United States and the EU member states shared little common ground in their approach to Middle East peacemaking and differed in the way they dealt with the Palestinian issue. While the United States adopted a gradualist step-by-step tactic and concentrated on separate bilateral agreements, the EU member-states favoured multilateral negotiations that would involve all the parties concerned and would lead to an overall peace settlement. Moreover, whereas the United States left it to the parties directly involved to agree on solutions, the EU formulated itself what the final solution should be. The Venice declaration that was adopted by the EU heads of government in June 1980 and would be the basic EU position on the Middle East peace process for many years, was worked out without the parties involved. The EU member states themselves listed the necessary requirements for a comprehensive peace settlement and expected the people concerned to comply. They argued that the Palestinian issue is the core of the Arab-Israeli conflict and therefore should also be at the heart of the peace process. If the Palestinian problem was solved, Israel and its Arab neighbours could easily reach a peace settlement. Consequently, they demanded that in a peace settlement the Palestinians must exercise fully their right to self-determination and that the PLO has to be involved in the peace negotiations.[39]

When the EU launched shortly after the Venice declaration an independent European peace initiative it was faced with a hostile Israeli attitude, as Israel interpreted the Venice declaration as a pro-Arab statement. From the Israeli perspective the EU was a self-serving mediator instead of a neutral honest broker as the EU member-states were driven by egoistic economic considerations rather than a concern about Israel's security. The clear-cut Israeli message to European diplomats who visited the region in two EU fact-finding missions was that if a mediator is needed, it could be only the United States. This made any European attempt to fulfil a mediating role, in fact, a non-starter. It took the EU more than a decade to get a foothold in Middle East peacemaking during the Madrid peace process. From the start the EU tried to become fully involved in the conduct of the peace conference but to its disappointment neither the United States nor Israel were willing to accept the EU as full participant. The United States kept the EU on the sidelines of the Madrid peace conference and choose to make the Soviet Union, not the EU, the cosponsor of the Madrid peace conference. The EU was invited to attend the Madrid conference but it was excluded from the separate bilateral negotiations, which were managed by the United States. However, the EU was given a more prominent role within the multilateral track of the Madrid peace process. As the American policy-makers expected the EU to contribute a substantial share in the funding of the peace process, it became chairman of the important Regional Economic Development Working Group. The significance of the working group diminished after the signing of the Oslo accords, but when the United States organized in October 1993 a donors conference in Washington to support the development of the Palestinian economy and the building of the Palestinian Authority in the West Bank and Gaza, the EU claimed for itself a leading role in the implementation of the economic dimension of the Oslo agreement.[40]

Although the EU still missed the clout to have a strong political role in the Oslo peace process, it exploited its economic power to increase its influence in the peace process through concrete financial contributions. The large financial assistance to the Palestinians in the West Bank and Gaza created pressures for deeper involvement of the EU in the peace process. Being by far the first donor placed the EU in a position to demand participation alongside the United States in all the bilateral negotiations between the parties. The fact that the EU has become the most important financial source of the Palestinian Authority, has given the EU indeed the power to influence the policies of the Palestinian Authority. Its ability to use its leverage with the Palestinians actually led to an informal division of labor between the

EU and the United States, whereby American peace diplomacy would focus much more on Israel and the EU would concentrate on the Palestinians. It would ultimately result in making the EU full member of the Quartet on the Middle East that was established by the United States in 2002 to deal with further Middle East peacemaking.

The Mutual Wish of Separation

A major driving force behind the Oslo accords was the wish on both sides to replace the Hobbesian anarchical logic of kill or be killed by the Lockean anarchical logic of live and let live. The Labor government and the PLO leadership wanted to change the practice of their inter-action by mutual recognition of each other's right to exist and to live in two states, a Palestinian state alongside Israel. The acceptance of this two-state solution was reinforced by a strong desire of the population on both sides to separate and live in two different states. Large parts of the Israelis and Palestinians began to adhere to the notion: we here, and they there. It reflected, though in a negative way, a belief in the logic of live and let live. This desire for separation or disengagement, as some preferred to call such a physical separation, was, in fact, the final acceptance of partition by Israelis and Palestinians.

Rabin has always been in favor of separation between Israel and the Palestinians in the occupied territories. He believed that such a sepa-ration would not only reduce terrorist acts against Israeli citizens and improve the sense of personal security, but that it would also cure the Israeli society from its dependency on Arab labor and decrease the level of unemployment among the Israeli population. Rabin was less worried about the consequences that such a separation would have for the dependency of Palestinians for their income on their work in Israel, as he believed that a real separation between Israel and the occupied territories and the creation of a de-facto Palestinian entity would make it easier for the Palestinians to attract investments from abroad that, in turn, would create employment for the local population. It would also make the Palestinian Authority financially and economically less dependent on Israel. Separation was for Rabin not simply a practical answer to the problem of terrorism, but part of a permanent political solution to the Israeli-Palestinian conflict.[41] When Rabin came to power in 1992 he was determined to use the framework of the Madrid peace conference to realize a separation between Israel and the Palestinians. He preferred to create such a separation through agreements with the Palestinians, but if this was not possible he was prepared to separate from the Palestinians unilaterally.[42]

But Rabin did not act in a vacuum. He recognized a deep desire for separation among the Israeli population. Public opinion polls demonstrated, in particular after the signing of the Oslo accords, that a vast majority of the Israeli population wanted a clear-cut border between Israel and a Palestinian entity. Only a small minority rejected such a separation. The political division among the Israeli public became actually less relevant on the issue of separation, since many Likud voters supported the separation as well.[43] The remarkable desire in the national mood for separation was clearly caused by the lack of personal security during the first Palestinian uprising and the terror acts after the signing of the Oslo accords. The *intifada* and the suicide bombs attacks left clearly their impact on the Israeli public. As Ben-Ami argues, the arrogance of power so firmly established in the collective mind of the Israelis after the June War was broken by the military setbacks of the October War, the South Lebanese quagmire, the vulnerability of the home front during the Gulf War, and the ongoing *intifada*. They had all demonstrated that the era of quick and elegant victories was definitely over. The daily television pictures of the *intifada* that showed the ugly side of the occupation reinforced the change of heart. It raised questions among Israelis whether their stay in the territories was a human occupation, and weakened their resolve to remain in the occupied territories. The growing perception of the *intifada* as a David and Goliath battle, but this time with the Palestinians in the role of David demonstrated that Israel's obsession with an exclusive military answer to what were essentially political challenges was no longer sustainable.[44]

The Palestinian uprising in the occupied territories taught many Israelis that the military occupation of the West Bank and the Gaza Strip could not go on forever. They began to understand that a new policy was badly needed, a policy that would relieve them from the heavy burden of the occupied territories and would give them normal life and economic well-being; in other words, a policy that will bring peace. The secular majority of Israeli society did not share the territorial vision of a greater Israel, and lacked an understanding of the settlers who would do anything to fulfill their dream. They had little regard for their pain and were ready to pay the price of a Palestinian entity alongside Israel in most of the West Bank and Gaza. This pragmatic majority was ready to accept a territorial compromise with the Palestinians and questioned the logic of the religious messianic obsession with Judea and Samaria of the nationalist camp and the refusal to come to terms with the need to compromise and moderation.[45] The labor leadership responded to the new reality.

Rabin's slogan during the 1992 elections campaign that it was time for a change of national priorities reflected, in fact, the public mood of many Israelis. As Ilan Peleg argues, the decision of Rabin to redefine Israel's policies on Israel's relationship with the historical enemy, the Palestinians, the organization representing them, the PLO, and Israel's attitude toward the occupied territories, broke all taboos regarding the Palestinian issue. The redefinition of the relationship with the Palestinian "other," symbolized by shaking Arafat's hand, was a quantum leap in the Israeli-Palestinian relationship. While a Labor prime minister, Golda Meir, had declared in the 1970s that there was no Palestinian nation, in the 1990s a labor prime minister had negotiated and reached an agreement with the representatives of that non-nation.[46]

The Palestinians, and in particular the PLO, had also gradually changed their thinking about the inherent conflict with Israel. The PLO gave up the idea of the establishment of a state in all of Palestine by a continuous armed struggle already in 1974, when the PNC decided to establish a Palestinian state on any part of the West Bank and the Gaza Strip that Israel evacuated. By the adoption of this so-called phased strategy it only redefined its territorial aspirations. It did not imply recognition of the Jewish state.[47] However, this change of focus to the occupied West Bank and Gaza Strip brought the PLO in direct competition with Jordan about the future possession of these territories. It forced the PLO to get involved in the Middle East peace process that started after the October War in an attempt to implement resolutions 242 and 338, and became the forum in which the Arab states tried to regain their territories by diplomatic negotiations rather than war.

In order to get a foothold in this peace process the PLO leadership moderated its position toward Israel. The PLO stated in 1977 that it would accept the right of Israel to exist, if Israel recognized Palestinian rights. It emphasized that the PLO's goal was to establish an independent state in the occupied territories, which would present no threat to Israel. The PLO leadership expressed its willingness to live in peace with Israel and declared its readiness to accept an amended version of resolution 242. At that time the PLO leadership still insisted on a modification of resolution 242 so that it would refer to the Palestinian issue not only as a refugee problem, but also as one of self-determination. The culmination of the gradual process toward the acceptance of the idea of the existence of a Palestinian state alongside Israel, was the PNC meeting in Algiers in November 1988 that proclaimed the establishment of an independent state, based on the UN partition resolution, accepted resolutions 242 and 338 with a provision on Palestinian rights, and condemned terrorism. Arafat repeated these declarations before the UN General Assembly in December 1988. On American insistence, he was ready to say again that the PLO accepted resolutions 242 and 338, this time without making any reservations, stated unequivocally that the PLO recognized Israel's right to exist, and not only condemned but renounced all forms of terrorism.[48] The PLO restated all these declarations in the Oslo accords, to which Israel responded with recognition of the PLO as the representative of the Palestinian people and a legitimate negotiating partner. Once the Oslo negotiations started the Palestinians wanted to be recognized as a nation and to have the perspective of an independent Palestinian state alongside Israel.

However, the incentive for moderation came not only from the international community. The Palestinians in the occupied territories pressed the PLO leadership as well to move toward further moderation of its positions. The local PLO leaders in the occupied territories demanded that the PLO leadership find a political formula that would translate the willingness of Israel to end the uprising into political and diplomatic gain. The Palestinian uprising failed to force Israel to retreat from the occupied territories, but the Israeli desire to end the *intifada* gave the Palestinians in the West Bank and Gaza Strip a real sense of achievement against the undefeatable Israeli army. After the collapse of the Palestinian entity in Lebanon, the *intifada* created a feeling of success and restored Palestinian pride and honor. From the perspective of the local PLO leaders the Palestinians could now agree to compromises that would end the occupation and put an end to their daily suffering by a political separation. Pressed by Israeli repression the local PLO leaders called for the need to move from stones and violence to a political initiative. They asked the PLO leadership to show political flexibility and came up with the suggestion to set up a Palestinian state alongside Israel. In the PNC meeting in 1988, Arafat hailed the glorious *intifada* and its martyrs and declared the establishment of a Palestinian state coexisting with Israel.[49]

In an analysis of the Oslo accords Gazit has rightly argued that the Oslo accords had revolutionary significance. It signaled the mutual recognition by Israel and the Palestinians of each other's national rights, and the end of the "all or nothing" approach as the only and exclusive goal of each side to resolving the conflict. But the Oslo accords, he further says, launched a political process whose outcome was neither agreed upon nor defined in advance. The Oslo accords, for example, did not promise the Palestinians the achievement of establishing a Palestinian state, or a commitment to Israel to end the process of hostility and violence. The Oslo agreement also failed to initiate confidence-building measures that would lift barriers and change attitudes, or to start a dialogue that would lead to a real psychological turnabout. Gazit reminds us of Anwar Sadat, the Egyptian president who started his successful peace initiative in 1977 with two statements: the first one was, "No more war!" the second was, "seventy percent of the conflict is the psychological barrier, my visit to Israel toppled it!"[50]

CONCLUSION

MORE THAN ONE STORY TO TELL

In the preceding chapters I have focused on two crucial events in the long history of the Israeli-Palestinian conflict: the partition of Palestine in 1947, and the signing of the Oslo accords in 1993. With the help of three different lenses that represent a range of theoretical perspectives, the empirical cuts have produced three different insights into the Israeli-Palestinian conflict. Applying alternative international relations perspectives and choosing among different assumptions about foreign policy-making, has offered different accounts of why the Jewish community in Palestine accepted partition and the Palestinian Arabs rejected partition, and has provided different explanations of why Israel and the PLO decided in 1993 to reach an agreement on the Oslo accords.

The first theoretical lens focuses on the way the beliefs and images of individual leaders and other key foreign policy-makers influences the choices they make in order to deal with the problem they face. The first empirical cut has demonstrated that the personal beliefs of Ben-Gurion had played a crucial role in the way he dealt with the dilemma of partition. His decision to accept the UN partition plan and to proclaim an independent Jewish state were clearly influenced by his deep belief that the conflict between Jews and Palestinians was a zero-sum game, and that the Arab community will never settle for a political compromise. His image of the basic enmity of the Palestinian Arabs toward the Jews, and his firm belief that the conflict between the two national movements would be decided by war, in combination with his belief in the utility of military force, was an important drive for his effort to make the Jewish community as strong as possible and well prepared for such a confrontation. His belief that the Jewish community, and later Israel, should never operate without at least one great power ally and avoid diplomatic isolation, paved the way for the broad support in the UN General Assembly for the partition plan. His intense conviction in the obligation of a leader to seize the historical chances that can change the fate of a nation was a major motivation for his decision to approve the UN partition plan. Although he believed in the justified claim of the Jewish people to the whole land of Palestine, Ben-Gurion did not want to miss the opportunity offered by the partition plan to establish a Jewish state. Ben-Gurion's strong belief that people can influence historical outcomes inspired him to proclaim an independent Jewish state regardless of the certainty that this would cause an all-out war with the Palestinian Arabs and the Arab countries. The presence of a strong Jewish leader whose definition of the situation determined the choice in favor of partition, and the lack of a Palestinian Arab leader who could influence the course of events in 1947 when the Palestinian Arabs faced the challenge of partition illustrated the relevance of leadership.

The individual beliefs and images of Rabin, Peres, and Arafat also played a crucial part in the way they dealt with the fundamental problem they faced at Oslo: mutual recognition and acceptance of the principle of a two-state solution. The decision of Rabin to sign the Oslo accords was clearly influenced by his changing perception of the conflict and his traumatic experience of war and desire for peace. Rabin's belief in the responsibility of a leader to exploit a historical opportunity when it occurs was an important reason for his decision to break the taboo of not dealing with the PLO. He not only recognized a former enemy, but also treated the PLO and Arafat as a legitimate negotiations partner. His motivation to put an end to the conflict with the Palestinians was also motivated by his conviction that military power and economic strength were two sides to the coin, and that a peaceful environment would stimulate economic expansion. Peres shared many of these beliefs with Rabin. But his motivation to break all taboos and to search for a deal with the PLO was also driven by his image of a peaceful and prosperous Middle East in which Israel had a leading role. For Peres this was not a misperception or wishful thinking. He truly believed in the absolute necessity to reach a settlement of the Palestinian problem in order to realize his vision of a borderless Middle East. This image was clearly influenced by analogical reasoning, as he referred time after time to the European Union as an historical example.

The fundamental belief in the need to build a Palestinian state was for Arafat an overall motivation for his political handling. Only an independent Palestinian state could end the suffering of the Palestinian refugees in the Arab countries and the Israeli repression of the Palestinian population in the occupied territories. In realizing that goal Arafat was guided by a fundamental belief in the importance of historical timing and need for political pragmatism. It led him to adapt his strategy for achieving a Palestinian state to the changing regional and international circumstances. After the October War, which reinforced the perception that Israel was militarily undefeatable, he actually gave up the strategy of armed struggle. His wish to get involved in the diplomatic process of Middle East peacemaking compelled him to revise his position regarding the creation of a Palestinian state in the whole of Palestine. The ending of the cold war, which established the United States as the sole superpower, forced him to make further concessions and recognize Israel's existence in order to become a legitimate negotiating partner for the United States and Israel. As the establishment of an independent Palestinian state in the West Bank and Gaza Strip was only a remote possibility at the time of the Oslo negotiations, a further concession of the acceptance of limited autonomy in the West Bank and the Gaza Strip in exchange for formal recognition from Israel was perceived by Arafat as a deal he could not resist. The Oslo agreement was not the perfect outcome, but it offered a chance to start the realization of his national aspirations and could serve as springboard for Palestinian statehood.

The second theoretical lens stresses the impact of the drive for domestic political survival and the incentive for consensus building on the foreign policy choices made by political leaders and ruling groups. The second empirical cut has shown that Ben-Gurion managed to build a broad coalition in favor of partition, in spite of the internal divisions within the Jewish community regarding the issue of partition. He used the formula of a viable Jewish state without a demarcation of its borders to avoid a debate about partition within his own party between moderates and activists. The same tactic and the use of the rally around the flag effect helped him also to bring other parties into the domestic consensus. The Palestinian Arabs were less divided about partition, which they rejected almost unanimously. But they were unable to organize themselves in one unified front with a cohesive and centralized leadership to resist partition, as a result of the domestic political structure and the failure to form self-governing institutions.

The Oslo accords were only possible by the coming to power in 1992 of a Labor government. The new elected prime minister, Rabin, made his political survival dependent on an agreement with the Palestinians on self-rule in the occupied territories by promising to reach such an agreement within nine months. With this promise he won the elections, as a majority of the Israeli electorate supported his conviction that the ongoing *intifada* could not be solved by military means and needed a political solution, which the former Likud government refused to consider. However, when he reached such an agreement in secret negotiations with the PLO leadership at Oslo, the Labor government had to deal with the absence of broad domestic support for the Oslo accords. Rabin was faced with a significant challenge for staying in office. To maintain the support of a minimal majority in parliament the ruling Labor party had to accommodate the opposition of a small group of hawkish Labor parliament members who opposed further territorial concessions. It led to a split in the Labor faction in parliament, as a result of which the Labor government lost its blocking majority in parliament. Rabin hoped to attract broad public support for the continuation of the Oslo peace process to compensate for the eroding parliamentary support, but public support for the Oslo accords declined continuously as a result of terrorist suicide attacks on Israeli civilians. To survive politically, after Rabin's assassination by an opponent of the Oslo accords, Peres tried to win back public support. He postponed further progress in the Oslo peace process until after the elections and stalled the peace negotiations with Syria. To demonstrate his toughness he authorized the murder of a Hamas leader and started heavy bombardments against guerrilla positions in south Lebanon. Peres, however, was unable to turn the tide and lost the elections.

An important reason for Arafat to conclude the Oslo agreement with Israel was the emergence of a radical local young Fatah leadership in the occupied territories that had led the *intifada*, and challenged the old leadership of the PLO that surrounded Arafat in the PLO headquarters in Tunis. Although Arafat had complete control of the PLO, the threat for the political survival of the ruling PLO leadership became more serious when the United States and Israel began to treat the local Palestinian leaders as potential negotiating partners over the future of the occupied territories. The ruling PLO leadership managed to neutralize the local leaders during the Madrid peace process by signaling to Israel that they were the only ones who had the authority to conclude an agreement. The signing of the Oslo accords triggered opposition from within the PLO as well as in the occupied territories. Arafat survived the opposition within the PLO executive committee thanks to the resignation and self-imposed absence of some members of the committee. To avoid a clash with the PNC he bypassed this highest decision-making body of the PLO and ratified the Oslo accords in Fatah's central committee, his home base. In his new role as head of the PA he faced an internal power struggle between the ruling PLO leaders who came with Arafat from Tunis and wanted to continue the Oslo peace process, and the more radical local Fatah leaders who wanted to increase the pressure on Israel in order to end the occupation. He survived it by balancing the interests of both groups. A more serious political threat was Hamas that competed for political influence with the PLO, and continued the confrontation with Israel. He accommodated Hamas by an agreement in which Hamas promised to operate from areas that were not controlled by the PLO.

The third theoretical lens consists, in fact, of three alternative lenses. The first one conceives the choices of leaders and the actions of states as resulting from the national wish to survive. The second emphasizes that international institutions that change the conceptions of self-interest and promote mutual cooperation influence these choices. The third stresses that these choices are influenced by the beliefs and expectations that states have about each other as a result of their interaction and that may change over time. The third empirical cut has illustrated that both the Jewish community and the Palestinian Arabs were clearly driven in their choice whether to accept or reject the UN partition plan by arguments of national survival. But to ensure national survival the Jewish community considered self-help to be the main rule of conduct while the Palestinian Arabs relied on the help of the Arab states. International institutions, in this case the UN, were instrumental in the search for a solution to the Jewish-Palestinian conflict in Palestine by proposing a solution in the form of a partition plan for Palestine. The international community, including the two superpowers, also approved this plan by a decision of the UN General Assembly. But the UN and the entire international community failed to implement this decision on partition. It failed completely in changing the conceptions of self-interest and in generating cooperation between the two sides before and after the 1947–1948 War. The success of the Jewish community to establish its own state and the failure of the Palestinian Arabs to set up an independent Palestinian Arab state in the remaining parts of Palestine, led to a vicious circle of violence that deepened the Israeli-Palestinian hostility and created a relationship that was dominated by the logic of Hobbesian anarchy, kill or be killed.

The issue of national survival played no role in Israel's decision to reach agreement on the Oslo accords. The *intifada* undermined the sense of national security but it did not present a threat to Israel's existence or control of the occupied territories. For the PLO, by contrast, it was a matter of national survival after its expulsion from Beirut, the failure of the *intifada* to end the Israeli occupation, and the Israeli intensive settlement policy in the occupied territories. The outcome of the Oslo accords clearly reflects the imbalance of power between Israel and the PLO. But in spite of this asymmetry in power they were willing to cooperate and produce the Oslo accords. This readiness was clearly motivated by their conception of self-interest and the expectations that Israel and the PLO had about their absolute gains.

Two explicit ground rules: the principle of land for peace and the principle of Palestinian self-determination, were developed by the international community to set out the conditions for an Israel-Palestinian settlement. Both ground rules were an important factor in changing the conception of self-interest on both sides. It was the combination of these ground rules and American diplomatic pressure that pushed Israel and the PLO gradually toward a two-state solution. But a major driving force behind the Oslo accords was also the wish on both sides to replace the logic of kill or be killed by the logic of live and let live. The Labor government and the PLO were driven toward the conclusion of the Oslo agreement by the wish to change the practice of their interaction by mutual recognition of each other's right to exist, as well as a strong desire for separation among Israelis and Palestinians. It was the final acceptance of partition by Israelis and Palestinians.

Hence, breaking the Israeli-Palestinian conflict down into its components demonstrates that there is indeed more than one story to tell about the dynamics of the Israeli-Palestinian conflict. It is also clear that there are relationships between phenomena at different levels-of-analysis. Factors that are influenced by human cognition, rooted in domestic politics or result from the characteristics of the international system, clearly interact in shaping Israeli and Palestinians policies toward the central issue of the conflict: the acceptance of a two-state solution. However, any attempt to show how these factors interact and are an unmistakable part of a whole, touches upon the level-of-analysis controversy.

Jervis has argued that there is no single answer to the question of which level is most important. Rather than one level containing the factors that are most significant for all problems, the importance of each level may vary from one issue area to another. But the choice of which level one focuses on is, in Jervis's view, not arbitrary or a matter of taste. It is the product of beliefs about the nature of the factors that influence the phenomena that concern one. Jervis himself takes the position that the state's internal politics and external environment or the working of the bureaucracy cannot explain state behavior. To explain crucial decisions and policies, he says, it is necessary to examine the perceptions and beliefs of the top decision-makers about the world and their images of others. Such analysis is necessary, he asserts, because people in the same situation behave differently. This is often the case, he explains, because people differ in their perceptions of the world in general and of other actors in particular.[1]

Waltz, holds an opposite position: international political theory does not include factors at the level of the state. As Waltz wants to explain how external factors shape states' behavior, he says nothing about the effects of internal forces. He has formulated a theory that shows how the interaction of states generates a structure that then constrains them from taking certain actions and disposes them toward taking others. As Waltz states, the theory is based on the assumption that states are unitary actors with a single motive: the wish to survive. It explains why states similarly placed behave similarly despite their internal differences. He maintains that the explanation of states' behavior is found at the international level, and not at the national level. In debates with his critics, Waltz has acknowledged that under most circumstances such a theory is not sufficient for making predictions about states' behavior, but as he says, his theory makes no claim to explain foreign policy or international events. The most satisfying way, he admits, would be to formulate a unified theory of internal and external politics, capable of explaining the behavior of states, their interactions, and international outcomes. However, he says, no one has even suggested how such a single theory can be constructed.[2]

Indeed, says Randall Schweller, no one has attempted such a task because it is an impossible one.[3] As Fareed Zakaria, for example, has argued, a good account of a nation's foreign policy should include systemic, domestic, and other influences, specifying what aspects of the policy can be explained by what factors. A good explanation of Germany's foreign policy in the Nazi period, he says, has to include both the general systemic impulses and the more specific domestic, cultural, and personal ones.[4]

With these observations in mind, let me therefore round up by saying that the former chapters serve solely as building blocks to provide a multilevel insight into the determinants and dynamics of the Israeli-Palestinian conflict. They have shown that any attempt to resolve this conflict by disregarding the connection between cognitive, domestic, and systemic factors is simplistic and not realistic.

NOTES

INTRODUCTION: UNTYING THE GORDIAN KNOT

1. Singer, "The Level-of-Analysis Problem," 20–29.
2. Allison, *Essence of Decision*, 249–251.
3. Bruce Bueno de Mesquita, "Domestic Politics and International Relations," 8.
4. Gilpin, *War and Change in World Politics*, 17–18.
5. Schweller, "The Progressiveness of Neoclassical Realism," 326.
6. Gilpin, *War and Change in World Politics*, 17–18.
7. Krasner, *Sovereignty*, 14–16.
8. See also: Bruter, "Diplomacy Without a State," 185.
9. Segev, *One Palestine, Complete*, 494–495.
10. Laqueur and Rubin, *The Israel-Arab Reader*, 30–31.
11. Ibid., 41–43.
12. Ibid., 43–50.
13. Ibid., 65–77.
14. Laqueur and Rubin, *The Israel-Arab Reader*, 116; and Morris, *Righteous Victims*, 346.
15. Laqueur and Rubin, *The Israel-Arab Reader*, 223–225; and Morris, *Righteous Victims*, 472–474.
16. Laqueur and Rubin, *The Israel-Arab Reader*, 335–357; and Morris, *Righteous Victims*, 606–608.
17. Quandt, *Peace Process*, 311, 323.
18. Laqueur and Rubin, *The Israel-Arab Reader*, 413–425.
19. Ibid., 442–455, 502–521.

1   A FIRST LENS: INDIVIDUAL INFLUENCES IN WORLD POLITICS

1. Morgan, *Theories and Approaches to International Politics*, 42.
2. Snyder, Bruck, and Sapin, *Foreign Policy Decision-Making*, 59.
3. Kegley, "Decision Regimes," 249; and Kegley and Wittkopf, *American Foreign Policy*, 502.
4. Rosati, "The Power of Human Cognition," 47.
5. Snyder, Bruck, and Sapin, *Foreign Policy Decision-Making*, 59.

6. Boulding, "National Images and International Systems," 422.
7. Holsti, "The Belief System and National Images," 544.
8. Little and Smith, *Belief Systems and International Relations*, 44.
9. Rosati, "The Power of Human Cognition," 52; and George, *Presidential Decisionmaking*, 56–57; and Steinbruner, *The Cybernetic Theory of Decision*, 91.
10. Young and Schafer, "Is there Method in Our Madness," 64.
11. Stein, "Psychological Explanations of International Conflict," 293.
12. George, *Bridging the Gap*, 17 and 132; George, "The Causal Nexus," 101–104; Holsti, "Foreign Policy Formation," 34–35.
13. Cited in: Holsti, "Foreign Policy Formation," 20; and George, *Presidential Decisionmaking*, 57.
14. George, *Presidential Decisionmaking*, 56–57; and Holsti, "Foreign Policy Formation," 19–20; Vertzberger, *The World in their Minds*, 113–114; Little and Smith, *Belief Systems and International Relations*, 47–48; and Jervis, *Perceptions and Misperceptions*, 28–31.
15. Larson, "The Role of Belief Systems and Schemas," 19.
16. Steinbruner, *The Cybernetic Theory of Decision*, 95–100; Walker, "Operational Code Analysis as a Scientific Research Program," 251–252; Vertzberger, *The World in their Minds*, 137; Rosati, "The Power of Human Cognition," 56; and Rosati, "A Cognitive Approach," 52.
17. Jervis, *Perceptions and Misperceptions*, 117–118.
18. Ibid., 143; and George, *Presidential Decisionmaking*, 63.
19. Janis, *Groupthink*, 80–81.
20. Vertzberger, *The World in their Minds*, 46, 60–61, 61, 142, 152.
21. George, "The Causal Nexus," 100; Walker, "Operational Code Analysis," 251; and Rosati, "A Cognitive Approach," 56.
22. George, "The Operational Code," 197–220; Vertzberger, *The World in their Minds*, 115–116; Voss and Dorsey, "Perception and International Relations," 13; and Walker, "Operational Code Analysis," 252.
23. George, "The Causal Nexus," 100; and Walker, "Operational Code Analysis," 250–251.
24. George, "The Operational Code," 191; George, "The Causal Nexus," 99, 101; and George, *Presidential Decisionmaking*, 45.
25. George, "The Causal Nexus," 102–103.
26. Vertzberger, *Risk Taking and Decisionmaking*, 67.
27. Walker, "The Interface between Beliefs and Behavior," 135–153.
28. Steinbruner, *The Cybernetic Theory of Decision*, 101–102.
29. Ibid.
30. Rosati, "The Power of Human Cognition," 56; Levy, "Political Psychology and Foreign Policy," 264; Voss and Dorsey, "Perception and International Relations," 8; Lau, "Models of Decision-Making," 30; and Young and Schafer, "Is There Method in Our Madness," 81.
31. Voss and Dorsey, "Perception and International Relations," 9; and Herrmann, "Image Theory and Strategic Interaction," 286–287.
32. Herrmann, "Image Theory and Strategic Interaction," 288.

33. Herrmann, "Image Theory and Strategic Interaction," 289; Voss and Dorsey, "Perception and International Relations," 9; Lau, "Models of Decision–Making," 30; and Fiske, "Stereotyping, Prejudice, and Discrimination," 362.

34. Herrmann, "Image Theory and Strategic Interaction," 289, 291.

35. Tetlock, "Social Psychology and World Politics," 880; Levy, "Political Psychology and Foreign Policy," 264–265; and Herrmann, "Image Theory and Strategic Interaction," 291.

36. Rosati, "The Power of Human Cognition," 55–56.

37. Holsti, "The Belief System and National Images," 545–550.

38. Ibid., 548.

39. Lau, "Models of Decision-Making," 30; and Larson, "The Role of Belief Systems and Schemas," 18.

40. Lau, "Models of Decision-Making," 30; Larson, "The Role of Belief Systems and Schemas," 22–23; and Vertzberger, *The World in their Minds*, 157.

41. Larson, "The Role of Belief Systems and Schemas," 29.

42. Cited in: George, *Presidential Decisionmaking*, 43.

43. Voss and Dorsey, "Perception and International Relations," 12; George, *Presidential Decisionmaking*, 43; Jervis, *Perceptions and Misperceptions*, 217–282; and Vertzberger, *The World in their Minds*, 300, 309–319.

44. Kissinger, *Diplomacy*, 310–315; and Vertzberger, *The World in their Minds*, 36.

45. Eban, *The New Diplomacy*, 380–381; Kissinger, *Diplomacy*, 641–642; and Jervis, *Perceptions and Misperception*, 223.

46. George, *Presidential Decisionmaking*, 44; and Jervis, *Perceptions and Misperceptions*, 229.

47. Rosati, "The Power of Human Cognition," 71.

48. Voss and Dorsey, "Perception and International Relations," 19.

49. Sullivan, *Theories of International Relations*, 26.

50. Ibid.

51. Winter, "Personality and Foreign Policy," 92–93.

52. Voss and Dorsey, "Perception and International Relations," 19; and Byman and Pollack, "Let Us Now Praise Great Men," 140–143.

53. Hermann, Preston, Korany, and Shaw, "Who Leads Matters," 83–93.

54. Ibid., 94–100. Hermann, "Explaining Foreign Policy Behavior," 7–14.

55. Allison, *Essence of Decision*, 10–32. See also: Allison and Zelikow, *Essence of Decision*, 26–54.

56. Allison, *Essence of Decision*, 32–35; Allison and Zelikow, *Essence of Decision*, 24–25; Stein and Tanter, *Rational Decision–Making*, 27; and Ferguson and Mansbach, *The Elusive Quest*, 146.

57. George, *Presidential Decisionmaking*, 40. Stein and Tanter, *Rational Decision-Making*, 33; and Ferguson and Mansbach, *The Elusive Quest*, 151.

58. Cited in: Allison and Zelikow, *Essence of Decision*, 20.

59. Levy, "An Introduction to Prospect Theory," 179–184; Jervis, "Political Implications of Loss Aversion," 187–192; and Farnham,

Avoiding Losses / Taking Risks, 1–5. See also: Levy, "Prospect Theory, Rational Choice, and International Relations," 88–94.

60. Chollet and Goldgeier, "The Scholarship of Decision-Making," 160.

61. See also: Hollis and Smith, *Explaining and Understanding International Relations*, 146; Rosati, "The Power of Human Cognition," 72—75; and Vertzberger, *The World in their Minds*, 109–110.

2   A FIRST CUT: THE RELEVANCE OF LEADERSHIP

1. George, "The Causal Nexus," 104–110; Walker, "The Interface between Beliefs and Behavior," 130–132; Holsti, "Foreign Policy Formation Viewed Cognitively," 29–30; Hermann, "How Decision Units Shape Foreign Policy," 58.

2. Ben-Ami, *Scars of War, Wounds of Peace*, 12; and Shlaim, *The Iron Wall*, 28.

3. Brecher, *The Foreign Policy System of Israel*, 251–290; and Shlaim, *The Iron Wall*, 95–98.

4. Ben-Ami, *Scars of War, Wounds of Peace*, 53.

5. Cited in Ben-Ami, *Scars of War, Wounds of Peace*, 19.

6. Ben-Ami, *Scars of War, Wounds of Peace*, 2, 4–5, 12–13, 19; and Seliktar, *New Zionism and the Foreign Policy of Israel*, 62–63.

7. Seliktar, *New Zionism and the Foreign Policy of Israel*, 62–64.

8. Cited in Seliktar, *New Zionism and the Foreign Policy of Israel*, 62.

9. Cited in Ben–Ami, *Scars of War, Wounds of Peace*, 13; and Shlaim, *The Iron Wall*, 18.

10. Ben-Ami, *Scars of War, Wounds of Peace*, 14–15; and Heller, *The Birth of Israel*, 86.

11. Morris, "Revisiting the Palestinian Exodus of 1948," 41–48; and Morris, *The Birth of the Palestinian Refugee Problem Revisited*, 588–589.

12. Morris, "Revisiting the Palestinian Exodus of 1948," 49.

13. Ben-Ami, *Scars of War, Wounds of Peace*, 54–55; Shlaim, *The Iron Wall*, 18, 97; and Brecher, *The Foreign Policy System of Israel*, 284.

14. Heller, *The Birth of Israel*, 114.

15. Ben–Ami, *Scars of War, Wounds of Peace*, 37; and Shlaim, *The Iron Wall*, 36–39.

16. Ben-Ami, *Scars of War, Wounds of Peace*, 14–15; Shlaim, *The Iron Wall*, 18–19, 96; Seliktar, *New Zionism and the Foreign Policy of Israel*, 66–68; and Brecher, *The Foreign Policy System of Israel*, 284; Aronson, *The Politics and Strategy of Nuclear Weapons in the Middle East*, 51.

17. Aronson, *The Politics and Strategy of Nuclear Weapons in the Middle East*, 51.

18. Ben-Ami, *Scars of War, Wounds of Peace*, 18.

19. Cited in Ben-Ami, *Scars of War, Wounds of Peace*, 27.

20. Ibid., 27–28; and Heller, *The Birth of Israel*, 114–120.
21. Cited in Heller, *Birth of Israel*, 24.
22. Ibid., 23–24.
23. Cited in Shlaim, *The Iron Wall*, 98.
24. Brecher, *The Foreign Policy System of Israel*, 257–258; and Ben–Ami, *Scars of War, Wounds of Peace*, 37.
25. Shlaim, *The Iron Wall*, 59–61, 87.
26. Ben-Ami, *Scars of War, Wounds of Peace*, 12; and Heller, *The Birth of Israel*, 124–125, 289–290.
27. Ben-Ami, *Scars of War, Wounds of Peace*, 25.
28. Ibid; and Shlaim, *The Iron Wall*, 21.
29. Cited in Ben-Ami, *Scars of War, Wounds of Peace*, 34.
30. Ibid., 37; and Heller, *The Birth of Israel*, 90, 92.
31. Ben-Ami, *Scars of War, Wounds of Peace*, 38.
32. Ibid., 26.
33. Morris, "Revisiting the Palestinian Exodus of 1948," 49, 52; and Morris, *The Birth of the Palestinian Refugee Problem Revisited*, 588.
34. Kimmerling and Migdal, *The Palestinian People*, 89–90, 95; Pappe, *a History of Modern Palestine*, 85; and Khalidi, "The Palestinians and 1948," 23.
35. Kimmerling and Migdal, *The Palestinian People*, 113, 114, 144–145, 154; and Pappe, A *History of Modern Palestine*, 107, 125–126; and Khalidi, "The Palestinians and 1948," 28–29.
36. Khalidi, "The Palestinians and 1948," 28–29.
37. Cited in Oren, *Six Days of War*, 313.
38. Ibid.
39. Laqueur and Rubin, *The Israeli-Arab Reader*, 426.
40. Ben-Ami, *Scars of War, Wounds of Peace*, 123, 152.
41. Bar-On, *In Pursuit of Peace*, 221; and Gazit, *Trapped Fools*, 294–296.
42. Gazit, *Trapped Fools*, 300–303.
43. Ben-Ami, *Scars of War, Wounds of Peace*, 211.
44. Ross, *The Missing Peace*, 94.
45. Hazan, *The Labor Party and the Peace Process*, 24–25; and Ben-Ami, *Scars of War, Wounds of Peace*, 208.
46. Hazan, *The Labor Party and the Peace Process*, 25; and Shlaim, *The Iron Wall*, 503.
47. Ben-Ami, *Scars of War, Wounds of Peace*, 210–211; Ross, *The Missing Peace*, 91–92; and Oren, *Six Days of War*, 81.
48. Gazit, *Trapped Fools*, 48, 56–57.
49. Peres, *Battling for Peace*, 301–302.
50. Gazit, *Trapped Fools*, 154–155.
51. Peres, *Battling for Peace*, 297–298, 318–320, 355, 358.
52. Ibid., 314, 317; and Kay, B*eyond the Handshake*, 48, 82, 114, 127, 156–157.
53. Peres, *Battling for Peace*, 320–333.

54. Sayigh, *Armed Struggle*, 84–85, 88–90.
55. Ibid., 87, 89, 91, 104–108, 119–120, 123, 141.
56. Sayigh, *Armed Struggle*, 156; Kurz, *Fatah and the Politics of Violence*, 46–47.
57. Kurz, *Fatah and the Politics of Violence*, 47–49, 51–63; Sayigh, *Armed Struggle*, 155– 156, 174–179; and Cobban, *The Palestinian Liberation Organization*, 37–38.
58. Khalidi, *Under Siege*, 20–36; and Sayigh, *Armed Struggle*, 447–463.
59. Lukacs, *The Israeli-Palestinian Conflict*, 308–309, 464.
60. Quandt, *Decade of Decisions*, 275; Sayigh, *Armed Struggle*, 344, 368, 622–624; Kurz, *Fatah and the Politics of Violence*, 121–123; and Lukacs, *The Israeli-Palestinian Conflict*, 411–434.
61. Sayigh, *Armed Struggle*, 574, 643; and Kurz, *Fatah and the Politics of Violence*, 125, 128–129.
62. Sayigh, *Armed Struggle*, 654–656; see also Kurz, *Fatah and the Politics of Violence*, 1.

3   A SECOND LENS: DOMESTIC ROOTS OF WORLD POLITICS

1. Sullivan, *Theories of International Relations*, 67–93; and Hudson, "Foreign Policy Analysis,"18–19.
2. Bueno de Mesquita, "Domestic Politics and International Relations," 2.
3. Wendt, *Social Theory of International Politics*, 2.
4. Neustadt, *Presidential Power*; Hilsman, *The Politics of Policy Making*; Allison, *Essence of Decision*; and Halperin, *Bureaucratic Politics and Foreign Policy*.
5. Putnam, "Diplomacy and Domestic Politics," 432.
6. Hagan, *Political Opposition and Foreign Policy*, 2–3.
7. Bueno de Mesquita, "Domestic Politics and International Relations," 7.
8. Ibid.
9. Ibid., 4, 8.
10. Hagan, "Domestic Political Explanations," 124; and Hagan, "Regimes, Political Oppositions," 346.
11. Bueno de Mesquita, Morrow, Siverson, and Smith, "Policy Failure and Political Survival," 148.
12. Ibid., 148–150.
13. Ibid., 147–149, 160.
14. King, *Running Scared*, 3–5.
15. Ibid., 29–43.
16. Ibid.
17. Ibid., 30–33.
18. Manin, *The Principles of Representative Government*, 202–226.

19. Bueno de Mesquita, Morrow, Siverson, and Smith, "Policy Failure and Political Survival," 150; and Hagan, "Regimes, Political Oppositions," 343.
20. Hagan, *Political Opposition and Foreign Policy*, 82–84.
21. Ibid., 80–82, 84–88.
22. Russett, *Controlling the Sword*, 26–27; and 88–90.
23. Hagan, "Domestic Political Explanations," 124.
24. Fearon, "Domestic Political Audiences," 577–581, 586–587.
25. Morgenthau, *Politics Among Nations*, 576–578.
26. Ibid., 578.
27. Bueno de Mesquita and Lalman. *War and Reason*, 13–14; and Skidmore and Hudson, "Establishing the Limits of State Autonomy," 9–13.
28. Snyder, *Myths of Empire*, 14–18.
29. George, *Presidential Decisionmaking*, 2.
30. Hagan, "Domestic Political Explanations," 122–124.
31. Farnham, "Political Cognition and Decision-Making," 97.
32. Hagan, *Political Opposition and Foreign Policy*, 68.
33. Neustadt, *Presidential Power*, 10–11, 33–58.
34. Hilsman, *The Politics of Policy Making*, 64–65, 69–75.
35. Ibid., 65.
36. Allison and Halperin, "Bureaucratic Politics," 40–79.
37. Allison, *Essence of Decision*, 144–147, 162–176; and Allison and Zelikow, *Essence of Decision*, 255–258, 294–307.
38. Halperin, *Bureaucratic Politics and Foreign Policy*, 312–313.
39. Hagan, *Political Opposition and Foreign Policy*, 68–69.
40. Ibid., 70–74; Hagan, "Domestic Political Regime Change," 151–155; and Hagan, "Regimes, Political Oppositions," 344–346.
41. Hagan, *Political Opposition and Foreign Policy*, 74–76.
42. Ibid., 76–78.
43. Ibid., 6–8, and, 93–97; Hagan, "Domestic Political Explanations," 127–132; Hagan, "Regimes, Political Opposition," 348–350; and Hagan, "Domestic Political Systems and War Proneness," 194–197.
44. Putnam, "Diplomacy and Domestic Politics," 435–450.
45. Evans, Jacobson, and Putnam, *Double Edged Diplomacy*, 399–400.
46. See: Allison and Zelikow, *Essence of Decision*, 255–313.
47. Hermann, "How Decision Units Shape Foreign Policy," 47–81.
48. Hermann, Stein, Sundelius, and Walker, "Resolve, Accept or Avoid," 133–168.
49. Hagan, Everts, Fukui, and Stempel, "Foreign Policy by Coalition," 169–216.
50. Cohen, *The Public's Impact on Foreign Policy*, 26.
51. Russett, *Controlling the Sword*, 52–54.
52. Ibid., 48.
53. Ibid., 47–48.
54. Ibid., 54–86; 110; and, 154–155.

55. See: Bueno De Mesquita and Lalman, *War and Reason*, 14–15.
56. Ellsberg, *Papers on the War*, 49–50 and 71–74.
57. Ibid., 100–127.

4 A Second Cut: Choosing Stalemate

1. Hermann, "How Decision Units Shape Foreign Policy," 56.
2. Heller, *The Birth of Israel*, 90.
3. Ibid., 256–259, 273–275; Shlaim, *The Iron Wall*, 12; and Ben-Ami, *Scars of War, Wounds of Peace*, 19–20.
4. Heller, *The Birth of Israel*, 132–134; and Ben–Ami, *Scars of War, Wounds of Peace*, 9.
5. Heller, *The Birth of Israel*, 198–201, 212–215; and Ben-Ami, *Scars of War, Wounds of Peace*, 26, 31.
6. Heller, *The Birth of Israel*, 217–220, 225–226; and Ben-Ami, *Scars of War, Wounds of Peace*, 18, 26, 31–32.
7. Ben-Ami, *Scars of War, Wounds of Peace*, 16–17.
8. Ibid., 34.
9. *Ibid.*, 17, 36–37, 45–47.
10. Ibid., 37.
11. Heller, *The Birth of Israel*, 131–133.
12. Ibid., 132.
13. Ibid., 134.
14. Ibid., 136.
15. Ibid., 227–228.
16. Ibid., 135–136, 143, 260, 263–264.
17. Morris, *The Birth of the Palestinian Refugee Problem Revisited*, 18–21.
18. Khalidi, "The Palestinians and 1948," 21–24; and Morris, *The Birth of the Palestinian Refugee Problem Revisited*, 21–22.
19. Sayigh, *Armed Struggle*, 4–6; Khalidi, "The Palestinians and 1948," 17–21; and Morris, *The Birth of the Palestinian Refugee Problem Revisited*, 22–23.
20. Pappe, *A History of Modern Palestine*, 98, 104.
21. Sayigh, *Armed Struggle*, 7, 9; and Khalidi, "The Palestinians and 1948," 28.
22. Khalidi, "The Palestinians and 1948," 30–31.
23. Makovsky, *Making Peace with the PLO*, 12; and Hazan, *The Labor Party and the Peace Process*, 4.
24. Makovsky, *Making Peace with the PLO*, 193.
25. Bar-On, *In Pursuit of Peace*, 27–30, 36–44; Seliktar, *New Zionism and the Foreign Policy System of Israel*, 157–159; Flamhaft, *Israel on the Road to Peace*, 118–122; and Peretz, "Israeli Peace Proposals," 26–27.
26. Gazit, *Trapped Fools*, 154–156.
27. Hazan, *The Labor Party and the Peace Process*, 16–17.
28. Flamhaft, *Israel on the Road to Peace*, 122–123; and Gazit, *Trapped Fools*, 267–270.
29. Quandt, *Camp David*, 256, 378; and Gazit, *Trapped Fools*, 211–215.

30. Yaniv, *Dilemmas of Security*, 101; Feldman and Rechnitz-Kijner, *Deception, Consensus and War*, 19–21; Rabinovich, *The War for Lebanon*, 133; and Schiff and Ya'ari, *Israel's Lebanon War*, 43.

31. Ben-Ami, *Scars of War, Wounds of Peace*, 187.

32. Cited in Eisenberg and Caplan, *Negotiating Arab-Israeli Peace*, 81.

33. Hazan, *The Labor Party and the Peace Process*, 3, 5–6.

34. Laqueur and Rubin, *The Israel-Arab Reader*, 403–407.

35. Ibid., 413–425.

36. Bar-Siman-Tov, *Peace Policy as Domestic and as Foreign Policy*, 22.

37. Bar-On, *In Pursuit of Peace*, 80–82; and Gazit, *Trapped Fools*, 260–271.

38. Sprinzak, *The Israeli Right and the Peace Process*, 18–22.

39. Hazan, *The Labor Party and the Peace Process*, 21; and Shlaim, *The Iron Wall*, 516.

40. Hazan, *The Labor Party and the Peace Process*, 11–12; and Rabinovich, *Waging Peace*, 68–69.

41. Hazan, *The Labor Party and the Peace Process*, 13–14.

42. Arian, *The Second Republic*, 203–204, 231–233; Bar-Siman-Tov, *Peace Policy as Domestic and as Foreign Policy*, 23; and Shlaim, *The Iron Wall*, 521.

43. Hazan, *The Labor Party and the Peace Process*, 11, 22–25; and Bar-Siman-Tov, *Peace Policy as Domestic and as Foreign Policy*, 23.

44. Ben-Ami, *Scars of War, Wounds of Peace*, 215.

45. Arian, *The Second Republic*, 107, 204, 233; Rabinovich, *Waging Peace*, 74–81; and Shlaim, *The Iron Wall*, 553–563.

46. Cobban, *The Palestinian Liberation Organization*, 15; and Miller, *The PLO and the Politics of Survival*, 55.

47. Miller, *The PLO and the Politics of Survival*, 42–51.

48. Sayigh, *Armed Struggle*, 322, 420–421, 433–434, 440–444.

49. Kurz, *Fatah and the Politics of Violence*, 129–130, 133; and Sayigh, *Armed Struggle*, 654–656, 658.

50. Brown, *Palestinian Politics after the Oslo Accords*, 67–72.

51. Shikaki, "Palestine Divided," 93–94; Shikaki, "Changing the Guards," 32–33; Sayigh, *Armed Struggle*, 656, 658; and Gazit, *Trapped Fools*, 299.

52. Shikaki, "Palestine Divided," 95–98; and Shikaki, "Changing the Guards," 33–34.

53. Shikaki, "Palestine Divided," 91.

54. Mishal and Sela, *The Palestinian Hamas*, 2–4, 36, 59, 102.

55. Ibid., 68–71.

5   A Third Lens: Underlying Rules of World Politics

1. Wendt, *Social Theory of International Politics*, 11–12.

2. Walt, "The Enduring Relevance of the Realist Tradition," 199; and Schweller, "The Progressiveness of Neoclassical Realism," 322.

3. Gilpin, "No One Loves a Political Realist," 7, 26; Gilpin "The Richness of the Tradition of Political Realism," 304–305; and Gilpin, *War and Change in World Politics*, 17–18.
4. Waltz, *Theory of International Politics*, 95.
5. Waltz, *Theory of International Politics*, 94–95; and Gilpin, "No One Loves a Political Realist," 25.
6. Keohane and Nye, *Power and Interdependence*, 24–26; Keohane, *International Institutions and State Power*, 1, 8; and Nye, *Understanding International Conflicts*, 8–9.
7. Wendt, *Social Theory of International Politics*, 8–9.
8. Waltz, *Theory of International Politics*, 88; Gilpin, "No One Loves a Political Realist," 8; Grieco, "Realist International Theory," 164; and, Mearsheimer, "The False Promise of International Institutions," 10.
9. Waltz, *Theory of International Politics*, 88–89, 95–96.
10. Waltz, *Man, the State and War*, 159–160; and Waltz, *Theory of International Politics*, 91–92, 102, 111, 113.
11. Mearsheimer, *The Tragedy of Great Power Politics*, 3; and Mearsheimer, "The False Promise of International Institutions," 9–12.
12. Morgenthau, *Politics among Nations*, 5.
13. Ibid., 31, 37–38. See also: Grieco, "Realist International Theory," 188.
14. Thucydides, *The Peloponnesian War*, 331.
15. Waltz, *Theory of International Politics*, 97–99, 118, 126, 131, 192.
16. Jervis, "Realism, Neoliberalism, and Cooperation," 289–290; and Walt, "The Enduring Relevance of the Realist Tradition," 204–206.
17. Glaser, "Realists as Optimists," 71.
18. Ibid., 60–64.
19. Jervis, "Realism, Neoliberalism, and Cooperation," 291–292; and Jervis, "Realism in the Study of World Politics," 346–347.
20. Grieco, "Anarchy and the Limits of Cooperation," 485; and Grieco, "Understanding the Problem of International Cooperation," 302.
21. Waltz, *Man, the State, and War*, 198; and Waltz, *Theory of International Politics*, 105–107.
22. Grieco, "Anarchy and the Limits of Cooperation," 487, 498–499, 502–503; and Mearsheimer, "The False Promises of International Institutions," 12–13.
23. Grieco, "Understanding the Problem of International Cooperation," 331.
24. Ibid., 331–335.
25. Mearsheimer, "The False Promises of International Institutions," 13.
26. Ibid., 13–14.
27. See Keohane, "Theory of World Politics," 194; Keohane, *After Hegemony*, 9; and Keohane "Institutional Theory and the Realist Challenge," 271.
28. Simmons and Martin, "International Organizations and Institutions," 194.
29. Keohane, *International Institutions and State Power*, 3.
30. See Keohane, *International Institutions and State Power*, 3–4, 162–166; Krasner, *International Regimes*, 1–3; Ruggie, *Multilateralism Matters,*

3–7; and Simmons and Martin, "International Organizations and Institutions," 192–194.

31. Keohane, *International Institutions and State Power*, 8.

32. Keohane, *International Institutions and State Power*, 2, 11; Axelrod and Keohane, "Achieving Cooperation under Anarchy," 87; and Keohane, *After Hegemony*, 244.

33. Keohane, *After Hegemony*, 27.

34. Russet, Starr, and Kinsella, *World Politics*, 228–236; and Axelrod and Keohane, "Achieving Cooperation under Anarchy," 88, 103–104.

35. Axelrod and Keohane, "Achieving Cooperation under Anarchy," 91–94, 104–106; and Keohane "Theory and World Politics," 196.

36. Keohane, *After Hegemony*, 243–247; Keohane, *International Institutions and State Power*, 2, 108–113, 117–124; Keohane "Institutional Theory and the Realist Challenge," 273–274; Axelrod and Keohane, "Achieving Cooperation under Anarchy," 99; and Krasner, *International Regimes*, 2.

37. Stein, *Why Nations Cooperate*, 44.

38. Stein, *Why Nations Cooperate*, 39; and Stein, "Coordination and Collaboration," 140.

39. Keohane "Institutional Theory and the Realist Challenge," 274–275.

40. Haas, *The Uniting of Europe*, 13.

41. Soetendorp, *Foreign Policy in the European Union*, 3–7.

42. Bull, *The Anarchical Society*.

43. Wendt, "Anarchy is What States Make of It," 395.

44. Buzan, Jones, and Little, *The Logic of Anarchy*, 152.

45. Bull, *The Anarchical Society*, 13; Bull and Watson, *Expansion of International Society*, 1; and Watson, *The Evolution of International Society*, 4.

46. Bull, *The Anarchical Society*, 42, 46–52.

47. Ibid., 16–19, 53–57, 65–74.

48. Hurrell, "International Society and the Study of Regimes," 53–61.

49. Wendt, *Social Theory of International Politics*, 1; and Wendt, "Collective Identity Formation," 385.

50. Wendt, *Social Theory of International Politics*, 20, 366; Wendt, "Collective Identity Formation," 387–388; and Wendt, "Anarchy is What States Make of It," 395–397.

51. Wendt, *Social Theory of International Politics*, 246–268.

52. Ibid., 279–297.

53. Ibid., 297–307.

54. Wendt, *Social Theory of International Politics*, 336–337; and Wendt, "Anarchy is What States Make of It," 419–422.

55. Katzenstein, *The Culture of National Security*, 1–32.

56. Finnemore, "Constructing Norms of Humanitarian Intervention," 153–161.

57. Ibid., 161–185.

58. Tannenwald, "The Nuclear Taboo," 442–462; and Price and Tannenwald, "Norms and Deterrence," 115–126, 134–141.
59. Ibid.
60. Ruggie, *Constructing the World Polity*, 22–25; Kratochwil, *Rules, Norms, and Decisions*, 26; and Dessler, "What's at Stake in the Agent-Structure Debate?" 454–455.
61. Tannenwald, "The Nuclear Taboo," 437, 463; and Price and Tannenwald, "Norms and Deterrence," 116, 145.

6   A Third Cut: Conflicting International Pressures

1. Ben-Ami, *Scars of War, Wounds of Peace*, 6, 7, 48.
2. Ibid., 15.
3. Heller, *The Birth of Israel*, 89–90, 143; and Morris, *Righteous Victims*, 192–193.
4. Heller, *The Birth of Israel*, 129, 141–142.
5. Morris, *Righteous Victims*, 236; and Shlaim, *The Iron Wall*, 35.
6. Heller, *The Birth of Israel*, 84, 129.
7. Morris, *Righteous Victims*, 192–196; and Shlaim, *The Iron Wall*, 34–36.
8. Heller, *The Birth of Israel*, 85, 119, 130.
9. Safran, *Israel, the Embattled Ally*, 37–39; Heller, *The Birth of Israel*, 22, 33, 35; and Christison, *Perceptions of Palestine*, 61–94.
10. Heller, *The Birth of Israel*, 58, 60–61; and Kochavi, "Indirect Pressure", 60–73.
11. Cited in Bregman and El-Tahri, *The Fifty Years War*, 26.
12. Shlaim, *The Iron Wall*, 27.
13. Morris, *Righteous Victims*, 237, 249–252; and Shlaim, *The Iron Wall*, 41–47.
14. Shlaim, *The Iron Wall*, 57–59; and Morris, *Righteous Victims*, 262.
15. Morris, *Righteous Victims*, 252–258; and Shlaim, *The Iron Wall*, 47, 49.
16. Morris, *Righteous Victims*, 269–279; and Shlaim, *The Iron Wall*, 81–93.
17. Cited in Morris, *Righteous Victims*, 287–288.
18. Ross, *The Missing Peace*, 759–760.
19. Gazit, *Trapped Fools*, 298.
20. Sayigh, *Armed Struggle*, 643.
21. Rothstein, "Oslo and the Ambiguities of Peace," 30–31; Ben-Ami, *Scars of War, Wounds of Peace*, 210–212; and Rabinovich, *Waging Peace*, 56–57.
22. Rothstein, "Oslo and the Ambiguities of Peace," 30.
23. Quandt, *Decade of Decisions*, 64–65; and Laqueuer and Rubin, *The Israel-Arab Reader*, 116.
24. Quandt, *Peace Process*, 202.
25. Ibid., 255.
26. Cited in Quandt, *Peace Process*, 296.

27. Ross, *The Missing Peace*, 82–84; Ball and Ball, *The Passionate Attachment*, 149–150; and Quandt, *Peace Process*, 307, 312–313.
28. Quandt, *Peace Process*, 201–202, 217.
29. Sayigh, *Armed Struggle*, 421–422.
30. Quandt, *Camp David*, 213, 246, 255; Quandt, *Peace Process*, 182; and Laqueuer and Rubin, *The Israel-Arab Reader*, 221.
31. Laqueuer and Rubin, *The Israel-Arab Reader*, 223–225.
32. Rabinovich, *Waging Peace*, 56.
33. Sayigh, *Armed Struggle*, 420.
34. Laqueuer and Rubin, *The Israel-Arab Reader*, 262.
35. Quandt, *Decade of Decisions*, 275;Quandt, *Peace Process*, 278;
36. Quandt, *Peace Process*, 278–285; and Sayigh, *Armed Struggle*, 624.
37. Golan, *Soviet Policies in the Middle East*, 263, 269,
38. Ibid., 273–278.
39. Soetendorp, "The EU's Involvement in the Arab-Israeli Peace Process," 284–285; and Soetendorp, *Foreign Policy in the European Union*, 100–103.
40. Soetendorp, "The EU's Involvement in the Arab-Israeli Peace Process," 285–287; and Soetendorp, *Foreign Policy in the European Union*, 103–109.
41. Schueftan, *Disengagement*, 46–47.
42. Ross, *The Missing Peace*, 797.
43. Schueftan, *Disengagement*, 55, 60.
44. Ben-Ami, *Scars of War, Wounds of Peace*, 203, 209; and Gazit, *Trapped Fools*, 298–299.
45. Ben-Ami, *Scars of War, Wounds of Peace*, 208–210.
46. Peleg, "The Peace Process and Israel's Political Culture," 14–15.
47. Sayigh, *Armed Struggle*, 322.
48. Ibid., 420–422, 624.
49. Morris, *Righteous Victims*, 605–607; and Gazit, *Trapped Fools*, 299.
50. Gazit, *Trapped Fools*, 314–318.

CONCLUSION: MORE THAN ONE STORY TO TELL

1. Jervis, *Perception and Misperception*, 15–31.
2. Waltz, "International Politics is not Foreign Policy," 54–57.
3. Schweller, "The Progressiveness of Neoclassical realism," 311.
4. Zakaria, "Realism and Domestic Politics," 198; and Zakaria, *From Wealth to Power*, 18.

BIBLIOGRAPHY

Allison, Graham T. *Essence of Decision: Explaining the Cuban Missile Crisis*. Boston: Little, Brown and Company, 1971.

Allison, Graham T., and Morton A. Halperin. "Bureaucratic Politics: A Paradigm and Some Policy Implications." *World Politics* 24 (1972): 40–79.

Allison, Graham T., and Philip Zelikow *Essence of Decision: Explaining the Cuban Missile Crisis*, 2nd ed. New York: Longman, 1999.

Arian, Asher. *The Second Republic: Politics in Israel*. Chatham, N J: Chatham House Publishers, 1998.

Aronson, Shlomo. *Conflict & Bargaining in the Middle East: An Israeli Perspective*. Baltimore: The Johns Hopkins University Press, 1978.

———. *The Politics and Strategy of Nuclear Weapons in the Middle East: Opacity, Theory, and Reality, 1960–1991, An Israeli Perspective*. Albany: State University of New York Press, 1992.

Axelrod, Robert, and Robert O. Keohane. "Achieving Cooperation under Anarchy: Strategies and Institutions." In *Neorealism and Neoliberalism: The Contemporary Debate*, edited by David A. Baldwin, 85–115. New York: Columbia University Press, 1993.

Baldwin, David A. "Neoliberalism, Neorealism, and World Politics." In *Neorealism and Neoliberalism: The Contemporary Debate*, edited by David A. Baldwin, 3–25. New York: Columbia University Press, 1993.

Ball, George W., and Douglas B. Ball. *The Passionate Attachment: America's Involvement with Israel, 1947 to the Present*. New York: W.W. Norton & Company, 1992.

Bar-On , Mordechai. *In Pursuit of Peace: A History of the Israeli Peace Movement*. Washington: United States Institute of Peace Press, 1996.

Bar-Siman-Tov, Yaacov. *Peace Policy as Domestic and as Foreign Policy*. Jerusalem: The Hebrew University Jerusalem, 1998.

Ben-Ami, Shlomo. *Scars of War, Wounds of Peace: The Israeli-Arab Tragedy*. Oxford: Oxford University Press, 2006.

Boulding, Kenneth E. "National Images and International Systems." In *International Politics and Foreign Policy: A Reader in Research and Theory*, edited by James N. Rosenau, 422–431. New York: The Free Press, 1969.

Brecher, Michael. *The Foreign Policy System of Israel: Setting, Images, Process*. London: Oxford University Press, 1972.

Bregman, Ahron, and Jihan El-Tahri. *The Fifty Years War: Israel and the Arabs*. London: Penguin Books, 1998.

Brown, Nathan J. *Palestinian Politics after the Oslo Accords: Resuming Arab Palestine*. Berkeley: University of California Press, 2003.

Bruter, Michael. "Diplomacy without a State: The External Delegations of the European Commission." *Journal of European Public Policy* 6, no. 2 (June 1999): 183–205.

Bueno de Mesquita, Bruce. "Domestic Politics and International Relations." *International Studies Quarterly*, 46, no. 1 (March 2002): 1–9.

Bueno de Mesquita, Bruce, and David Lalman. *War and Reason: Domestic and International Imperatives*. New Haven: Yale University Press, 1992.

Bueno de Mesquita, Bruce, James D. Morrow, Randolph M. Siverson, and Alastair Smith. "Policy Failure and Political Survival." *Journal of Conflict Resolution* 43, no. 2 (April 1999): 147–161.

Bull, Hedley. *The Anarchical Society: A Study of Order in World Politics*. London: Macmillan, 1977.

Bull, Hedley, and Adam Watson, eds. *The Expansion of International Society*. Oxford: Oxford University Press.

Buzan, Barry. "From International System to International Society: Structural Realism and Regime Theory Meet the English School." *International Organization* 47, no.3 (Summer 1993): 327–352.

Buzan, Barry, Charles Jones, and Richard Little. *The Logic of Anarchy: Neorealism to Structural Realism*. New York: Columbia University Press, 1993.

Byman, Daniel L., and Kenneth M. Pollack. "Let Us Now Praise Great Men: Bringing the Statesman Back In." *International Security* 25, no. 4 (Spring 2001): 107–146.

Chollet, Derek H., and James M. Goldgeier. "The Scholarship of Decision-Making: Do We Know How We Decide?" In *Foreign Policy Decision-Making (Revisited)*, edited by Richard C. Snyder, H. W. Bruck, and Burton Sapin, 153–180. New York: Palgrave Macmillan, 2002.

Christison, Kathleen. *Perceptions of Palestine: Their Influence on U.S. Middle East Policy*. Berkeley: University of California Press, 1999.

Cobban, Helena. *The Palestinian Liberation Organisation: People, Power and Politics*. Cambridge: Cambridge University Press.1984.

Cohen, Bernard C. *The Public's Impact on Foreign Policy*. Boston: Little, Brown and Company, 1973.

Dessler, David. "What's at Stake in the Agent-Structure Debate?" *International Organization* 43, no 3 (Summer 1989): 441–473.

Destler, I. M. *Presidents, Bureaucrats and Foreign Policy: The Politics of Organizational Reform*. Princeton: Princeton University Press, 1972.

Dunn, Timothy. "The Social Construction of International Society." *European Journal of International Relations* 1, no. 3 (1995): 367–389.

Eban, Abba. *The New Diplomacy: International Affairs in the Modern Age*. New York: Random House, 1983.

Eisenberg, Laura Zittrain, and Neil Caplan. *Negotiating Arab-Israeli Peace: Patterns, Problems, Possibilities*. Bloomington: Indiana University Press, 1998.

Ellsberg, Daniel. *Papers on the War.* New York: Simon and Schuster, 1972.

Evans, Peter B., Harold K. Jacobson, and Robert D. Putnam, eds. *Double-Edged Diplomacy: International Bargaining and Domestic Politics.* Berkeley: University of California Press, 1993.

Farnham, Barbara. "Political Cognition and Decision-Making," *Political Psychology* 11, no. 1 (1990): 83–111.

———, ed. *Avoiding Losses / Taking Risks: Prospect Theory and International Conflict.* Ann Arbor: The University of Michigan Press, 1994.

Fearon, James D. "Domestic Political Audiences and the Escalation of International Disputes." *American Political Science Review* 88, no.3 (September 1994): 577–592.

Feldman, Shai, and Heda Rechnitz-Kijner. *Deception, Consensus and War: Israel in Lebanon.* Tel Aviv: Tel Aviv University, 1984.

Ferguson, Yale H., and Richard W. Mansbach. *The Elusive Quest: Theory and International Politics.* Columbia: University of South Carolina Press, 1988.

Finnemore, Martha. "Constructing Norms of Humanitarian Intervention." In *The Culture of National Security: Norms and Identity in World Politics,* edited by Peter J. Katzenstein, 153–185. New York: Columbia University Press, 1996.

Fiske, Susan T. "Stereotyping, Prejudice, and Discrimination." In *The Handbook of Social Psychology,* Vol. 2, 4th ed., edited by Daniel T. Gilbert, Susan T. Fiske, and Gardner Lindzey, 357–392. Boston: McGraw-Hill, 1998.

Flamhaft, Ziva. *Israel on the Road to Peace: Accepting the Unacceptable.* Boulder: Westview Press, 1996.

Flapan, Simha. *Zionism and the Palestinians.* London: Croom Helm, 1979.

Gazit, Shlomo. *Trapped Fools: Thirty Years of Israeli Policy in the Territories.* London: Frank Cass, 2003.

Gelb, Leslie H., and Richard K. Betts. *The Irony of Vietnam: The System Worked.* Washington: The Brookings Institution, 1979.

George, Alexander L. *Bridging the Gap: Theory and Practice in Foreign Policy.* Washington: United States Institute of Peace Press, 1993.

———. "The Causal Nexus between Cognitive Beliefs and Decision-Making Behavior: The 'Operational Code' Belief System." In *Psychological Models in International Politics,* edited by Lawrence S. Falkowski, 95–124. Boulder: Westview Press, 1979.

———. "The 'Operational Code': A Neglected Approach to the Study of Political Leaders and Decision-Making." *International Studies Quarterly* 13, no. 2 (June 1969): 190–222.

———. *Presidential Decisionmaking in Foreign Policy: The Effective Use of Information and Advice.* Boulder: Westview Press, 1980.

Gilpin, Robert G. "No One Loves a Political Realist." *Security Studies* 5, no. 3 (Spring 1996): 3–26.

———. "The Richness of the Tradition of Political Realism." In *Neorealism and its Critics,* edited by Robert O. Keohane, 301–321. New York: Columbia University Press, 1986.

Gilpin, Robert G. *War and Change in World Politics*. Cambridge: Cambridge University Press, 1981.

Glaser, Charles L. "Realists as Optimists: Cooperation as Self-Help." *International Security* 19, no. 3 (Winter 1994 / 95): 50–90.

Golan, Galia. *Soviet Policies in the Middle East: From World War Two to Gorbachev*. Cambridge, Cambridge University Press, 1990.

Grieco, Joseph, M. "Anarchy and the Limits of Cooperation: A Realist Critique of the Newest Liberal Institutionalism." *International Organization* 42, no. 3 (Summer 1988): 485–507.

———. "Realist International Theory and the Study of World Politics." In *New Thinking in International Relations Theory*, edited by Michael W. Doyle and G. John Ikenberry, 163–201. Boulder: Westview Press, 1997.

———. "Understanding the Problem of International Cooperation: The Limits of Neoliberal Institutionalism and the Future of Realist Theory." In *Neorealism and Neoliberalism: The Contemporary Debate*, edited by David A. Baldwin, 301–338. New York: Columbia University Press, 1993.

Haas, Ernst B. *The Uniting of Europe: Political, Economic, and Social Forces, 1950–1957*. Stanford: Stanford University Press, 1958.

Hagan, Joe D. "Domestic Political Explanations in the Analysis of Foreign Policy." In *Foreign Policy Analysis: Continuity and Change in its Second Generation*, edited by Laura Neack, Jeanne A. K. Hey, and Patrick J. Haney, 117–143. Englewood Cliffs: Prentice Hall, 1995.

———. "Domestic Political Regime Change and Foreign Policy Restructuring." In *Foreign Policy Restructuring: How Governments Respond to Global Change*, edited by Jerel A. Rosati, Joe D. Hagan, and Martin W. Sampson, 138–163. Columbia: University of South Carolina Press, 1994.

———. "Domestic Political Systems and War Proneness." *Mershon International Studies Review* 38 (October 1994): 183–207.

Hagan, Joe D. *Political Opposition and Foreign Policy in Comparative Perspective*. Boulder: Lynne Rienner Publishers, 1993.

———. "Regimes, Political Oppositions, and the Comparative Analysis of Foreign Policy." In *New Directions in the Study of Foreign Policy*, edited by Charles F. Hermann, Charles W. Kegley, Jr., and James N. Rosenau, 339–365. Boston: Allen & Unwin, 1987.

Hagan, Joe D., Philip P. Everts, Haruhiro Fukui, and John D. Stempel. "Foreign Policy by Coalition: Deadlock, Compromise, and Anarchy." *International Studies Review* 3, no. 2 (Summer 2001): 168–216.

Halperin, Morton H. *Bureaucratic Politics and Foreign Policy*. With the assistance of Priscilla Clapp and Arnold Kanter. Washington: The Brookings Institution, 1974.

Hazan, Reuven Y. *The Labor Party and the Peace Process: Partisan Disintegration Amid Political Cohesion*, Jerusalem: The Hebrew University Jerusalem, 1998.

Heller, Joseph. *The Birth of Israel, 1945–1949: Ben–Gurion and his Critics*. Gainesville: University of Florida Press, 2003.

Hermann, Margaret G. "Explaining Foreign Policy Behavior Using the Personal Characteristics of Political Leaders." *International Studies Quarterly* 24, no. 1 (March 1980): 7–46.

————. "How Decision Units Shape Foreign Policy: A Theoretical Framework." *International Studies Review* 3, no. 2 (Summer 2001): 47–81.

Hermann, Margaret, G., and Charles F. Hermann. "Who Makes Foreign Policy Decisions and How: An Empirical Inquiry." *International Studies Quarterly* 33, no. 4 (December 1989): 361–387.

Hermann, Margaret, G., Charles F. Hermann, and Joe D. Hagan. "How Decision Units Shape Foreign Policy Behavior." In *New Directions in the Study of Foreign Policy*, edited by Charles F. Hermann, Charles W. Kegley, Jr., and James N. Rosenau, 309–336. Boston: Allen & Unwin, 1987.

Hermann, Margaret G., Thomas P. Preston, Baghat Korany, and Timothy M. Shaw. "Who Leads Matters: The Effects of Powerful Individuals." *International Studies Review* 3, no. 2 (Summer 2001): 83–131.

Hermann, Charles F., Janice Gross Stein, Bengt Sundelius, and Stephen G. Walker. "Resolve, Accept, or Avoid: Effects of Group Conflict on Foreign Policy Decisions." *International Studies Review* 3, no. 2 (Summer 2001): 132–168.

Herrmann, Richard K. "Image Theory and Strategic Interaction in International Relations." In *Oxford Handbook of Political Psychology*, edited by David O. Sears, Leonie Huddy, and Robert Jervis, 285–313. Oxford: Oxford University Press, 2003.

Herrmann, Richard K., and Michael P. Fischerkeller. "Beyond the Enemy Image and Spiral Models: Cognitive-Strategic Research after the Cold War." *International Organization* 49, no. 3 (Summer 1995): 415–450.

Hill, Christopher. *The Changing Politics of Foreign Policy*. Houndmills: Palgrave Macmillan: 2003.

Hilsman, Roger. *The Politics of Policy Making in Defense and Foreign Affairs: Conceptual Models and Bureaucratic Politics*, 2nd ed. Englewood Cliffs: Prentice Hall, 1990.

Hollis, Martin, and Steve Smith. *Explaining and Understanding International Relations*. Oxford: Clarendon Press, 1991.

Holsti, Ole R. "The Belief System and National Images: A Case Study." In *International Politics and Foreign Policy: A Reader in Research and Theory*, edited by James N. Rosenau, 543–550. New York: The Free Press, 1969.

————. "Foreign Policy Formation Viewed Cognitively." In *Structure Of Decision: The Cognitive Maps of Political Elites*, edited by Robert Axelrod, 18–54. Princeton: Princeton University Press, 1976.

Hudson, Valerie M. "Foreign Policy Analysis: Actor Specific Theory and the Ground of International Relations." *Foreign Policy Analysis* 1, no. 1 (March 2005): 1–30.

Hurrell, Andrew. "International Society and the Study of Regimes: A Reflective Approach." In *Regime Theory and International Relations*, edited by Volker Rittberger and Peter Mayer, 49–72. Oxford: Clarendon Press, 1995.

Janis, Irving L. *Groupthink: Psychological Studies of Policy Decisions and Fiascoes*, 2nd ed. Boston: Houghton Mifflin company, 1982.

Jervis, Robert. *Perception and Misperception in International Politics.* Princeton: Princeton University Press, 1976.

———. "Realism, Neoliberalism, and Cooperation." In *Progress in International Relations Theory: Appraising the Field,* edited by Colin Elmam and Miriam Fendius Elman, 277–309. Cambridge: MIT Press, 2003.

———. "Political Implications of Loss Aversion." *Political Psychology,* 13, no.2 (1992): 187–204.

———. "Realism in the Study of World Politics." In *Exploration and Contestation in the Study of World Politics,* edited by Peter J. Katzenstein, Robert O. Keohane, and Stephen D. Krasner, 331–351. Cambridge, MA: MIT Press, 1999.

Katzenstein, Peter J., ed. *The Culture of National Security: Norms and Identity in World Politics.* New York: Columbia University Press, 1996.

Kay, Dalia Dassa. *Beyond the Handshake: Multilateral Cooperation in the Arab-Israeli Peace Process, 1991–1996.* New York: Columbia University Press, 2001.

Kegley, Charles W. Jr. "Decision Regimes and the Comparative Study of Foreign Policy." In *New Directions in the Study of Foreign Policy,* edited by Charles F. Hermann, Charles W. Kegley, Jr., and James N. Rosenau, 247–268. Boston: Allen & Unwin, 1987.

Kegley Charles W., and Eugene R. Wittkopf. *American Foreign Policy: Pattern and Process.* New York: St. Martin's Press, 1996.

Keohane, Robert O. *After Hegemony: Cooperation and Discord in the World Political Economy.* Princeton: Princeton University Press, 1984.

———. "Institutional Theory and the Realist Challenge After the Cold War." In *Neorealism and Neoliberalism: The Contemporary Debate,* edited by David A. Baldwin, 269–300. New York: Columbia University Press, 1993.

———. *International Institutions and State Power.* Boulder: Westview Press,1989.

———. "Theory and World Politics: Structural Realism and Beyond." *Neorealism and its Critics,* edited by Robert O. Keohane, 158–203. New York: Columbia University Press, 1986.

Keohane, Robert O. and Lisa L. Martin. "Institutional Theory as a Research Program." In *Progress in International Relations Theory: Appraising the Field,* edited by Colin Elmam and Miriam Fendius Elman, 71–107. Cambridge: MIT Press, 2003.

Keohane, Robert O., and Joseph S. Nye. *Power and Interdependence.* 2nd ed. New York: Harper Collins, 1989.

Khalidi, Rashid. "The Palestinians and 1948: The Underlying Causes of Failure." In *The War for Palestine: Rewriting the History of 1948,* edited by Eugene L. Rogan and Avi Shlaim, 12–36. Cambridge: Cambridge University Press, 2001.

Khalidi, Rashid. *Under Siege: P.L.O. Decisionmaking during the 1982 War.* New York: Columbia University Press, 1986.

Kimmerling, Baruch, and Joel S. Migdal. *The Palestinian People: A History.* Cambridge, MA: Harvard University Press, 2003.

King, Anthony. *Running Scared: Why America's Politicians Campaign Too Much and Govern Too Little.* New York: The Free Press, 1997.

Kissinger, Henry. *Diplomacy.* New York: Simon & Schuster, 1994.

Kochavi, Arieh J. "Indirect Pressure: Moscow and the End of the British Mandate in Palestine." In *Israel: The First Hundred Years, Volume IV, Israel in the International Arena,* edited by Efraim Karsh, 60–76. London: Frank Cass, 2004.

Krasner, Stephen D. *International Regimes.* Ithaca: Cornell University Press, 1983.

———. *Sovereignty: Organized Hypocrisy.* Princeton: Princeton University Press, 1999.

Kratochwil, Friedrich V. *Rules, Norms, and Decisions: On the Conditions of Practical and Legal Reasoning in International Relations and Domestic Affairs.* Cambridge: Cambridge University Press, 1989.

Kurz, Anat, N. *Fatah and the Politics of Violence: The Institutionalization of a Popular Struggle.* Brighton: Sussex Academic Press, 2005.

Laqueur, Walter, and Barry Rubin, eds. *The Arab-Israeli Reader: A Documentary History of the Middle East Conflict,* 6th revised ed. New York: Penguin Books, 2001.

Larson, Deborah. "The Role of Belief Systems and Schemas in Foreign Policy Decision-Making." *Political Psychology* 15, no. 1 (March 1994) 17–74.

Lau, Richard R. "Models of Decision-Making." In *Oxford Handbook of Political Psychology,* edited by David O. Sears, Leonie Huddy, and Robert Jervis, 19–59. Oxford: Oxford University Press, 2003.

Levy, Jack S. "An Introduction to Prospect Theory." *Political Psychology,* 13, no. 2 (1992): 171–186.

———. "Political Psychology and Foreign Policy." In *Oxford Handbook of Political Psychology,* edited by David O. Sears, Leonie Huddy, and Robert Jervis, 253–283. Oxford: Oxford University Press, 2003.

———. "Prospect Theory, Rational Choice, and International Relations." *International Studies Quarterly* 41 (March, 1997): 87–112.

Little, Richard, and Steve Smith, eds. *Belief Systems and International Relations.* Oxford: Basil Blackwell, 1988.

Lukacs, Yehuda, ed. *The Israeli-Palestinian Conflict: A Documentary Record.* Cambridge: Cambridge University Press,1992.

Makovsky, David. *Making Peace with the PLO: The Rabin Government's Road to the Oslo Accord.* Boulder: Westview Press, 1996.

Manin, Bernard. *The Principles of Representative Government.* Cambridge: Cambridge University Press, 1997.

Mearsheimer, John J. "The False Promise of International Institutions." *International Security* 19 no. 3 (Winter 1994/95): 5–49.

———. *The Tragedy of Great Power Politics.* New York: W.W. Norton, 2001.

Miller, Aaron David. *The PLO and the Politics of Survival.* New York: Praeger, 1983.

Mishal, Shaul, and Avraham Sela. *The Palestinian Hamas: Vision, Violence, and Coexistence.* New York: Columbia University Press, 2000.

Moravcsik, Andrew. "Liberal International Relations Theory." In *Progress in International Relations Theory: Appraising the Field*, edited by Colin Elmam and Miriam Fendius Elman, 160–204. Cambridge: MIT Press, 2003.

Morgan, Patrick M. *Theories and Approaches to International Politics: What Are We to Think?* New Brunswick: Transaction books, 1984.

Morgenthau, Hans J. *Politics Among Nations: The Struggle for Power and Peace.* 6th ed. Revised by Kenneth W. Thompson. New York: McGraw-Hill, 1985.

Morris, Benny. *The Birth of the Palestinian Refugee Problem Revisited.* Cambridge: Cambridge University Press, 2004.

———. "Revisiting the Palestinian Exodus of 1948." In *The War for Palestine: Rewriting the History of 1948*, edited by Eugene L. Rogan and Avi Shlaim, 37–59. Cambridge: Cambridge University Press, 2001.

———. *Righteous Victims: A History of the Zionist-Arab Conflict, 1881–2001.* New York: Vintage Books, 2001.

Neustadt, Richard E. *Presidential Power: The Politics of Leadership.* New York: John Wiley and Sons, Inc., 1960.

Nye, Joseph S. *Understanding International Conflicts: An Introduction to Theory and History.* 5th ed. New York: Pearson/Longman, 2005.

Oren, Michael B. *Six Days of War: June 1967 and the Making of the Modern Middle East.* Oxford: Oxford University Press, 2002.

Pappe, Ilan. *A History of Modern Palestine: One Land, Two Peoples.* Cambridge: Cambridge University Press, 2004.

Peleg, Ilan. "The Peace Process and Israel's Political Cultures: The Intensification of a Kulturkampf." In *The Role of Domestic Politics in Israeli Peacemaking*, 13–24. Jerusalem: The Hebrew University Jerusalem, 1998.

Peres, Shimon. *Battling for Peace: Memoirs.* Edited by David Landau. London: Weidenfeld & Nicolson, 1995.

Peretz, Don. "Israeli Peace Proposals." In *Middle East Peace Plans*, edited by Willard A. Beiling, 11–36. London: Croom Helm, 1986.

Powell, Robert. "Anarchy in International Relations Theory: The Neorealist-Neoliberal Debate." *International Organization* 48, no. 2 (Spring 1994): 313–344.

Price, Richard, and Nina Tannenwald. "Norms and Deterrence: The Nuclear and Chemical Weapons Taboos." In *The Culture of National Security: Norms and Identity in World Politics*, edited by Peter J. Katzenstein, 114–152. New York: Columbia University Press, 1996.

Putnam, Robert D. "Diplomacy and Domestic Politics: The Logic of Two-Level Games." *International Organization* 42, no. 3 (Summer 1988): 427–460.

Quandt, William B. *Camp David: Peacemaking and Politics.* Washington: The Brookings Institution, 1986.

———. *Decade of Decisions: American Policy towards the Arab-Israeli Conflict, 1976–1976.* Berkeley: University of California Press, 1977.

———. *Peace Process: American Diplomacy and the Arab-Israeli Conflict since 1967.* Washington: The Brookings Institution, 2001.

Rabinovich, Itamar. *Waging Peace: Israel and the Arabs at the End of the Century.* New York: Farrar, Straus and Giroux, 1999.

———. *The War for Lebanon, 1970–1985.* Ithaca: Cornell University Press, 1984.

Rosati, Jerel A. "A Cognitive Approach to the Study of Foreign Policy." In *Foreign Policy Analysis: Continuity and Change in its Second Generation,* edited by Laura Neack, Jeanne A. K. Hey, and Patrick J. Haney, 49–70. Englewood Cliffs: Prentice Hall, 1995.

———. "The Power of Human cognition in the Study of World Politics." *International Studies Review* 2 (Fall 2000): 45–75.

Ross, Dennis. *The Missing Peace: The Inside Story of the Fight for Middle East Peace.* New York, Farrar, Straus, and Giroux, 2004.

Rothstein, Robert L. "Oslo and the Ambiguities of Peace." In *The Middle East Peace Process: Vision Versus Reality,* edited by Joseph Ginat, Edward J. Perkins, and Edwin G. Corr, 21–38. Brighton: Sussex Academic Press, 2002.

Rubin, Barry. *The Transformation of Palestinian Politics: From Revolution to State-Building.* Cambridge, Mass.: Harvard University Press, 1999.

Rubinstein, Amnon. *From Herzl to Rabin: The Changing Image of Zionism.* New York; Holmes & Meier, 2000.

Ruggie, John Gerard. *Constructing the World Polity: Essays on International Institutionalization.* London: Routledge, 1998.

———, ed. *Multilateralism Matters: The Theory and Praxis of an Institutional Form.* New York: Columbia University Press, 1993.

Russet, Bruce. *Controlling the Sword: The Democratic Governance of National Security.* Cambridge, MA: Harvard University Press, 1990.

Russett, Bruce, Harvey Starr, and David Kinsella. *World Politics: The Menu for Choice,* 6th ed. Boston: Bedford / St. Martin's, 2000.

Safran, Nadav. *Israel, the Embattled Ally.* Cambridge, MA: Harvard University Press, 1978.

Sayigh, Yezid. *Armed Struggle and the Search for State: The Palestinian National Movement 1949–1993.* Oxford: Oxford University Press, 1997.

Schiff, Ze'ev and Ehud Ya'ari. *Israel's Lebanon War.* New York. Simon and Schuster, 1984.

Schueftan, Dan. *Disengagement: Israel and the Palestinian Entity.* Tel Aviv: Zmora-Bitan, 1999. (In Hebrew)

Schweller, Randall, L. "The Progressiveness of Neoclassical Realism." In *Progress in International Relations Theory: Appraising the Field,* edited by Colin Elmam and Miriam Fendius Elman, 311–347. Cambridge: MIT Press, 2003.

Segev, Tom. *One Palestine, Complete: Jews and Arabs under the British Mandate.* New York: Henry Holt and Company, 2000.

Seliktar, Ofira. *New Zionism and the Foreign Policy of Israel.* London: Croom Helm, 1986.

Shikaki, Khalil. "Changing the Guards—From Old to New." In *Israel, The Middle East and Islam: Weighing The Risks and Prospects*, edited by Oded Eran and Amnon Cohen, 31–36. Jerusalem: Harry S. Truman Research Institute, 2003.

———. "Palestine Divided." *Foreign Affairs*, 81, no.1(January/ February 2002): 89–105.

Shlaim, Avi. *The Iron Wall: Israel and the Arab World*. New York: W. W. Norton & Company, 2001.

———. "Israel and the Arab Coalition." In *The War for Palestine: Rewriting the History of 1948*, edited by Eugene L. Rogan and Avi Shlaim, 79–103. Cambridge: Cambridge University Press, 2001.

Simmons, Beth A. and Lisa L. Martin. "International Organizations and Institutions." In *Handbook of International Relations*, edited by Walter Carlsnaes, Thomas Risse, and Beth A. Simmons 192–211. London: Sage Publications, 2002.

Skidmore, David, and Valerie M. Hudson. "Establishing the Limits of State Autonomy: Contending Approaches to the Study of State-Society Relations and Foreign Policy-Making." In *The Limits of State Autonomy: Societal Groups and Foreign Policy Formulation*, edited by David Skidmore, and Valerie M. Hudson, 1–22. Boulder: Westview Press, 1993.

Snyder, Jack. *Myths of Empire*. Ithaca: Cornell University Press, 1991.

Snyder, Richard C., H. W. Bruck, and Burton Sapin. *Foreign Policy Decision-Making (Revisited)*. New York: Palgrave Macmillan, 2002.

Soetendorp, Ben. "The EU's Involvement in the Israeli-Palestinian Peace Process: The Building of a Visible International Identity." *European Foreign Affairs Review*, 7 no. 3 (Autumn 2002): 283–295.

———. *Foreign Policy in the European Union*. London: Longman, 1999.

Sprinzak, Ehud. *The Israeli Right and the Peace Process, 1992–1996*. Jerusalem: The Hebrew University Jerusalem, 1998.

Sprout, Harold, and Margaret Sprout. "Environmental Factors in the Study of International Politics." In *International Politics and Foreign Policy: A Reader in Research and Theory*, edited by James N. Rosenau, 41–56. New York: The Free Press, 1969.

Stein, Arthur A. "Coordination and Collaboration: Regimes in an Anarchic World." In *International Regimes*, edited by Stephen D. Krasner, 115–140. Ithaca: Cornell University Press, 1983.

———. *Why Nations Cooperate: Circumstances and Choice in International Relations*. Ithaca: Cornell University Press, 1990.

Stein, Janice Gross. "Psychological Explanations of International Conflict." In *Handbook of International Relations*, edited by Walter Carlsnaes, Thomas Risse, and Beth A Simmons 292–308. London: Sage Publications, 2002.

Stein, Janice Gross, and Raymond Tanter. *Rational Decision-Making: Israel's Security Choices, 1967*. Columbus: Ohio State University Press, 1976.

Steinbruner, John D. *The Cybernetic Theory of Decision: New Dimensions of Political Analysis*. Princeton: Princeton University Press, 1974.

Sullivan, Michael P. *Power in Contemporary International Politics*, Columbia, S.C.: University of South Carolina Press, 1990.

———. *Theories of International Relations: Transition vs. Persistence*. New York: Palgrave, 2001.

Tannenwald, Nina. "The Nuclear Taboo: The United States and the Normative Basis of Nuclear Non-Use." *International Organization* 53 no. 3 (Summer 1999): 433–468.

Tetlock, Philip E. "Social Psychology and World Politics." In *The Handbook of Social Psychology*, Vol. 2, 4th ed., edited by Daniel T. Gilbert, Susan T. Fiske, and Gardner Lindzey, 868–902. Boston: McGraw-Hill, 1998.

Thucydides. *The Peloponnesian War*. Translated by John H. Finley, Jr. New York: Random House, 1951.

Vertzberger, Yaacov Y. I. *Risk Taking and Decisionmaking: Foreign Military Intervention Decisions*. Stanford: Stanford University Press, 1998.

———. *The World in their Minds: Information Processing, Cognition, and Perception in Foreign Policy Decisionmaking*. Stanford: Stanford University Press, 1990.

Voss, James F., and Ellen Dorsey. "Perception and International Relations: An Overview." In *Political Psychology and Foreign Policy*, edited by Eric Singer and Valerie Hudson, 3–30. Boulder: Westview Press, 1992.

Walker, Stephen G. "The Evolution of Operational Code Analysis." *Political Psychology* 11, no. 2 (1990): 403–418.

———. "The Interface between Beliefs and Behavior: Henry Kissinger's Operational Code and the Vietnam War." *Journal of Conflict Resolution* 21, no. 1 (March 1977): 129–163.

———. "Operational Code Analysis as a Scientific Research Program: A Cautionary Tale." In *Progress in International Relations Theory: Appraising the Field*, edited by Colin Elmam and Miriam Fendius Elman, 245–276. Cambridge: MIT Press, 2003.

Walt, Stephen M. "The Enduring Relevance of the Realist Tradition." In *Political Science: The State of the Discipline*, edited by Ira Katznelson and Helen V. Milner, 197–230. New York: W.W. Norton & Company, 2002.

Waltz, Kenneth N. "International Politics is not Foreign Policy." *Security Studies* 6, no. 1 (Autumn 1996): 54–57.

———. *Man, the State and War: A Theoretical Analysis*. New York: Columbia University Press, 1959.

———. "Reflections on Theory of International Politics: A Response to my Critics." In *Neorealism and its Critics*, edited by Robert O. Keohane, 322–345. New York: Columbia University Press, 1986.

———. *Theory of International Politics*. Reading, MA: Addison-Wesley, 1979.

Watson, Adam. *The Evolution of International Society: A Comparative Historical Analysis*. London: Routledge, 1992.

Wendt, Alexander E. "The Agent-Structure Problem in International Relations Theory." *International Organization* 41 no. 3 (Summer 1987): 335–370.

Wendt, Alexander E. "Anarchy is what States Make of it: The Social Construction of Power Politics." *International Organization* 46 no. 2 (Spring 1992): 391–425.

———. "Bridging the Theory / Meta-Theory Gap in International Relations." *Review of International Studies* 17 (1991): 383–392.

———. "Collective Identity Formation and the International State." *The American Political Science Review* 88 no. 2 (June 1994): 384–396.

———. *Social Theory of International Politics.* Cambridge: Cambridge University Press, 1999.

Winter, David G. "Personality and Foreign Policy: Historical Overview of Research." In *Political Psychology and Foreign Policy,* edited by Eric Singer and Valerie Hudson 79–101. Boulder: Westview Press, 1992.

Yaniv, Avner. *Dilemmas of Security: Politics, Strategy, and the Israeli Experience in Lebanon.* New York: Oxford University Press, 1987.

Young, Michael D. and Mark Schafer. "Is there Method in Our Madness? Ways of Assessing Cognition in International Relations." *Mershon International Studies Review* 42 (May 1998): 63–96.

Zakaria, Fareed. *From Wealth to Power: The Unusual Origins of America's World Role.* Princeton: Princeton University Press, 1998.

———. "Realism and Domestic Politics." *International Security* 17, no. 1 (Summer 1992): 177–198.

INDEX

Printed in the United States
79134LV00001B/139-234